Selected Writings on Ethics and Politics

STUDIEN ZUR ÖSTERREICHISCHEN PHILOSOPHIE
Herausgegeben von Rudolf Haller

BAND XL

Selected Writings on Ethics and Politics

Bernard Bolzano

Translated by

Paul Rusnock
&
Rolf George

Amsterdam - New York, NY 2007

The paper on which this book is printed meets the requirements of "ISO 9706:1994, Information and documentation - Paper for documents - Requirements for permanence".

ISBN-13: 978-90-420-2154-9

Printed in the Netherlands

For Ann and Elizabeth

Acknowledgements

We would like to thank Wolfgang Künne, Edgar Morscher, and Jan Sebestik for a number of helpful suggestions concerning the contents of this collection. Thanks also to Anna Ezekiel, who has been a great help in the preparation of this volume. Linda Daniel and Ethan Toombs were both kind enough to proofread the introduction. Finally, we gratefully acknowledge the generous support provided by the Social Sciences and Humanities Research Council of Canada.

Contents

Introduction

Vaclav Havel used the phrase "living in truth" to describe a way of keeping faith in justice and human decency alive within a thoroughly corrupt and corrupting state.[1] It is a phrase that may rightly be applied to Bernard Bolzano's life as a public intellectual in early nineteenth-century Bohemia. For the similarities between the communist regime in Czechoslovakia and the administration of Austria under the Emperor Francis run deep. Both were characterised by corruption, abuse of power, and injustice. In both, a rigorous ideological control was exercised, and dissidence systematically, often violently, suppressed. In view of the consequences, to criticise existing arrangements required a great deal of courage. Bolzano, like Havel, possessed this courage in large measure, and took it upon himself to speak up on behalf of his oppressed fellow-citizens.

In October 1881 a group of Czech-Bohemian politicians, professors, scholars, artists and many students gathered in Prague to honour Bolzano on the centenary of his birth. The principal speaker, Dr. Durdik, after praising Bolzano's social activism in difficult times and his ethical teaching, ended his speech with these words:

> His example and his writings will always speak to us. Take them to hand and read... Honour the memory of this man and in him the spirit of humanity, of nobility, of light and peace! [Enthusiastic applause that does not want to end].[2]

"Take them to hand and read" [*tolle lege*] is a reference, well understood by the audience, to St. Augustine's deliverance, *Confessions* viii, 12, and thence leading to Romans XIII, 12:

> The night is far spent, the day is at hand: let us therefore cast off the works of darkness, and let us put on the armour of light.

---

[1] Vaclav Havel, *Living in Truth* (London: Faber and Faber, 1990).

[2] "Bolzano-Feier" in Politik 287, Prague, 16.10.1881, p. 5 f. Cited from Wolfgang Künne, "Geschichte der philosophischen Bolzano-Rezeption," in *Bernard Bolzano und die Politik*, ed. Helmut Rumpler, Vienna, Cologne, Graz: 2000. Vol 61 of *Studien zur Politik und Verwaltung*, p. 319 f.

This occasion, to which we shall return, one of many commemorative events in Prague over the years, focused on Bolzano's contributions to Bohemia's political landscape, his political wisdom, and his unfaltering commitment to the common good. Even during the dark days of Soviet occupation after the Prague Spring of 1968 flowers and candles on Bolzano's grave were not an unusual sight.

Today, Bernard Bolzano is best known and mentioned in histories of philosophy for his contributions to mathematics, logic and the philosophy of science. He was the first to propose and systematically investigate set theory as a foundation for mathematics, one of the pioneers of modern real analysis, and one of the great logicians of the modern period, who invented formal semantics and a wealth of other things set out in the monumental *Theory of Science* of 1837.[3]

In his own day, few appreciated Bolzano's contributions to theoretical philosophy and mathematics; only a small number were even aware that he had done this work. He was renowned, rather, for his work as "catechist", professor of religious science (*Religionswissenschaft*), at the Charles University in Prague from 1805 to 1819. In this highly visible position, Bolzano had become one of the most prominent advocates of social justice and reform in his homeland, a national philosopher who was the "social and political conscience of Bohemia."[4]

Bernard Placidus Johann Nepomuk Bolzano was born in Prague in September 1781 to middle-class parents. He was educated both at home and in school in the spirit of the Bohemian Catholic Enlightenment, with its emphasis on clarity of thought, the cultivation of useful knowledge, and promotion of the common good. After preparatory studies at the Piarist Gymnasium, he entered the Charles University, where he distinguished himself in several disciplines, notably philosophy, theology and mathematics. Toward the end of his studies he spent much time deliberating on his choice of profession. Starting with the supreme moral law—"which demands nothing but the advancement of the common

[3]B. Bolzano, *Wissenschaftslehre* (Sulzbach: Seidel, 1837).

[4]W. Künne, "Bernard Bolzano über Nationalismus und Rassismus in Böhmen," p. 97-139 in E. Morscher and O. Neumaier ed. *Bolzanos Kampf gegen Nationalismus und Rassismus*, Beiträge zur Bolzano-Forschung 4 (Sankt Augustin: Academia, 1996), p. 97.

good”[5]—he deduced the utility of various professions and concluded that only as a priest could he fulfill his duty to advance the progress of humanity.[6] He became a secular priest rather than joining a religious order since he did not want to be bound to a superior by a special vow of obedience. He saw his role not as steward of the sacraments or intermediary between God and man, but as teacher and advocate of the cause of progress.

Soon after finishing his studies, he applied for two posts at the Charles University, one in mathematics, the other a newly instituted chair in religious science. Highly recommended for both posts, he expressed his preference for the latter with little hesitation. In April 1805, only twelve days after his ordination and two days after receiving his doctorate, he assumed his duties. The new chairs were introduced in all universities as well as Latin (or secondary) schools and placed in the Faculty of Philosophy. This was the “low” faculty of basic studies that all students had to attend for three years before entering the “higher” disciplines of Theology, Law or Medicine. Bolzano was required to deliver two weekly lectures to each of the three classes, and to deliver exhortations (*Erbauungsreden*) during Sunday services. His position would thus allow him to address and counsel all students of the university, thereby influencing the future intellectual elite of Bohemia and impressing upon them the need for the reform of society. Despite opposition in Vienna, the wishes of the university officials in Prague prevailed, and his appointment was confirmed.

His view of the nature of religion and religious commitment made it difficult to perform the duties that came to be expected of the holders of these new chairs. These had been established in the course of the so-called Austrian Catholic Restoration with the purpose of providing religious instruction for lay students, and to reverse deistic and atheistic tendencies. Accordingly, Bolzano was expected to give government approved interpretations of religious dogma in his lectures, which he was to base upon a book by the Emperor’s confessor Jakob Frint.

Bolzano’s homeland, Bohemia, was then a province of the Austrian Empire, which for most of his life was ruled by the Emperors Joseph II

[5] *Wissenschaftslehre* Vol. 4, p. 27.

[6] From his autobiography: *Lebensbeschreibung des Dr. B. Bolzano*, ed. M. Fesl, (Sulzbach: Seidel, 1836), p. 27.

(1780-1790) and Francis II (1792-1835).[7] Joseph, the very model of the enlightened absolute mon- arch, had begun his term as ruler of Austria in 1780 with a package of sweeping reforms. Censorship was relaxed, the legal system reformed, torture and serfdom abolished. Limited religious tolerance was proclaimed: Protestants were free to attend their own services, even if they still had to pay taxes to support the Catholic clergy, and Jews were granted important, if still limited, civil rights. Radical reforms were prescribed for the institutions of the Catholic Church with the intention of transforming them into instruments for the betterment of society. Many monasteries were closed, the so-called contemplative or "inactive" orders abolished, and control over the education of priests transferred to the state. In Joseph's plans, the enlightened priest was to be a key figure in the transformation of society, playing a central part especially in the education of the people. It was for just such a role that Bolzano was prepared in his youth.

Joseph died in 1790, and his successor, Leopold, who was broadly sympathetic to Joseph's aims if not to his political methods, died shortly afterwards. He was followed by Francis II, who could not have been more hostile to Josephinian projects. Terrified by the French Revolution, harassed and humiliated by Napoleon, Francis wished above all to put an end to the reform movement, indeed to all *thought* of reform within his realm. The ideals of the Enlightenment, now seen as fomenting revolution, were to be fought with all available means. Over time rigorous censorship was reimposed, the secret police greatly expanded, and strict ideological controls placed upon educators and intellectuals. The Church, in a perfect reversal, was expected to stamp out enlightenment rather than to serve as the principal agent of its spread. But these measures, not introduced as fast as intended, were much delayed by the pressure of secular forces and adverse events: Austria lost several wars against France (1797, 1800, 1805 and 1809), was occupied by the French (who had no interest in Francis's religious policies), and forced to join Napoleon's continental system. To cement this alliance, Francis

[7]As the Emperor of the "Holy Roman Empire of the German Nation" he was Francis II. When the Empire was dissolved in 1803 under the pressure of Napoleon's conquests, he became Francis I of the Habsburg Empire—Austria, Bohemia, Moravia, Slovakia, Hungary, parts of Italy, Poland and Ukraine, and other bits scattered through the west of Germany.

married his daughter Marie Louise to Napoleon. In addition, Francis's chief minister Clemens Metternich had no interest in things spiritual.

As a consequence, many professors of religious science in Latin schools and universities were in fact appointed by local authorities, who still favoured the Joseph- inian reforms. Bolzano was by no means a revolutionary, but it was clear from the start that he did not measure up to the expectations which the government in Vienna, the capital, attached to his post. A fearless and dogged critic of both ecclesiastical and civic institutions and authorities, he managed, with the help of the Prague archbishop and others, to fend off trouble until strict new policies led to his dismissal in 1819. Bolzano's homilies, of which one volume was published in 1813 (and placed on the Index of Forbidden Books in 1828), were tangible proof of his unsuitable opinions, and were a focal point of the conflict. These weekly sermons became immensely popular, often drawing as many as 1000 listeners,[8] and were a central part of a movement which combined a rationally reconstructed Catholic faith with a programme for social and political reform that became known as the "Bohemian Enlightenment." It was partly this popularity, partly the ferment of the Napoleonic wars that kept him in this position for such a long time.

Karl Postl, later known as Charles Sealsfield, who had studied in Prague, and had escaped the Austrian Empire in 1823 to become a prolific author in America and England, wrote in an acerbic volume *Austria as it is:*

> By an Imperial decree ... the chair of the Religious Philosophy was erected, and attached to the philosophical studies. The most erudite men were selected to fill this chair, its effects were astonishing. An intellectual progress was felt

[8]Nearly every student must have attended, if we can trust Sealsfield's numbers: "Of the 30,000 students who are said to have crowded, in the times of Charles the Fourth [1316-1378] and his successors, the salons of the renowned university at Prague, but 1000 remain. These are trained according to the pleasure of his Imperial Majesty." Charles Sealsfield–Karl Postl, *Austria as it is* (London, 1828; reprinted and ed. Primus-Heinz Kucher [Vienna, Cologne, Weimar: Böhlau, 1994]), p. 42. There had been more students a couple of decades earlier. Enrollment 1802/3: Philosophy 795, Theology 471, Law 278, Medicine 70 (Jan Havránek, "Das politische Klima an der Prager Universität zur Zeit Bolzanos" in *Bernard Bolzano und die Politik*, pp. 77-86, p. 81).

> throughout, far above what can be imagined. The Austrian academical youth became, through these lectures, in fact, Protestants in mind, though professing Catholicism.[9]

Sealsfield extrapolated from his own experiences in Prague where he had attended Bolzano's lectures and noted their effect on the audience of young students—in the rest of the Austrian Empire the effect was not so pronounced. His description of the youth as "Protestants in mind" would not have pleased Bolzano, who firmly believed in the "perfectibility" of Catholicism and its profoundly rational structure, and found much to criticise in Protestantism.[10] But Sealsfield was close to the opinion held by the authorities at the imperial court.

To engage in social criticism, as Bolzano claimed in an exhortation of 1810, was only to fulfill one of the most basic duties of a priest:

> Is it not his profession to curb and oppose vice and disorder wherever they are found? Does he not have the arduous obligation, in the confessional, at the sick bed, the pulpit and wherever he properly can, fearlessly to call any person of rank and power a villain if he has violated his duty? Should he not point out to him in clear and precise terms what he must do, what use he must make of his wealth, his power and his prestige so that he is not merely *called* a nobleman, but actually is one? Does it not require courage, high courage to dare all this, everywhere to speak the truth freely and without reservation? Does this not attract the hatred of exactly those persons whose mere *desire* can cause the most grievous harm?[11]

Bohemia, a principal laboratory of the anti-Enlightenment Restoration, was claimed to be a most Catholic country. This would be a very good thing were it so, according to Bolzano, but only the most deluded

---

[9] *Austria as it is*, p. 111.

[10] Cf. the selections on the "Right of the Clergy," below, pp. 143–167.

[11] "Über den Muth" [On courage] (1810), *Erbauungsreden* (Prague, 1813), p. 148 (Also in the *Bernard Bolzano Gesamtausgabe* [hereafter, **BBGA**], (Stuttgart–Bad Cannstatt: Frommann–Holzboog, 1969–), Volume I.2, p. 111-112).

or hypocritical could fail to see the sharp contrast between Catholic doctrine and Bohemian practice.

We can begin with the Church itself. For Bolzano one of the most important teachings of Catholicism, indeed its very essence, is the requirement of universal consensus of the members of the Church in matters of faith:

> [Jesus] was the first to realize that it is not the arbitrary will of a single person, but the general agreement of all that must decide what is true or false in matters of religion. He therefore founded a church that allowed as God's revelation only what can be the united opinion of all.[12]

Yet if one had to judge from the conduct of Church leaders, one would never have guessed that this was a fundamental part of their teaching: decisions tended to be autocratic, even the most mildly critical works were promptly proscribed, and dissent was systematically suppressed. Far from fostering open discussion among the faithful, they had a tendency to confuse the Church with themselves, much as political rulers have a tendency to confound the best interests of states with their own. This is, as Bolzano repeatedly pointed out, to get things exactly backwards. It is not the Pope, nor even councils of Bishops, who determine the content of Catholicism, but rather the entire body of the faithful. Individual Catholics owe obedience to Church leaders, just as they do to any legitimately constituted authority, but, like any other human authority, the leaders of the church are fallible. They can, and indeed frequently do, make mistakes. If the mistakes are serious enough, then it is not only permissible but in some cases even a duty to oppose them. The leaders will not like this, he recognised, but that is no reason to remain silent:

> The *leaders* of the Church are quite happy to call *their own* judgment the judgment of the *entire Church*, and anyone who contradicts them must expect that they will call him heterodox. Whether he in fact ceases to deserve to be called a good Catholic is another matter. Here things stand much

[12]"Richtiges Verhältniß des bloß Verdienstlichen zum Pflichtmäßigen," *Erbauungsreden*, Vol. II (Prague, 1850), p. 23-24.

> as they do with the name of a *good citizen* in a state. The leaders of our states are not generally inclined to apply this name to someone who disobeys even a single one of their decrees, although he may do so with the best intentions, and precisely because he strives most conscientiously to do everything that the promotion of the common good requires, that is, because he is one of the *best* citizens in the state.[13]

If Bolzano did not counsel revolution, he nonetheless preached both the possibility and the desirability of change. This alone was enough to gain him enemies at the Imperial court. The passion with which he denounced the powerful made it virtually certain, however, that he would be silenced as soon as a suitable opportunity presented itself. This came in March of 1819, when a theology student, Carl Friedrich Sand, stabbed to death the conservative writer August von Kotzebue in Mannheim, Germany. Kotzebue, a Russian diplomat and author of mediocre plays, had made a name for himself by mocking reformists, especially student radicals like Sand. His murder was used as a pretext for the general anti-republican crackdown in Germany and Austria embodied in the so-called Carlsbad Decrees: delegates from Austria and the German states met in that spa to put an end to all thoughts of progress and republicanism.

Among the first casualties was a former student of Bolzano's, Michael Joseph Fesl, who was caught running a secret society in the seminary at Litoměřice (Leitmeritz). Even though the society aimed at nothing more than the moral perfection of its members, it was lumped together with the revolutionary student movements then widespread in German universities. Sealsfield says this:

> [Fesl] ... asserted ... in one of his lectures, that those doctrines, which are incompatible with human reason, cannot be founded on divine precepts. This daring speech resounded in Vienna, and a few weeks afterwards the confessor of his majesty, M. Frint, arrived with two commissaries from Vienna, arrested the poor director, and carried him under escort to Vienna, where he was imprisoned....

---

[13] B. Bolzano and J. Stoppani, *Über die Perfektibilität des Katholicismus* (Leipzig, 1845), Vol. I, 74; also in **BBGA**, Vol. I.19/1, p. 93.

> The bishop, under whose eyes this *ne plus ultra* of infidelity took place, was deprived of his see, and sent into a capuchin monastery.[14]

Fesl's statement was an echo of Bolzano's teaching:

> Whatever contradicts reason, whatever does not advance morality, what is indifferent to the purposes of virtue and happiness cannot belong to revealed doctrine, no matter who proclaims it.[15]

Proclaiming the enlightenment doctrine of the compatibility of reason and revelation was anathema. As he must have expected, Bolzano's turn came soon after, when he and a number of other university professors in Germany and Austria were summarily dismissed, often on the thinnest of pretexts. Charges of heterodoxy and political unreliability had been placed against Bolzano much earlier, and personal grievances also seem to have played a role.[16] As early as 1806, the ever present Frint had complained that his prescribed textbook did not sell well in Prague, and later Bolzano was expressly asked to justify himself for lecturing from his own notes rather than Frint's book. Now that the wars were over, and Francis had consolidated his power, Frint and others made presentations to the Emperor, excerpting objectionable passages from Bolzano's exhortations.

In a memorandum to the Emperor dated 13 December 1819, Baron von Stifft set out the charges:[17] Bolzano, he claims, wants to explain everything in religion, even the mysteries, philosophically; he maintains that general councils do not determine what is to count as revelation, but only the general agreement of all the members of the Church, that there may be more than one religion that is maximally beneficial for a man in certain circumstances, that the world is infinite in space and time; that

[14]*Austria as it is*, p. 43.

[15]*Über die Perfektibilität des Katholicismus* (Leipzig, 1845), p. 292 (**BBGA** I.19/2, p. 298).

[16]These matters are discussed in W. Künne, "Die theologischen Gutachten in den Verfahren gegen den Professor und den Priester Bolzano," in W. Löffler ed. *Bernard Bolzanos Religionsphilosophie und Theologie* (Sankt Augustin: Akademia Verlag, 2002), Beiträge zur Bolzano-Forschung, Volume 12.

[17]Reproduced in E. Winter, *Der Bolzanoprozeß* (Brno, 1944), p. 139-150.

Jesus was merely a man; and that one of the highest goals of humanity is the elimination of distinctions of rank. Von Stifft continued:

> This was taught in France by the Jacobins, and the German demagogues preached the same. But it is mind-boggling that in our country a priest and teacher of religion can give such a lecture from a holy pulpit.... Bolzano conveyed his doctrines to the students of philosophy who are always most prone to catch fire. He lectured them at a time when minds are so much inclined to uproot all existing order, at a time of zealous agitation through twisted religious-political principles, to turn the youth at our universities into fanatics who would think every means permitted, indeed mandatory, if it led to the desired goal.... By casting Christianity as a mere religion of reason, by leaving to *dark feeling* and *mere human reason* the concept of legitimate governance and opening to doubt the duty of obedience and at the same time advocating the *equality* of different peoples and new *constitutions* as the *highest* goal of human happiness, Bolzano's efforts are well-suited to create in our country the kind of fanatic that already exists in German universities in great number.[18]

The Chancellor, Prince von Saurau, stated that Bolzano's "innovations" could not be justified. In *German* universities, he pointed out, where professors must live on students' fees, novel doctrines are an economic necessity; but in *Austria* professors are paid by the state:

> They must therefore teach propositions that are approved by the church and the civil administration. It is a dangerous error for a professor to think that he can instruct the youth entrusted to his care according to the drift of his individual convictions or according to his own views.[19]

---

[18]E. Winter, *Der Bolzanoprozeß*, p. 148-149. Von Stifft was the Emperor's physician and responsible for the administration of public health. Since he did not believe cholera to be contagious, no precautions were taken when that disease arrived in Vienna in 1830. Two thousand died.

[19]E. Winter, *Der Bolzanoprozeß*, p. 35 f.

This echoed the Emperor's opinion:

> New ideas that I cannot condone have now found currency. Abstain from them and embrace the positive: I do not need scholars, but obedient citizens. It is your obligation thus to form our youth. Who serves me must teach what I command. Whoever cannot do this, or pesters me with new ideas can walk or I shall remove him.[20]

Evidently, independent thought was by itself grounds for dismissal.[21]

An imperial decree suspending Bolzano was issued on December 24, 1819, and the Emperor ordered that ecclesiastical charges be laid. A commission was appointed to examine his writings, and great pressure was put upon Church authorities in Prague to convict—the punishment contemplated was that which had been meted out to Fesl, namely solitary confinement in a monastery. The examination of Bolzano's religious writings, however, found them to fall well within the limits of orthodoxy. In addition, Josef Dobrovský,[22] a famous champion of Czech autonomy and an influential Churchman, had got wind of the plan to convict Bolzano and threatened to publish the entire story, including Bolzano's own statements of defense as well as Frint's role in the affair.

---

[20]Quoted after Friedrich Anton von Schoenholz, *Traditionen zur Charakteristik Oesterreichs* (Munich, 1914), Vol. 1. p. 255, note 1.

[21]On this, compare the comments of Karl Postl/Charles Sealsfield (*Austria as it is*, p. 131): "The Bohemians, Moravians, Hungarians, and Poles, are not Englishmen, nor even Germans, in point of enlightened information; but they have infinitely more strength of mind and national feeling than the latter. The silence which reigns throughout Austria is compulsory; but the '*aqua tofana*' of Metternich's system is too complicated not to excite the attention and the indignation even of the most stolid human being. To reduce the youth of an empire of thirty millions to that low degree of idiotism which befits the views of his Majesty, it is not sufficient to write schoolbooks in Vienna, by Messrs. Frint and Co., and to send them to the different universities and colleges: there have been, and still are, men upright and learned; they must be removed and replaced by faithful slaves. This has been done with the universities of Prague, Vienna, Olmutz, Laybach, etc."

[22]Dobrovský (1753-1829), famous patriarch of Slavic studies, was not a professor at the university but was sought out by many students for instruction in the Czech language.

This was apparently enough to ensure that the tribunal's decision went in Bolzano's favour.

The Emperor was not amused. He wrote to the Archbishop of Prague:

> With sadness of heart I gather from your report that matters with the priest Bernard Bolzano still stand about where they stood six years ago, and that in an affair so important for religion, church and state nothing has actually happened.[23]

Despite his acquittal, Bolzano was still forbidden to teach or to publish, even on purely technical matters like mathematics and logic. He accepted his lot, indeed one might say he even welcomed it in certain respects. Given his extremely poor health—throughout his life he suffered from lung disease, which was so bad during the years 1813-16 that he was unable to lecture—it is unlikely he would have lived much longer had he continued to teach and counsel, keeping an open door to hundreds of students. For the next thirty years his health was preserved thanks in large part to the care of his good friend Anna Hofmann, at whose country estate in Těchobuz he spent much time. He could now devote himself to his scholarly works, among them the *Theory of Science* (*Wissenschaftslehre*, 1837), *Athanasia* (a tract on immortality, 1827), *On the Best State*, the never-finished mathematical treatise (*Größenlehre*), work on infinite sets and a host of other topics ranging from physics to religion to aesthetics and the history of philosophy.

Austrian governance is sometimes described as despotism tempered by inefficiency. Despite official disapproval, liberal-enlightened intellectual life managed to continue in Prague. When Bolzano returned to live there in 1841, he often met with friends for discussion, lectured at the Royal Bohemian Academy of Sciences, to which he had been elected in 1815, served as president in 1818 and again in 1842. He was, however, not able to publish his work in the Habsburg Empire; his books had to be launched in Germany. An active force in Bohemian society until the end of his life, Bolzano died in Prague in December of 1848.

[23] Winter, *Der Bolzanoprozeß*, p. 197.

Bolzano's writings on Ethics and Politics

While professor at the Charles University, Bolzano composed over 600 "Exhortations" or "homilies", (*Erbauungsreden*)—Sunday sermons for all students of the university—a great many of them dealing with ethical and political topics. Some of these were published during his lifetime,[24] a larger number just after his death,[25] another volume in the late nineteenth century,[26] and several more in the past few years.[27] He also wrote systematic treatments of both ethical and political theory. Bolzano's ethics is presented under the title "Natural Morality" in the *Treatise of the Science of Religion*,[28] his political philosophy in the treatise *On the Best State*, which dates from around 1830. Finally, Bolzano published a number of occasional works on political topics later in his life, among them *Opinions of a Liberal Catholic Theologian on the Relations between Church and State*,[29] *On the Right of the Clergy to obtain their Livelihood from Persons not of their Faith*,[30] *On the Perfectibility of Catholicism*,[31] and *On Charity*.[32]

Our goal in putting together this volume has been to provide a representative selection of these works. You will find here complete transla-

[24] *Erbauungsreden* (Prague,1813 = **BBGA** Vol. I.2; 2nd ed., Prague, 1839).

[25] *Bernard Bolzano's Erbauungsreden an die akademische Jugend*, 4 Volumes (Prague/Vienna, 1849–1852).

[26] *Erbauungsreden*, n. F. (Vienna, 1884).

[27] *24 Erbauungsreden 1808–1820*, ed. K. Strasser (Vienna: Böhlau, 2001). For details on all of Bolzano's *Erbauungsreden*, see K. Strasser, *Bernard Bolzanos Erbauungsreden. Prag 1805–1820* (Sankt Augustin: Academia, 2004).

[28] *Lehrbuch der Religionswissenschaft*, Part I, §§86-95; In part III of the same work, Bolzano presents a systematic exposition of Catholic teachings on ethics under the heading "Catholic Morality".

[29] *Ansichten eines freisinnigen katholischen Theologen über das Verhältnis zwischen Kirche und Staat* (Sulzbach, 1834).

[30] "Über das Recht der Geistlichkeit, ihren Lebensunterhalt von Personen zu beziehen, welche nicht ihres Glaubens sind. Eine Abhandlung nach B. Bolzanos Ansichten von einem seiner Schüler bearbeitet." [actually by Bolzano] Freimüthige Blätter (Stuttgart, 1838) Vol. 11, pp. 291-331 and Vol. 12, pp. 5-47.

[31] *Über die Perfektibilität der Katholicismus* (Leipzig, 1845).

[32] *Über die Wohltätigkeit. Dem Wohle der leidenden Menschheit gewidmet von einem Menschenfreunde* (Prague, 1847)

tions of *On the Best State* as well as "Natural morality," selections from the essay "On the Right of Clergy...," and a number of exhortations. As important as religion is to Bolzano's conception of both ethics and politics, we have not attempted to represent his writings on this subject. To do so would require at least another large volume, and must be left to other translators or at least to another day. We have included some small selections of his writings on religion with the presentation of his ethics, enough to give the reader some small idea of his general approach. We recognize that by so doing we run the risk of giving an incomplete or misleading picture of his work in the field. We accept the risk, and point out here once and for all that Bolzano's views on religion extend far beyond the matters discussed in the selections translated here.

Exhortations

We include only a small selection of Bolzano's exhortations, but one large enough, we hope, to communicate something of his teaching and his personality: the integration of social reform with Christian teaching, his understanding of enlightenment, why he thinks education must be looked upon as the ultimate moving force of improvement, at least for the present moment, and how society can and must be peacefully transformed from within.

The first of our selections is a homily preached on April 20, 1817. In the introduction, Bolzano refers to the hardships the people were then experiencing. If the reports from the country are true, he says, "they make it impossible to understand how people who have been reduced to such a state of misery have not had recourse to the law of necessity, and taken with force what they need and what he is indeed there for the taking."[33] Bolzano here refers to the great famine of 1816/17.

Germany, the Habsburg Monarchy, and most countries of northern latitudes had been blanketed by a cloud of volcanic debris from an eruption of the volcano Tomboro on the Indonesian island Sumbawa in 1815, the largest volcanic eruption in recorded history. The effect was that in 1816 New England and northern Europe experienced "the year we had

---

[33]"Mangel an Aufklärung (Unwissenheit und Irrthum) ist als die wahre Ursache der Übel anzusehen, die unser Vaterland bedrücken," *Erbauungsreden*, Vol. I (Prague, 1849), p. 1; below, p. 45.

no summer," which led to disastrous harvests, and famine in the following year. There are reports of people in Germany, Austria and Switzerland eating cats, rats, grass and straw; columns of refugees headed east to Russia, where food was still available. Even without the famine, most early nineteenth-century cities were death-traps, and the poor economic organization, particularly of agriculture, multiplied the effects of natural disasters.[34] Added to this were the consequences of the Napoleonic wars. Bolzano had said in a homily of the previous year:

> These are especially hard and evil times, my friends.... The frequent wars conducted with unprecedented brutality that swept over Europe from one end to the other have visited on us innumerable evils of all kinds. For centuries there have not been as many unfortunates who were robbed of their property, of their limbs, who crawl about gruesomely mutilated; there have not been as many mothers and fathers who mourn a beloved son who was to be their support in old age; or children who cry for their father and supporter.... The beautiful progress in the arts and sciences that raised such hopes at the end of the last century, how suddenly was it stopped and pushed back! In almost all countries war has caused the instruction of our youth visibly to decline and ignorance and irrational superstition to spread again.... Neither can it be denied that in the last decades dishonesty in commerce, fraud and treachery, excessive sensual pleasures, voluptuous dissipation, theft, robbery and murder have become more and more common and ordinary occurrences.[35]

---

[34]The high prices of 1817, for instance, encouraged many small land-owners to mortgage their holdings against expected profits in the next year. But overproduction in 1818 made prices collapse, and about half of them lost their properties. While disastrous for them, these developments were not even slightly uncomfortable for the upper class on their vast estates.

[35]"Durch die vereinigte Bemühung nur weniger Männer kann in jedem Zeitalter eine verbesserte Gestalt der Dinge herbeigeführt werden," (read on the 27th Sunday after Pentecost, 1816); *Erbauungsreden* Vol. I (Prague, 1849), p. 73-74.

One of the most basic teachings of Christianity, Bolzano observed, was the essential equality of all people. Yet this precept was systematically violated in every aspect of Bohemian life. For despite the reforms of the eighteenth century, the ways of Bohemian society were still predominantly feudal. Throughout the Austrian Empire, and especially in Bohemia, power and wealth were distributed in the most arbitrary way imaginable. The vast majority lived in abject poverty, a condition exacerbated by the effects of war, famine and the early stages of industrialization. In their midst, however, lived a small group of incredibly rich families, passing on their wealth from one generation to the next. This inequality, indeed the very conception of property that underlies it, was, Bolzano taught, in flagrant contradiction with the teachings of Christianity. In a homily of 1809, based on Acts, 4, 32-37,[36] he contrasts the attitudes towards property in the early Christian communities with those current in his homeland:

> Jerusalem was the city that harboured in its midst the first larger congregation of true Christians. Despite much external pressure from mighty and numerous enemies it was a happy society! There was not a single poor and destitute person among them, for those who previously owned fields and houses sold them and placed the proceeds at the feet of the Apostles, and all those in need received a share. O! what a difference, my friends, what a deplorable difference in this and many other respects between that congregation in Jerusalem and our congregations that call themselves Christian! There one found the freest communality of all goods that could be shared by a neighbour, and the cold little words "mine" and "thine" had almost been banished from the language of the early Christians. In the Christian countries of our period the extreme inequality of wealth, the jealous fixing of boundaries between the properties of different persons must insult the humane observer wherever he looks. Then charitable support was as active as it has ever been among people. Now we see abject stingi-

[36]"The whole body of believers was united in heart and soul, not a man of them claimed any of his possessions as his own, but everything was held in common. . . ."

> ness in the support of needy persons that appears even more deplorable when donors expect public praise for giving less than a ten-thousandth of their abundance to the poor, and perhaps only because their labour would no longer return a profit if they starved to death.[37]

Distinctions of rank were all-pervasive, marked by a variety of external signs, titles, dress, shows of opulence, etc., reinforced by an elaborate code of conduct, and backed, as often required, by violence. Each higher station enjoyed its own set of privileges:

> Over time, distinctions of rank were introduced for almost all of our special offices and occupations and, what is the worst, were not only tolerated as custom, but encoded in law. Secular as well as ecclesiastical authorities were induced to determine in law in what order the thousandfold offices and ways of life should be sorted into ranks. Laws were concocted that determined with highest precision the titles and tributes with which the members of a higher estate were to be glorified by all inferiors.[38]

The vast majority found themselves at the bottom of the hierarchy, subject to many abuses with little chance of redress:

> How many unfortunates are there not in even the best of the currently existing states that are kept in such a condition of oppression that almost their whole life is an uninterrupted string of sufferings. It appears that they were admitted into society as citizens only to work for others and be spectators of their amusements, but never allowed themselves to enjoy any of the many goods.[39]

The rigid structures of authority encouraged servility, sycophancy, and especially hypocrisy: vices alarmingly prevalent among those in positions of power, and especially in the church.

---

[37]"Über den Begriff des Eigenthums und von den Pflichten gegen das eigene Besitzthum,"*Erbauungsreden*, Vol. I (Prague, 1849), p. 264.

[38]"Über die Rangsunterschiede" (*Erbauungsreden*, I. 36).

[39]"Von den Vortheilen, die uns die bürgerliche Gesellschaft (der Staat) bei aller Mangelhaftigkeit gewährt," *Erbauungsreden* I, p. 131.

> The hypocrite of our era approves, praises and admires whatever is done by persons of high rank and great power. But, so as not to lose favour with the lower classes, he shows himself as affable, condescending and engaging toward them. In administering his office he carefully avoids severity even if punishment is deserved for violations of duty. For although he knows that he could prevent much evil [by properly exercising his office], he also knows that this would gain him innumerable enemies. He therefore finds it advisable to tolerate and overlook much and this indulgence even earns him the reputation of a benevolent, mild and humanitarian man.[40]

The equality of women is the subject of the homily "Of the Mission and Dignity of Womanhood,"[41] again drawing on Bolzano's interpretation of Scripture. Jesus taught that women are the equals of men in wisdom, virtue and happiness, the three characteristics that matter most. But these views are hardly reflected in the treatment of women:

> It would be better for you, O! you oppressed woman-kind, if in our principles, customs, habits and civic institutions we acted in harmony with the precepts of Jesus. Then you would not be barred from all serious learning and higher knowledge that men now keep only for themselves; then no one would fancy that everything possible was done for your education as long as you are given some useless elocution training and are taught skills of a sort that entertain fools and annoy the wise; then we would not read in acclaimed writings that there can be no virtue in the female sex, that here all apparent virtue is only weakness, instinct or the effect of vanity; then men would not seize all rights

[40]"Von der Heuchelei—ihren Quellen und den Verwahrungsmitteln gegen dieselbe," *Erbauungsreden* Vol. II (Prague, 1850), p. 313: "[H]ow many hypocrites there are in the higher ranks of the civil service, and —it saddens me to say—they are found most of all in precisely the calling where hypocrisy should least be tolerated, the worthy calling of the priesthood!"

[41]Read on the Feast of the Ascension of Mary, Wednesday, August 15, 1810, *Erbauungsreden* IV, p. 174.

> and claims to earthly goods; then you would not be the afflicted part and without protection, whose lamentation no one hears, destined to live in pain and merely to serve the lust of others; then you would not tremble all days of your youth for fear that some evil fellow might fall on you in a weak and unarmed moment and rob you of all your happiness, then go unpunished while bringing upon your head the ridicule and derision of the whole town; nor would you have to fear being neglected in old age, after giving life and education to many a good citizen.[42]

Then there was the treatment reserved for the Czech-speaking majority of Bohemia. Ever since the Thirty Years' War (1618-1648), when the (mostly Protestant) Czech nobles had been defeated by the Habsburg armies, Czech had been a beleaguered language. The leaders and teachers of the Czechs had been forced into exile in large numbers, their places taken by foreigners from other parts of the Empire. Jesuits, brought in to re-establish orthodoxy, took it upon themselves to destroy any books written in Czech that they could lay their hands on, since it was believed that all of them were tainted with heresy.[43] Almost overnight, Czech was changed from a language of politics, commerce and learning to a language of peasants, not unlike the situation of Old English after the Norman Conquest. For centuries afterwards, Bohemia remained in effect an occupied country, whose German speaking ruling classes and the ruled Czechs lived together—in the memorable phrase of Ernst Renan—"like oil and water in a glass."[44]

By the early nineteenth century, as Bolzano pointed out in a sermon of 1816, relatively little had changed in this state of affairs:

> Is it not the case that the German-born, and those who are connected with them, are privileged in a hundred impor-

[42]"Von der Bestimmung und Würde des weiblichen Geschlechtes," *Erbauungsreden*, IV, p. 177f; below, p. 135.

[43]Josef Dobrovský, *Geschichte der böhmischen Sprache und Literatur* (1792; new ed. Halle: Max Niemeyer Verlag, 1955), p. 114; R. W. Seton-Watson, *A History of the Czechs and Slovaks* (Hamden: Archon, 1965), p. 116-117, 140.

[44]E. Renan, "Qu'est-ce qu'une nation?" *Œuvres complètes* ed. H. Psichari (Paris: Calmann-Lévy, 1949), t. 1, p. 892.

> tant ways? Is it not the German language that is used in all learned communication in the country? And has not German been elevated to serve as the language of business in all public matters? Must this not, however little it can be criticized in and of itself, be most unwelcome to the other part of the people? When they are thus set back, must this not be bitterly felt? But still more: Is it not the case that the great and high-ranking in the country, the rich and propertied, are all of them either German born or perhaps even foreigners, or else persons who, having long since abandoned the Czech language and customs, are counted among the Germans? Does not the entire Czech speaking part of the population live in a deplorable state of poverty and oppression? And—the most scandalous of all—have not their superiors always been either Germans, or persons who associate with them? Persons who, since they don't have the least ability to speak their language, are completely incapable of appreciating the appeals and complaints, the requests and petitions of the Czechs and the reasons with which they support them? People who have no heart for them, who do not consider them as equals, and consequently do not treat them in a fatherly way, but rather follow the example of that Egyptian taskmaster (Exodus 1, 8-13), and bleed them white? Who can have lived in our country, or even traveled for a short time, without having to acknowledge the truth of what I am saying?[45]

Religious minorities, finally, were treated any way but fairly. If this was already pronounced in the case of the Protestants, who were taxed to support the Catholic clergy, it was much more so for the Jews. Joseph II may have knocked down the walls surrounding the ghettoes, nevertheless the toxic anti-Semitism of centuries remained:

> Israel's scattered descendants not only enjoy no reputation among us, but are instead in almost every country treated with contempt and oppressed and abused in the most unbearable ways. Nor is it just the rabble of Christianity that

[45] *Erbauungsreden*, Vol. II (Prague, 1850), p. 163; below p. 103.

> allows itself to abuse them in this way: even persons who may lay claim to education, and whom in every other respect one must accord both insight and uprightness, give vent to the most bizarre ideas on this subject. How often one hears them without a second thought and in all seriousness claim that the Jews, every last one of them, are deceitful and evil! How contemptuously they are treated, the individual members of this nation, for no other reason than that they are Jews![46]

Bolzano was a severe critic of the faults of his age, but he was in no way inclined simply to bemoan the miserable condition of humanity. Rather, from the first his goal was to help bring about a better age. He firmly believed in the possibility, though not indeed the universal reality, of human progress. In the homily to his students on Epiphany (Jan. 6) 1811, he calls it a "great truth" that "inspired and wholly imbued the holy bard" (Isaiah), on whose text his sermon was based: "Arise, shine, for thy light is come, and the glory of the Lord is risen upon thee. . . ."[47] He thought it "highly probable" that from the early days humanity had much advanced in three important respects: wisdom (that is, science in aid of virtue and happiness), virtue and true happiness. Although he admits that "for several decades in our own beloved fatherland, instead of becoming wiser, better, and happier we have been moving backward in all these respects," he nevertheless believes that the overall tendency of humankind is towards improvement:

> In humanity as a whole there is visible over the centuries, and going to infinity, a progress not limited to certain arts and sciences, but a progress extending to the three most important matters: true practical wisdom, virtue and happiness.[48]

---

[46]*Erbauungsreden*, Vol. III (Prague/Vienna, 1851), p. 200; below, p. 124.

[47]Homily to students preached on Epiphany, January 6, 1811 in *Erbauungsreden 1813* ed. Jaromir Loužil, **BBGA** Series I, Vol. 2, (Stuttgart: Frommann-Holzboog, 1985), pp. 67-77, p. 69. The text for the sermon is Isaiah 60, 1-6.

[48]*Erbauungsreden* I, p. 79.

This view has been expressed many times. Most noted is Dr. Martin Luther King's "The arch of the moral universe is long, but it bends toward justice."[49]

The blame for many of the ills of his age surely lay with the rulers of Bohemia, yet Bolzano was under no illusions that simply knocking down the existing order would produce a better state. Although disobedience and even revolution are sometimes justifiable, it by no means follows that stupid or futile acts of rebellion are. Not only was revolution unlikely to succeed at that time and place, there was also nothing ready to replace the existing order:

> Do not expect me, my friends, to sound a signal for rebellion, to counsel you to overturn the present state of affairs the sooner the better. No: I have nothing of the sort in mind; on the contrary, I explicitly want to warn you against this error. What would it help if we broke down the present form of things before better ones have been thought of, or, if thought of, before they are generally accepted? Could the new arrangements, drawn up in haste, could they be better than the former ones? If they are not would we not make our fellow citizens more and more weary of all attempts at change?[50]

Things could change for the better, Bolzano taught, but not in that way. Rather, the first step had to be to educate the people. Matthew 9, 35-38 is the text for Bolzano's homily just referred to on April 20, the 2nd Sunday after Easter 1817. Jesus, observing the misery of a harassed and helpless people, says: "The harvest is truly plenteous, but the labourers are few." He then admonishes his disciples to go out and *teach*. Bolzano takes literally the description of the people as physically, not spiritually distressed, and Jesus' admonition as an appeal to *education*, "teaching, instruction, the dissemination of better concepts."

> I am of the opinion that we cannot do better than to follow the example of Jesus and even now seek the true cause of

---

[49] In *The Essential Writings and Speeches of Martin Luther King, Jr.* (New York: Harper Collins, 1986), p. 245.

[50] *Erbauungsreden* I, p. 113; below, p. 64.

> all calamities that afflict us in ignorance and prejudice or, in other words, in a lack of enlightenment. I do not want this interpreted as saying that I believe in no other cause of our suffering. I want to say only that it is most advisable to accustom ourselves as well as others to tracing everything back to this one cause.... Certainly it is necessary for us, in order to focus our efforts, to grasp from a single vantage point the sum of everything we have to strive for in order to introduce a better age; for he who aims at many goals at the same time usually attains none of them.[51]

He then gives several reasons for this policy: he denies the establishment view that it is enlightenment itself that lies at the root of the current suffering, rejecting at the same time a naïve trust in progress. Many a new opinion was acquired at the cost of giving up an older and wiser one, like the belief in immortality, or in the just compensation of virtue and the punishment of villainy.

Two Sundays later Bolzano lectured his students on the importance of teaching *logic*. People must be taught to think, not merely to accept truths that are impressed upon their memory rather than their understanding:

> Let us awaken them first of all from the stupor of their thoughtlessness, let us encourage them to take note of everything and to maintain their intellect for as long as possible in a condition of distinct consciousness. Let us instruct them to form clear concepts, to connect them into judgments, and from these to deduce conclusions. Let us train them to maintain their attention even during long series of deductions and teach them, with many examples, how to distinguish claims that are similar to each other and finally how to uncover and expose fallacies no matter how deceptive.... Once we have achieved this we have won everything. Persons whose understanding is properly developed are not only in a position correctly to grasp and rationally to apply truths they have heard from others but—and this is infinitely more valuable—they have the key with which

[51] *Erbauungsreden*, I, p. 4; below, p. 47 ff.

> they themselves can unlock the realm of truth. . . . It is thus: Truth will have salutary effects only once people's power of judgment is properly developed; then the blessings of enlightenment will spread upon the earth.[52]

At the present low level of knowledge one cannot with assurance say what is most needed, nor can one clearly convey one's insights to others. It follows that the most urgent task is to improve education and remedy error and ignorance. Further, one should think of evil in the world as usually the effect of folly rather than malice, since the alternative is to sink into a misanthropic funk. And, finally, it is actually within our power to improve education. Hence:

> We expect deliverance for our aggrieved fatherland as for the whole earth only in the battle against error and the spreading of deeper insight.[53]

Elsewhere, he describes enlightenment as:

> . . . the appropriate development of the power of judgment in each individual citizen, as well as a certain stock of useful knowledge, especially healthy, correct concepts of everything having to do with virtue and happiness, attention directed towards the common best, direction and instruction in correctly judging whether something is beneficial or harmful for the common best; knowledge of the rights a people possess, and the ability to tell the difference between wise and unwise measures; eagerness to follow the former and loathing and opposition directed towards the adoption of the latter. Enlightenment so understood, my friends, can have nothing but the most blessed consequences, and it is certain that there is no better way to promote the happiness and well-being of a people than by promoting such enlightenment to the full extent of one's powers.[54]

---

[52]"Von den Fehlern, die man bei Ausbreitung der Aufklärung zu begehen pflegt, und von der Art, ihnen auszuweichen," *Erbauungsreden*, I, p. 34.

[53]*Erbauungsreden*, I, p. 9; below, p. 52.

[54]*Erbauungsreden*, I, p. 62; below, p. 92.

Even if Bolzano counseled his students, some of them wealthy, in disaster relief, common savings banks, charitable giving and distribution of food, it must surprise that at so calamitous a period much time would be allotted to logic, an abstract science far removed from the needs of the hour. But we must note that Bolzano's conception of logic, stated more than once in the *Theory of Science*, makes it a necessary prerequisite for rational and humane social policy. In his view, conditions in Bohemia were in such disastrous disarray that only the most radical reconstruction of society could ameliorate the needs of the vast underclass. To create the new institutions, however, requires both an educated civil service and an educated populace. This is why Bolzano maintains that the first step towards reform must be education, enlightenment. He was confident that the education of the masses could in the end be set in motion through the action of only a few who are united in the will to improve things. The title of his sermon on the 27th Sunday after Pentecost of 1816 is "The united effort of only a few men can at all times create a better shape of things."[55] Scripture, experience and reason concur in assuring us of this truth.[56] Indeed, the very audience of his sermons were to be the vanguard of this change in his own land. For Bolzano had before him the future elite of Bohemia, her administrators and clergy, the propertied class. They would not only be able gradually to transform Bohemia's institutions from within as they took up positions of power, but would also serve as an example for the entire people. He expected that more enlightened thought, "better concepts", once adopted by them, would in time spread into the lowest huts. But he also knew that his unorthodox views would arouse much hostility in Vienna.[57]

Enlightenment was not only a necessary condition for social improvement, Bolzano taught, but in many cases, perhaps in all, even sufficient. Many an unjust institution is kept alive only through widespread ignorance, for instance, through the mistaken belief that the happiness

---

[55] *Erbauungsreden* I, p. 73 ff.

[56] *Ibid.*, p. 75.

[57] On Jan. 6 and 7, 1816 He preached a pair of sermons on "Right conduct toward the enemies of enlightenment" (*Erbauungsreden* IV No 28/29, p. 196–209; below pp. 71–84), where he bemoans the promotion of ignorance as a necessary condition for exploitation, and notes "woefully that all countries of Europe are now declining" (209), that is, promote ignorance, oppose enlightenment.

of certain people is infinitely more important than that of others, or that certain classes of people are intrinsically unworthy. Once the ignorance is dispelled, the institutions that owe their existence to it gradually lose their purchase on society. If sufficient numbers of people recognise that something is unjust, it can no longer stand. This is why rebellion is always the last resort:

> There is an easier, a more gentle means for overturning burdensome laws and for resisting the oppression of tyrannical authorities. And this means is—the general conviction of their injustice. When all citizens see that something is unjust, when the entire people speak with one voice on the matter, who, my friends, will want to try forcing it upon them? The villain may well command—no one obeys. Whom can he punish? He must punish everyone; and no one will lend him an arm to provide weapons for his fury and so to give power to his words. Thus he has to withdraw his commands, and resign himself to giving better ones. And all this happens without a single drop of blood being spilled.[58]

One can see the concrete application of Bolzano's programme in a series of three exhortations on the subject of Czech-German relations read in 1816 (below, pp. 96–122). The first step, as always, is to understand the way things stand. The relations between the two groups, he notes, are anything but amicable. Mutual hatred and suspicion prevails, the German-speaking inhabitants, who are generally better educated, look down upon the Czechs, finding them ignorant, wanting to have nothing to do with them, perhaps even believing them to be genetically inferior. The Czechs, understandably if not justifiably, repay this hatred and contempt in kind. As a rule, Germans do not learn Czech, even when their jobs put them in positions of authority over Czech-speaking people. Indeed, they look with such contempt upon the Czechs that they are actually ashamed of speaking their language. There is little inclination for members of the two groups to work together. On the contrary,

---

[58] "Von den Pflichten gegen ungerechte Obrigkeiten," *Erbauungsreden* I, p. 64; below, p. 94.

the mutual hostility makes it far more likely that they will work against each other:

> [Here] everyone looks out only for himself. He cares not if his neighbour is oppressed, perhaps he even rejoices in it. There a government can quickly place the entire people under the most humiliating yoke of slavery, it can abuse them however it likes, simply by being cunning enough never to take on everyone at the same time, but rather to play one side off against the other. Such a people will never manage to deliberate together, still less to achieve unity and work together—for each side is deaf to the suggestions of the other. Here too the government can make many unfair demands, for it finds no resistance at all, not even objections or reproaches. And if a few isolated voices are heard complaining, they are never taken seriously, because those complaining do not speak to one another, and thus are never in agreement. With such a people, all too conscious of its powerlessness, fear prevails, and as a consequence sycophancy and the most degrading servility take root. Out of mutual hatred, each side tries to belittle the other and to make it look dangerous to the authorities. [...] is it any wonder that the rulers of such a people learn to despise them, and finally to believe that they in fact deserve no better than they get?[59]

At the time Bolzano delivered these sermons, as surprising as it may sound, there was genuine and well-founded fear for the future of the Czech language. The major source of worry was the impact of Joseph the Second's programme of germanization, which had been introduced along with the other reforms of 1780. Joseph had decreed that beginning at the high school level the language of education in the Habsburg domains was to be German, the intention being to establish a single working language throughout the Empire. In Bolzano's time, German was dominant in the cities of Bohemia. It was the language of government, scholarship, and much business. One effect of Joseph's decree was to assimilate educated Czechs into the German-speaking culture of

[59] *Erbauungsreden*, Vol. II, p. 170; below, p. 112.

the Empire. It was left to a variety of private individuals, working on their own and with minimal support, to keep the Czech language and culture alive. The great Bohemian linguist and philologist Josef Dobrovský wrote in 1792 that there seemed to be little hope of success for these efforts, praiseworthy as they might be:

> I cannot predict, and only the future can tell if all of these recent efforts, undertakings and involvement of a few patriotic Bohemians will result in raising the Bohemian language to a greater level of perfection than it had attained during the golden age under the emperors Maximilian [1493-1519] and Rudolph II [1552-1612]. It is no longer likely because of the decree that has been in force since 1780 and excludes any Bohemian ignorant of the German language from the Latin schools.[60]

German was the mark of an educated man, and there was an undeniable stigma attached to speaking Czech. As late as 1823, František Palacký noted upon coming to Prague for the first time that "whoever wore a decent coat did not venture so readily to speak Czech in public places."[61] It was only over the course of decades that Czech "reawakeners" managed to establish a modern literary culture. And not until after Bolzano's death, in 1849, when agricultural reforms led to a massive influx of Czech-speaking people into the cities of Bohemia, did Czech begin to make a serious bid for equality with German in Prague.

Thus in 1816, when Bolzano addressed his audience (in German[62]), the future of the Czech language was believed to be anything but assured. Bolzano showed himself nevertheless to be a passionate advocate for Czech language and culture. His students must first understand their situation, know why it is that there are many languages on earth, why in particular Bohemia has two main language groups. They must understand that there is no reason to suppose Czechs to be intellectually

---

[60]Josef Dobrovský, *Geschichte der böhmischen Sprache und Literatur* (1792; new ed. Halle: Max Niemeyer Verlag, 1955), p. 126.

[61]J. F. Zacek, *Palacký: The Historian as Scholar and Nationalist* (The Hague: Mouton, 1970), p. 18.

[62]Bolzano, who had a wide-ranging knowledge of languages (Hebrew, Greek, Latin, German, French, English, among others), also spoke Czech.

inferior when there is a far more obvious explanation for their relative backwardness, namely the fact that they have been kept in a miserable condition and denied access to education for centuries, indeed ever since Prague, under the emperors just mentioned, was the cultural and spiritual centre of central Europe. Bolzano did not mention that educated Czechs, by virtue of being educated in German, were often counted among the Germans.

Once they have well understood the folly of linguistic prejudice, and indeed of their own attitudes, they must do what they can to bring about a better situation. To begin with, all the educated people in the country should learn Czech as well as German, especially if, as was often the case, their posts would put them into contact with people who spoke only Czech. Instead of feeling ashamed to speak Czech, they should feel shame for ever having felt such emotions. The Czech language should be revered, the written language gradually improved. Efforts should be made to produce more literary works in Czech, as well as to translate works from one language into the other. Those in charge of schools should take it upon themselves to ensure that both languages are taught to their students. A point should be made of frequently and publicly interacting and cooperating with people of the other language group. Finally, all, Czechs and Germans alike, should strive to attain the excellence of character that speaks louder than words, and in the face of which unfounded prejudice is rendered mute.

Bolzano's encouragement of the Czechs was not forgotten. We return to an event mentioned earlier (p. 1), the meeting of leading Czechs to honour Bolzano's memory. Durdik's speech also included the following remarks:

> He was a German but also a whole man ... and this raised him above all racial hatred. In the best sense of that word he was a citizen of the world .... From this vantage point he looked upon the relation between the two nationalities of Bohemia much like Goethe. From this vantage point this man demanded justice for the Bohemians as long as 70 years ago with such energy that even now we cannot express it more eloquently. For justice lay at the core of everything he strove for in his political life... Introduce institutions as you like, but always act with justice [applause].

> He clearly stated his view about the two peoples that inhabit our country, seeking the ideal solution for them in harmony and concord... Even today there are occasional individuals who seek to prove that our language and our brains are not suitable for higher learning. It is a bitter burden, but we shall not be provoked Therefore in this year 1881 it is all the more desirable that Bolzano's opinions about the relation between the two peoples of Bohemia be restored....[63]

On the Right of Clergy...

The essay "On the Right of the Clergy to obtain their Livelihood from Persons not of their Faith" was published in the Stuttgart journal *Freimüthige Blätter* in 1838. Because of his continuing problems with the authorities, Bolzano could not claim to be the author. In the foreground of the essay is the question whether the Anglican clergy in Ireland have a right to draw their living from taxes levied on Irish Catholics. With his usual thoroughness, Bolzano decides to deal with this particular case by addressing the general question adverted to in the title of the essay. In so doing, however, he was in part talking about Ireland in order to talk about Bohemia. For the condition of Irish Catholics was, as he pointed out, in many ways similar to that of Bohemian Protestants, as well as to that of Jews throughout Europe. There are also obvious connections to inherited titles and revenues.

As Bolzano makes clear in the essay, this is not a question of merely academic interest. For the taxation regime was in effect taking the last crumbs of food out of the hands of starving people. This was already ghastly enough, but even more so coming at the hands of people who profess Christian principles:

> I should not have to point out that the injustice is the more offensive the larger the emoluments that this clergy obtains, and the poorer the people from whom they are extorted. If

[63]"Bolzano-Feier" in Politik 287, Prague, 16.10. 1881, p. 5 f. Cited from Wolfgang Künne, "Geschichte der philosophischen Bolzano-Rezeption," in *Bernard Bolzano und die Politik*, ed. Helmut Rumpler, Vienna, Cologne, Graz 2000. Vol 61 of *Studien zur Politik und Verwaltung*, p. 319 f.

> only part of what eyewitnesses tell us is true, if those tithes are extorted from people who live in the most abject misery, of whom hundreds die every year of starvation, while the Protestant bishops luxuriously consume the extorted abundance in another country, O! then I ask if the cruelties for which a Christian clergy is responsible cannot be compared to the most atrocious horrors that history reports of any heathen priestly regime, not excepting the horrors of human sacrifice? For these human sacrifices take the lives of only a few who, if they were adults, could console themselves in dying that they were expiating angry gods through their death. The priest sacrificed them not for his own pleasure, but from a sense of duty, however erroneous, believing that he had to obey the strict will of the deity. For my part I find the deed that you, preachers of the gospel, here commit more abhorrent.[64]

Even if an action is morally abhorrent, however, someone may nevertheless be within his rights in performing it. The Anglican clergy in Ireland certainly had the law on their side, for instance. But is that enough to determine the rightness of their action? This is the question Bolzano finds himself obliged to decide.

The first part of "On the Right of Clergy" sets out Bolzano's ideas on the concept of rights. Although a utilitarian, he did not share Bentham's view of rights as nonsense, whether on stilts or not. Nor could he accept Hobbes' view—still popular in his day—according to which all rights derive from the sovereign who, for his part, cannot act unjustly. Instead, Bolzano sketches a utilitarian approach to rights which underpins the right to civil disobedience and even rebellion in certain cases.

According to his account, rights are coextensive with certain duties. These duties, however, do not attach to the possessor of a right, but rather to everyone else. When someone has a right to do something, namely, everyone else has a duty not to prevent him by force from doing it. When someone betrays the intention of acting unjustly (i.e. in a way that is not right), then, it would seem, others have a duty to prevent him from so acting, by force if necessary. Yet Bolzano is not satisfied with

---

[64] "On the Right of Clergy," §22; below, p. 157.

this attempted definition, because there are certainly cases where others do not have the force required to prevent injustice. And, he maintains, appealing to a commonly held principle, we cannot have a duty to do something impossible. Thus he adds the following refinement:

> It is undeniable, rather, that by the rightfulness or unrightfulness of our actions we think of certain properties that belong to their inner essence and are entirely detached from the circumstance whether at this time there is more or less power of resistance. It follows that a certain ingredient is missing from the explanation we gave above, and it is not difficult to guess what that is. For we say that an action is unrightful if its inner character is such that there would be a duty forcibly to oppose it if a sufficiently large number of people were present and willing to protect the victims of such a deed. By contrast, we call an action rightful if it may not be forcibly prevented even if a sufficient number of persons were present and willing to do this.[65]

He then proceeds to show that, based upon this definition of rights, there is a right of civil disobedience, and even a right of violent resistance to authority in certain cases—but one always governed by pragmatic considerations, such as the likelihood of success. Not surprisingly, he finds that the Anglican clergy in Ireland, as well as all other clergymen in similar circumstances, do not have a right to draw their living from taxes levied on those who do not share their faith.

Ethical Theory

The principle of utility was the cornerstone of Bolzano's practical philosophy, of his ethics, political philosophy, and also of his philosophy of religion. The text "Natural Morality," which contains the most complete treatment of ethics in Bolzano's writings, sets out a moral theory founded on this principle. "Natural Morality" is part of the *Treatise of the Science of Religion*, a work that was compiled by some of Bolzano's students, and published anonymously with very little input from him. Thus what we have here are his lecture notes on ethical theory, rather

[65]"On the Right of Clergy," §1; below, p. 145.

than a polished treatise. This being said, his lectures were clearly of a high calibre, and from these notes we get a good, clear presentation of his ethical thought.

We should note to begin with that, although Bolzano's ethics may fairly be called utilitarian, it is not a consequentialist moral theory. For obligations, in his view, attach to acts of will rather than to what these acts accomplish. That intention and outcome can be quite different is illustrated by an example Bolzano discusses. Suppose that one man resolves to kill another. Attempting to carry out his resolution, he stabs the other man, but instead of killing him, only wounds him. The wound, unexpectedly, turns out to be a blessing for the other man, since it lances a boil that otherwise would have killed him. The consequences, clearly, are good in this case, but we have no hesitation in condemning the intention behind them. Similarly, well-intentioned actions can produce bad consequences through no fault of the agent. We are tempted to make the consequences decisive of the goodness of actions in Bolzano's view, because in most cases there is a reliable connection between what is intended and what is accomplished. Examples such as the one just discussed, however, suggest that our moral judgments apply to the intentions rather than to their consequences.

This important point of detail resolved, Bolzano proceeds to argue that the highest moral law commands us to will the actions that, in our best judgment, most promote the happiness of the whole.

Several points are worth discussing in greater detail here. We note, first, that happiness is, as with Bentham and Mill, measured by pleasure and the absence of pain. This is not to say, however, that Bolzano was a hedonist in the vulgar sense of the term. For in the Malthusian world he lived in, pleasures were rare, suffering the norm. Worse still, the most common pleasures of the time were of the sort that tended to bring more pain in their wake. Second, the scope of Bolzano's moral law is not restricted to humans, but extends to all sentient beings, a point that he uses to contest Kant's "end-in-itself" formulation of the categorical imperative. For if the highest moral law only governed those of our acts that have impact on other rational beings, any impacts on non-rational animals would be morally indifferent in and of themselves. This, Bolzano remarks, seems obviously false. Third, when we say that a rational agent should will acts that in his best judgment most promote the well-being of the whole, we need further precision on just what is meant by "most promote". Does this mean "produce the greatest increase in the average well-being"? It does not, as Bolzano makes clear elsewhere in his treatise:

> In connection with the highest moral law, [...] we tend to say that the virtue and happiness of the whole comes out ahead when one or another part does, while the remaining parts lose nothing.[66]

From this, it seems clear that Bolzano has a criterion of Pareto-optimality in mind: the action is best which most increases the average benefit without reducing the well being of any individual. Should no action be available that meets this test, as he made clear in a letter to Franz Exner, we then fall back upon a straight average:

> I say that an action promotes the well being of the whole and also conforms to the objective moral law even if it raises the well being of a single or a few creatures without upsetting the well being of the rest, or if whatever the latter lose, taken together, is not as much as what the former gain; and if no other act is possible through which the happiness of the whole would gain more.[67]

Having presented his highest moral law, Bolzano defends it against a variety of objections, and gives lengthy consideration to differing views on the content of the law. He maintains that an act-utilitarian theory like his can in some cases (e.g. the duty to tell the truth under oath) be used to ground exceptionless rules. He also sketches an approach to the ethics of virtue compatible with his system. Finally, as mentioned above, in the text "On the Right of Clergy..." he shows how a certain conception of rights can be constructed within a utilitarian ethics.

---

[66]*Lehrbuch der Religionswissenschaft* (Sulzbach, 1834), I, §145.3 (**BBGA** I.6/2, p. 149-150.

[67]Bolzano to Exner, 17 June 1834, in E. Winter ed. *Der Briefwechsel B. Bolzano's mit F. Exner* (Prague, 1935), p. 55.

On the Best State

On the Best State, Bolzano's major treatise on politics, dates from around 1830. Although a great many of the ideas presented in this work had already been publicly discussed in his exhortations, Bolzano was reluctant to publish it. Admittedly, when it was written, Bolzano could not have published even the most innocuous of texts under his own name in Austria, still less a work like *On the Best State* that could only be viewed as incendiary by the authorities. Yet even in 1848, when the chance presented itself, Bolzano resisted others' attempts to print and distribute the work. An old-school intellectual, he believed that not every truth is suitable for every person. He feared, particularly in the tumult of 1848, that his work would be misunderstood, perhaps adopted as a guide for immediately restructuring society. This was the last thing he had in mind. He wrote the book, he tells us:

> . . . not in the expectation, and not even with the wish, that in a country where his thought became known people would immediately tear down its existing constitution and erect a new structure according to his plan. Such an undertaking he must rather declare in advance to be rash, and because of the disastrous consequences which it might entail, to be criminal.[68]

As he pointed out on many occasions, his intention was to contribute to the improvement of the political culture of Bohemia and, if possible, of the world in general. With public discussion forbidden, this was difficult, to say the least, and Bolzano was by no means confident that he had found all the solutions to political problems. His work was meant to be discussed, criticized, corrected, not clumsily and rashly implemented. This is why he "published" it in the traditional Bohemian way—by circulating manuscript copies among trustworthy people.

The goal of the work is to sketch the institutions that would be found in the best states, that is, in states that maximize the well-being of their members. Well aware of the disastrous course of Bohemian history, Bolzano held that a viable state must above all else be able to defend itself from hostile powers both within and without. Accordingly, all able-

[68] *On the Best State*, Foreword (**BBGA** IIA14, p. 21); below, p. 237.

bodied citizens are to be trained for military service, so that in cases of emergency, almost the entire population can be put under arms. Internal rebellion is to be avoided in his view especially by taking care to avoid dangerous inequalities of power and wealth.

In Bolzano's view, the best state will be a republic with no head of state. There shall be no distinctions of rank, especially not hereditary ones. Government offices shall be, as a rule, elective. Proposed legislation will be decided by direct democracy, subject to certain constraints. First, only those who have an interest in the outcome of a certain question and the knowledge required to judge it shall be granted a vote on it. Second, these plebiscites shall be subject to the oversight of a Council of Elders, namely:

> . . . a number of persons of both sexes who are elected to this honour by majority vote every three years in the municipalities in which they live. [. . .] Only persons who are more than, roughly, sixty should be chosen for this office, and among them only those who have through repeated tests given evidence of their uprightness as well as their insight, and who have shown themselves to be resistant to strong temptations. [. . .] People under sixty years of age who have given extraordinary proofs of their uprightness and extensive knowledge can be chosen for this office, but in no case should anyone under forty be chosen.[69]

The strict requirements for membership in this council are supposed to invest it with the moral authority required to overturn popular, but harmful, measures without risking rebellion. A further constraint requires near unanimity among the members of the Council in order to veto legislation approved by popular vote or to pass legislation on its own.

Bolzano's belief that such a Council of Elders was necessary was founded upon his assumption that the shockingly low average life expectancy of his time was a permanent feature of the human condition, so that young people, who lack experience and tend to be rash in their judgments, would always make up the majority in a state.

---

[69] *On the Best State*, Chapter 2; below, p. 253.

The basic equality of all citizens shall be recognised by the state, and women shall of course have the vote as well as the right to serve in government. There shall be no state religion and, except in extreme cases, the state shall take no steps to regulate religious practices or beliefs. Nor shall a person's religion prevent him from exercising any profession, inside or outside of government. A system of redistributive taxation will keep inequalities of wealth within reasonable limits, and 100% inheritance taxes will insure that wealth is not a function of one's parentage. A dense network of social services is also contemplated to ensure equal opportunity for the citizens of the best state, including universal public schooling, socialized health care, insurance schemes for the ill, infirm, and elderly, and the state's absorption of the costs of raising children.

Bolzano's conception of the best state is at its weakest, perhaps, when it comes to the organization of the economy. Not only housing and banking, but also the transportation, distribution, and selling of goods, is to be looked after by the state. Ideally, in his opinion, the state should decide upon the distribution of property among the citizens: who owns what, under what terms, who may give away property, who may lend it and so on. These suggestions strike us as both monstrously impractical and counterproductive. Why, we might wonder, does Bolzano not leave more room for private enterprise in his best states? Two answers suggest themselves: first, given the extreme poverty of Bohemia, there simply was not a whole lot of property to go around, and Bolzano might have thought, even reasonably, that this small amount could be usefully allocated in the way he describes.[70] Second, unlike the majority of nineteenth-century socialist thinkers, he was writing before, rather than after, the rise of industrial capitalism in his country. His economic institutions are conceived not so much as a countervailing response to the faults of private enterprise as to assume some of its beneficial functions, notably to distribute risk, pool resources, and increase production.

[70]We should also note in this context that Bolzano does not think the suggested measures should be pursued at any cost, as the following remarks indicate: "The state's authorized intervention in determining the citizens' property and its exchange is limited only by the concern that it should not go so far as to aggravate the citizens who find the attainment of their self-interested goals hampered by this intervention to a point where the peace and order of the whole is endangered." (*On the Best State*, Chapter 10 (**BBGA** IIA14, p. 87); below, p. 300).

When he suggested that the state provide insurance for a variety of risks, this was because the existing private schemes were far too small and fragile to be effective. It was with the image of peasants spending an entire day to bring a few eggs to market before his eyes that he wrote that the state should take over all transportation of goods—the free market, clearly, was not providing what was needed, and no other alternative seemed to be available.

Bolzano's concerns in economics and social policy were not the same as ours. We want to maintain a level of prosperity amazing by his standards, attain full employment, security in sickness and old age. During the great depression of the 1930s the focus was on the vast rate of unemployment. In Austria in the early 1800s the issues were famine, war, housing, roads to move food, the location of the trades. In these conditions it was not surprising to make governments ultimately responsible for the coordination of all economic activity. The so-called "Cameralist" economic theory spelled out the responsibilities of the state: to provide roads and secure food production, distribute the "commercial commodity trades" to the several regions, with textiles going to upper and lower Austria, Bohemia and Silesia, iron and steel to other parts of the country, fashion industries to Vienna, etc. where they were in fact located until the twentieth century.[71] At the time, Austria had not yet experienced the industrial revolution, and its condition made laissez faire economic policies very implausible. It is not surprising that in the treatise *On the Best State*[72] Bolzano prescribes state control over economic activities, and also an unusual extent of control over personal lives.

This was not as unreasonable as much current economic theory would suggest. Alternatives then discussed, especially in Britain, were the theories of Malthus and Ricardo. While Bolzano, in his essay on the best state, attends with serious concern to measures of disaster relief and redistribution of resources, he thought horrid the Malthusian and Ricardian doctrines of famine as population control. Malthus had argued that relief of the poor "relieves them for a short time, but leaves them afterwards in a condition worse than before," while Ricardo thought that funds raised for destitute people were wastefully diverted from "other

[71]Karl Pribram, *A History of Economic Reasoning*, (Baltimore: Johns Hopkins Press, 1983), pp. 89–93.

[72]Below, pp. 235–356.

productive employment."[73] This philosophy, with its astonishing conception of "natural prices" consequent upon deficiencies or surpluses dispensed by a merciful providence for inscrutable reasons informed British policies during the Irish potato famine of 1846-50. The destitute condition of the Irish peasantry is reflected in Bolzano's essay "On the Right of the Clergy to obtain their Livelihood from Persons not of their Faith" of 1838.[74] He was aware of the fact that the trebling of the Irish population in the preceding century allowed absentee landlords to lower wages and increase rents by reducing more and more the size of the allotments. This led to successive famines culminating in 1846-50. Irish poverty was notorious. In the year after Bolzano's essay, Gustave de Beaumont wrote:

> In all countries, more or less, paupers may be discovered; but an entire nation of paupers is what was never seen until it was shown in Ireland. To explain the social condition of such a country, it would be only necessary to recount its miseries and its sufferings; the history of the poor is the history of Ireland.[75]

Malthusian and Ricardian economics could be no more acceptable to Bohemia than to Ireland.

Bolzano's *Best State* is a worthwhile and interesting contribution to the political literature of the early nineteenth century, and deserves to be read alongside the other utopian works of the period. If for nothing else, it is valuable for providing a measure of what an intelligent, educated man thought the horizon of possibility was at the time. For even in the best states contemplated by Bolzano, there is not the slightest hint of the affluent society. There will indeed be adequate food, shelter, health care, and education for all. There shall be freedom, justice, the rule of

---

[73]T. Malthus, Evidence before the Select committee on Emigration from the United Kingdom, 1827. Parliamentary Papers 1827, Volume V. Public Records Office, London. D. Ricardo, Letter to Malthus. *Works and Correspondence* VII, ed. Piero Sraffa, Cambridge 1951. Cited from Patrick Webb, "Emergency Relief during Europe's Famine of 1817." Discussion paper No. 14 of the Gerald J. and Dorothy R. Friedman School of Nutrition Science, 2002.

[74]Below, pp. 143–167.

[75]Gustave de Beaumont, *Ireland: Social, Political, and Religious.* Ed. by W. C. Taylor (London: R. Bentley, 1839).

law, and a general, effective commitment to equality. Yet it is assumed, apparently as something that requires no justification, that many of the appalling aspects of the time are permanent features of human existence: low life expectancy, high levels of child mortality, and an especially hard life for women, who bear large numbers of children only to see most of them die.

Like most political philosophers, Bolzano is often better at detailing existing evils than in prescribing remedies. Yet there are a number of solid and practical suggestions, many of them well ahead of their time. Remarkable, too, is the modesty with which he puts forth his views, not only admitting the possibility that he might be mistaken, but even imploring others to correct his opinions when called for. Finally, his unwavering commitment to non-violent means of reform, to persuasion and measured civil disobedience, is admirable and—who knows—perhaps even practical. We leave the last word here to Vaclav Havel:

> In the 1980s, a certain Czech philosopher who lived in California published a series of articles in which he subjected the "anti-political politics" of Charter 77 . . . to crushing criticism. Trapped in his own Marxist fallacies, he believed that as a scholar he had scientifically comprehended the entire history of the world. He saw it as a history of violent revolutions and vicious power struggles. The idea that the world might actually be changed by the force of truth, the power of a truthful word, the strength of a free spirit, conscience, and responsibility—with no guns, no lust for power, no political wheeling and dealing—was quite beyond the horizon of his understanding. . . .
>
> Because his doctrine had taught him that the bourgeoisie would never voluntarily surrender its leading role, and that it must be swept into the dustbin of history through armed revolution, this philosopher assumed that there was no other way to sweep away the communist government either. Yet it turned out to be possible. Moreover, it turned out to be the only way to do it. Not only that, but it was the only way that made sense, since violence, as we know, breeds more violence. . . .

Communism was overthrown by life, by thought, by human dignity. Our recent history has confirmed that the Czech-Californian professor was wrong. Likewise, those who claim that politics is chiefly the manipulation of power and public opinion, and that morality has no place in it, are just as wrong.[76]

[76] *Summer Meditations* (New York: Knopf, 1992), pp. 5-6.

A note on the translations

All of the exhortations translated in this volume were published in a collection put together by Bolzano's friends shortly after his death: *Dr. Bernard Bolzano's Erbauungsreden an die akademische Jugend*, 4 Volumes (Prague and Vienna: 1849-1852). For this volume we have translated Vol. I, nos. 1-3, 7, Vol. 2, nos. 17-19, Vol. 3, no. 26, and Vol. 4, nos. 25, 28, and 29. The exhortations on the two peoples of Bohemia and the treatment of the Jews were also published, with commentary, in a recent separate edition: E. Morscher and O. Neumaier eds., *Bolzanos Kampf gegen Nationalismus und Rassismus* (Sankt Augustin: Academia Verlag, 1996). The essay "On the Right of clergy..." appeared anonymously in the journal *Freimüthige Blätter* **11**(1838) 291-331 and **12** (1838) 5-47. The *Treatise of the Science of Religion*, from which the selections on ethics and philosophy of religion have been taken, was originally published anonymously in 1834: *Lehrbuch der Religionswissenschaft: ein Abdruck der Vorlesungshefte eines ehemaligen Religionslehrers an einer katholischen Universität* (Sulzbach, 1834). A new edition by J. Loužil has been published in the *Bernard Bolzano Gesamtausgabe* (Stuttgart-Bad Cannstatt: Frommann-Holzboog, 1969–) Series I, Vols. 6-8. *On the Best State* was first published by the Bohemian Royal Society of Sciences in 1932: A. Kowalewski ed., *Von dem besten Staate*, Vol. 3 of *Spisy Bernarda Bolzana* (Prague, 1932). A new edition by J. Loužil appears in the Bolzano *Gesamtausgabe*, Series IIA, Volume 14. In the case of the *Treatise of the Science of Religion* and *On the Best State*, we have consulted both the original and the critical editions while making our translations, and would like to thank Frommann-Holzboog Verlag for their kind permission to work from the critical edition.

Part I

Selected Exhortations

Want of Enlightenment (Ignorance and Error) Must be Seen as the True Cause of the Evils that Beset our Fatherland

Read on the second Sunday after Easter, 1817 [April 20]

Introduction

A considerable number of you, my friends, have used the holidays we recently celebrated to visit your home regions. You have now returned, and are able to tell the rest of us about the situation of our fellow-citizens in all parts of the country. We would indeed be culpable if the condition of our countrymen were a matter of such indifference to us that we did not use this opportunity to find out about it. But how sorrowful are the responses to our queries we hear on all sides! Almost everyone we ask tells us that as great as want and misery where they live were half a year ago when they left to come to this capital city, things have now become still worse and more *critical*. Thus runs, I say, the usual answer. From some regions, however, we receive quite different, horrifying reports. If they are in fact true, they make it impossible to understand how people who have been reduced to such a state of desperation have not had recourse to the law of necessity, and taken with force what they need and what is indeed there for the taking. If the extent of the want was already great enough at the beginning of this unhappy year to oblige me to point out every means our little group might use to help one another, what must I not do now, and what must I not undertake, however unlikely success may be? The talks I gave at the beginning of the year, even if they did not accomplish as much as my heart wished, nevertheless, thanks to the grace of God, were by no means fruitless. For although I am not foolish enough to ascribe to my own encouragement all the good some of you have done in pursuit of more than one praiseworthy goal, I may well bear some indirect responsibility. However that may be, my friends, I rejoice and will rejoice in what you do, even if I had nothing to do with it. We ourselves indeed received some help, but how coldhearted it would be in a time when our fatherland is so severely distressed to think only of ourselves and not of how the so much more unfortunate situation of our fellow citizens might be improved. To be sure, it must be expected in advance that we can only do some rather insignificant things in this respect; but no matter how small our contribution may be, we should make it. And even if we should discover that we are unable to do even the slightest thing, we will have the *merit* of having been *ready and willing* to act, and not having shrunk from the work of reflecting on what might be done. In fact, such reflection will bear its greatest fruits in the future, my friends; for however great the need may now be in our land, and however it may pass, it is certainly not *the last* that this unhappy land will have to suffer. In the future, too, in the years when you yourselves will occupy the higher stations for which you are now preparing yourselves, our people will still have to withstand a great many and—though I hope I am mistaken in saying this—still *harder* blows of fate. Then it will depend on you, on your wisdom and your behavior (be it dutiful or disloyal), whether these unfortunate blows bring us to our senses so that we may redeem ourselves, or else make us sink into a deathly stupor and perish. Only if you now learn how to think rationally about the true *causes* of the misery in our fatherland and the most effective *means* for preventing it, can we expect the former. Nothing therefore prevents me from instructing you on this subject as much as I am able. Today I would like to speak about *what should be seen as the true cause of the evils that beset our fatherland.* The consequences that follow from the answer will form the subjects of our next two gatherings. I have often remarked that the condition in which our fatherland now finds itself is quite similar to that of the fatherland of Jesus in his time. We can therefore be all the more secure in learning how to judge our own situation by considering how he thought about his.

Matthew 9, 35 – 10, 1

> So Jesus went round all the towns and villages teaching in their synagogues, announcing the good news of the Kingdom, and curing every kind of ailment and disease. The sight of the people moved him to pity: they were like sheep without a shepherd, harassed and helpless; and he said to his disciples, "The crop is heavy, but labourers are scarce: you must therefore beg the owner to send labourers to harvest the crop." Then he called his twelve disciples and gave

them authority to cast out unclean spirits and to cure every kind of ailment and disease.

Discussion

It is remarkable (and deserves to be taken to heart especially by anyone who would gladly make a significant contribution to the benefit of mankind), that Jesus of Nazareth, the most gifted of all men, he who certainly saw best what had to be done to further the common good, never himself wanted to do anything but—*teach.* The offers that the people frequently made to him are sufficient proof that, had he wanted to, he could easily have amassed worldly power and then brought about through violence the greatest changes in the civil constitution of his own country as well as in neighboring states. Yet he refused to do that—but not because he believed that the existing institutions were well-constituted. On the contrary, no one saw more clearly than He that they deserved to be abolished—why else would today's text say that He found the people harassed and helpless, and that they seemed to him like a herd of sheep without a shepherd? But as moved as he was by the sad condition of these people, the only thing that He did was *travel* from one city to another and *teach* in the synagogues, announcing that the kingdom of heaven would soon arrive. Clearly he looked upon the healing of the sick, which he performed on these occasions, as a secondary thing, really only important insofar as it showed that his teachings truly came from God. And it was just this that He told his disciples to do, when He said: pray therefore the Lord of the harvest to send laborers into his harvest. For it is well known that by laborers he meant nothing other than teachers. We can therefore say that in order to relieve the misery that He found on earth at that time, Jesus applied no other means, and commanded his disciples to employ no other means than *teaching, instruction, the spreading of better ideas.* And it follows immediately from this that he must have found the cause of all these evils in nothing other than *ignorance* and *prejudice*. May not the same be said in our time?

I am of the opinion that we cannot do better than to follow the example of Jesus and even now seek the true cause of all calamities that afflict us in ignorance and prejudice or, in other words, in a *lack of enlightenment.* I do not want this interpreted as saying that I believe in no other cause of our suffering. I want to say only that it is most *advisable* to accustom ourselves as well as others to *tracing everything back to this one cause.* I will now present, in their proper order, the reasons I have for thinking this.

1. Certainly it is necessary for us, in order to focus our efforts, to grasp from a *single vantage point* the sum of everything we have to strive for in order to introduce a better age; for he who aims at many goals at the same time usually attains none of them. His attention is too divided, his powers scattered and thereby weakened, so that he cannot accomplish anything properly. So if we speak to people of a great many things as the grounds of the evils that oppress us in the present age, the result is either that they do not retain anything, or else have no idea where to begin. For this reason it is necessary for us to present only a single point of view from which all our efforts must proceed—if not forever, at least for *the present.* And herein lies the *first* reason why I demand that we look upon the lack of enlightenment as the single cause of all the sufferings that oppress us. At first glance many will perhaps feel inclined to claim the exact opposite, and to look for the causes of a significant portion of our present sufferings precisely in the enlightenment that has already been spread among us. For, they ask, were not our forefathers, although perhaps they knew less than we do, and were less enlightened, were they not better off all the same? Thus it is not the absence of enlightenment, but rather its presence, that makes us unhappy. Here we have a simple misunderstanding, my friends. Certainly our age knows many things of which previous ages were ignorant—but from this it follows by no means that we think more wisely and correctly than our forebears. Just as when a dark room is suddenly pierced by a bright ray of sunshine we often find ourselves blinded by the force of the light to which we are unaccustomed, and for a while cannot distinguish things well, in fact seeing less than we could before; so too is it with our judgments, when a new ray of truth illuminates the edifice of our previous knowledge. We indeed now see many new things—but many old things that we formerly knew, although only obscurely, become invisible, and it can often happen that the truths we reject in such moments are more important than the new one we have added to our store of knowledge. In that case, it would be wrong to say that we have become wiser and more enlightened. Rather, we should say that we have become more foolish. And

this is indeed the case with those of our enlightened contemporaries that people complain about. It is these men who are blinded by the light of a truth that they happen to have learned; and so comes it that we hear them boast that they do not believe that virtue is rewarded and vice punished, nor in the immortality of the soul, or indeed in any difference between right and wrong. Who would wish to call such men wiser than our forebears simply because the latter were ignorant of some things the knowledge of which has only brought harm to the former? Thus if we connect the proper concept with the word *enlightenment*, we can indeed reproach our age with a want of enlightenment, and say that it is precisely this lack that is responsible for a multitude of the most oppressive evils. For are there not in fact a great many pernicious errors that our contemporaries have either learned from their forebears or else added on their own? Even the few errors that I just mentioned, of which the falsely enlightened among our contemporaries boast, are not these alone sufficient to sink us in a sea of misery? Indeed, if we had the misfortune of seeing these errors more widespread among us, would we not see all the ties that bind people to each other dissolved, would we not annihilate each other, and grind each other down? How many evils are engendered, to mention only a couple of other examples, by the foolish opinions that wealth brings honour, that extravagance has merit? How much evil is brought forth by the prejudice that all the differences between the citizens of one and the same state, the disparity in hereditary rights, the layers upon layers of ranks, the inequalities in wealth, are absolutely necessary, so that society would necessarily perish were even the slightest thing changed! But what need have I to make clear through individual examples what you must already know as a fundamental principle of Christianity, namely, that we must seek the ground of all our suffering in *folly and vice*? And it is also certain that vice is always itself grounded in folly. One can only be vicious through error; sin only arises from blindness. Thus we must look upon errors, follies, as the *ultimate cause* from which all evil springs. Myriad painful sufferings that now torment us would immediately disappear as soon as we became wiser, and myriad others would thereby be prevented because those who inflict them upon us would no longer dare to do so. Am I not therefore right in wishing that *for the time being* we should all work together to dispel ignorance and error?

2. But there is a *second* reason that leads me to recommend this course. For it is difficult for us to judge what we most need precisely because we now find ourselves at such a low level of education. Even more difficult is it to make clear to *others* the views we think correct. But the most certain thing we can claim and prove to others is that we should strive to dispel ignorance and error. For precisely this reason, it is the most advisable course to limit oneself only to this. For admittedly, the thing that we want to point to as the source of all our sufferings, the thing we want to establish as the target against which all the strivings of our fellow men should be aimed, we must not only ourselves recognize with the most complete certainty as what we describe it as to others, we must also have reason to hope we shall succeed in convincing them that it is so. Without having engendered in them a truly solid and unshakeable conviction we cannot expect that they shall work with zeal against a monster that we alone find frightening and devastating. But as true as it may be that there are several monsters that plague mankind, I maintain that it is easiest to get everyone to *agree* that ignorance and error is *one of them*. For one can only maintain that liberation from ignorance and error, or enlightenment, might be harmful because of the misunderstanding I have just described. This misunderstanding disappears at once, however, as soon as it is pointed out that we are not speaking of the sort of enlightenment in which one error is removed only to be replaced by ten *other, more harmful ones*. Whoever keeps this condition in mind will be happy to agree with us that people should look upon ignorance and error as their greatest enemy. One does not meet with the same unanimity in other matters. One will claim that some institution is the source of all the ills of human society, while another counters that it is necessary, that although it has its faults and is open to many abuses, it nevertheless prevents still greater evils, and should never be abandoned. A third, perhaps the most modest, believes that the measure is indeed counterproductive, but that it is difficult to decide whether it could be abolished under the prevailing conditions without causing problems, when so many other things connected with it would remain. This last remark is only too true. For the most diverse things of this world stand in multifarious *connections* and exercise a mutual influence that is often hidden from our eyes. It is not so easy, therefore, to determine how a single thing should be arranged, even when all the others

are in the right place. How to begin, then, when many things are wayward and in the wrong place, maintained there by irrational institutions? Certainly, if we wish to be careful, we must leave it to a later, wiser age than our own to solve the difficult question how all that now appears inappropriate to us must be changed. For the present, it is enough that we work to *bring forth* this wiser age, that we strive towards the banning of error and ignorance, which are the greatest hindrances to all good.

3. *Thirdly*, this way of going about things will be the most suitable, not least because in finding the cause of all evil in human folly we are in less danger of falling into a dark misanthropy, than would be the case if we attributed these ills to *wickedness*. We neither can nor should blame God or the inalterable laws of nature for the evils that beset us here below. For should we do so, we shall believe evil to be inevitable, and thus expend no effort in opposing it. Neither God, therefore, nor nature, is to be looked upon as the true cause of these evils, but *only ourselves*, and indeed something in ourselves that can be *changed* in a variety of ways. Thus there remain only two options: evil either comes from the human mind or the human heart, is either the effect of our folly or our malice. Who does not feel that the latter, however true it may be in some cases, would be a most dispiriting thought? Who does not feel that all the sufferings we have to endure would become doubly painful and oppressive if we believed that human malice was their sole cause? Who does not see that this way of looking at things would gradually drive us into the darkest misanthropy? No—even if it be true that a considerable part of the sufferings on this earth are produced through malice, and endure through malice alone, we would still have to try to conceal this, and to convince ourselves that folly alone, mere stupidity, had produced all this and maintains it. For the sake of our peace of mind, and to avoid falling into a misanthropic funk, we must believe that ignorance and error alone are the ultimate cause of all evil.

4. But yet another reason speaks in favor of this way of looking at things, and it is by far the most important. To struggle against ignorance and error is what is *most in our power*, and is something that everyone can take a hand in. As I have said before, the unhappy state in which mankind as a whole and our fatherland in particular find themselves may indeed have several causes, but what good will it do to enumerate them,

when we can do nothing to remove them, when this lies only within the power of others who do not hear our voices and who, even should they hear them, might not do as we suggest? And how can we even begin, when in many places one is not even allowed frankly to discuss these causes? Thank heavens, to complain of ignorance and error, my friends, has not yet become an offense. One has certainly sought to hinder us in our attempts to control ignorance and error and to spread an appropriate enlightenment—but no one has yet made it impossible, and no one ever can. On the contrary, every citizen, not only those who occupy higher stations but also those of lower status, not only those who are wise and enlightened, but also the uneducated—everyone, I say, who is of good will, can contribute something to the enlightenment in our country. If he cannot do so by issuing commands, then through advice and requests; if he cannot do it by teaching, he can take instruction, or support and help others who are eager to learn. If he cannot fight against every harmful prejudice, perhaps because he is still in the grip of some of them, he can at least clearly show us the absurdity of others he has already seen. And since all truths stand in a friendly union, and because once one of them is found, others usually follow, a single wise word from someone can often awake several in us, and lead us to proceed even further in the knowledge of beneficial truths than he. So let us strive for this one thing, and this one thing alone, my friends, at least *for now*, for the spreading of beneficial truths, and the controlling of ignorance and error. We shall look upon this and this alone as the most pressing need of our time; we shall seek the *source of all evils* we suffer in *ignorance* and *error* alone, and teach others to do the same. We expect deliverance for our aggrieved fatherland as for the whole earth only in *the battle against error and the spreading of deeper insight.* And precisely for this reason shall we pray to our Father in heaven for nothing more fervently than for Him to help with this work by sending able laborers into His vineyard. Amen

Several Very Important Consequences and Duties that Follow from the Conviction that Want of Enlightenment (Ignorance and Error) is the Cause of the Evils that Beset our Fatherland

Read on the third Sunday after Easter, 1817 [April 27]

Matthew 15, 1-20

> Then Jesus was approached by a group of Pharisees and lawyers from Jerusalem, with the question: "Why do your disciples break the ancient tradition? They do not wash their hands before meals." He answered them: "And what of you? Why do you break God's commandment in the interest of your tradition? For God said 'Honour your father and mother,' and 'The man who curses his father or mother must suffer death.' But you say, 'If a man says to his father or mother, "Anything of mine which might have been used for your benefit is set apart for God," then he must not honour his father or his mother.' You have made God's law null and void out of respect for your tradition. What hypocrisy! Isaiah was right when he prophesied about you: 'This people pays me lip-service, but their heart is far from me; their worship of me is in vain, for they teach as doctrines the commandments of men.'" He called the crowd and said to them, "Listen to me, and understand this: a man is not defiled by what goes into his mouth, but by what comes out of it." Then his disciples came to him and said, "Do you know that the Pharisees have taken great offence at what you have been saying?" His answer was: "Any plant that is not of my heavenly Father's planting will be rooted up. Leave them alone; they are blind guides, and if one blind man guides another they will both fall into the ditch." Then Peter said, "Tell us what that parable means." Jesus answered, "Are you still as dull as the rest? Do you not see that whatever goes in by the mouth passes into the stomach and so is discharged into the drain? But what comes out

> of the mouth has its origins in the heart; and that is what defiles a man. Wicked thoughts, murder, adultery, fornication, theft, perjury, slander—these all proceed from the heart; and these are the things that defile a man; but to eat without first washing his hands, that cannot defile him."

Introduction

Throughout his entire life, my friends, Jesus of Nazareth fought against the power of error and ignorance with the same courage we admire in the evangelical text I have just read. He did not cease to use all his strength to spread beneficial truths until his vicious enemies had nailed him on the cross. But before they had succeeded in doing this, he had wisely taken care to ensure that the enlightenment of our species he had begun would not come to an end after his death. He had founded a unique society that would never die, and in which there would never be a lack of individuals ready to fight against error as long as it was found on earth. For doing this he merits more than any other man to be recognized as the light of the world and therefore also the saviour of the whole world. His first followers and disciples already declared him to be such, even though they were not yet able to see with their own eyes the great success his undertakings were to have—they could only faithfully hope for it. How much more fitting for us, who have before us the fruits his work has produced over a period of eighteen hundred years—how much more fitting it is for us to praise him as the light and the saviour of the whole world! Yet our praise is the least that he demands from us—for he wants us to imitate him. If someone is to have a right to bear the name He bore, he must fight against error and ignorance, and strive to spread truth with the same courage Jesus showed. That this is so cannot be denied; and whoever hinders the spread of truth and loves darkness, let him not hope at the end of his life to find mercy from Him who expressly declared at the end of his life that He had only come into the world in order to bear witness to the truth [John 18, 37]. This he declared when asked to set out clearly and in all frankness what the ultimate goal of all his activities was. And could he have answered otherwise? Is it not the case that according to Jesus' own views all evil found here on earth is the effect of two causes, namely, our *folly* and our *sins*? But are not our sins also grounded in our folly? When asked to mention only a single goal of all his striving, did he not therefore have to reply that it was the destruction of error, or, what amounts to the same, the expansion of the realm of truth? In our most recent gathering, I believe I showed that we will still do well in our days to adhere to this opinion of our Lord, that today too it is best to look for the *ultimate cause* of all the evils that oppress us in ignorance and error. If this is indeed the case, there follow several important *consequences* and *duties* for everyone. Those which are of greatest import to *us* I must set out in greater detail. This is precisely what I have chosen to do in today's gathering and, God willing, also on our next one. It will bring joy when you learn through these lectures that in fact you are already in a position to do *more than a little* to promote a beneficial enlightenment in our country. But you shall be able to do *far more* in later years, provided you make wise use of the present to prepare yourselves.

Discussion

1. Since it is true that we have incurred all evils whose increase we experience at certain times, and indeed all evils found on earth, only through ignorance and error, it obviously follows that every man has the *duty to strive with all his might to become more enlightened*, that is, to develop his understanding more and more, to separate himself from every false opinion, and to make the stock of his knowledge ever more complete by collecting new concepts, provided they are not useless. This, I say, is an unavoidable duty and obligation of every man—for what point is there in bemoaning our misery if we do nothing to remove its cause? Perhaps we wish for God to help us, giving us better times by remaking the order of nature, while we ourselves do nothing to develop our understanding so that we can improve matters? Perhaps we want God continually and forcibly to intervene in the natural course of events to prevent the evil consequences of our folly? No—although this is possible through His omnipotence, His wisdom would forbid it. Rather, He would use the mass of our sufferings, growing ever greater, and of which we ourselves

are the cause, to bring us to our senses, and would try to awaken in us the resolve to remove the true cause of all this misery. O may we do this just once! May we for once find our misery great enough so that we heed God's call to become wiser that he conveys through it. God calls each of us; each of us can, by becoming more enlightened, reduce the number of follies upon this earth and so reduce the sum of human sufferings. But if everyone can do this, if this duty lies upon all people no matter who they may be and under what conditions they live, it is doubly pressing upon you, my friends—in the first place, because in your present circumstances you have so many opportunities to gather wisdom, and further, because you intend to occupy the most important positions in the country in a few years. As much cause as you may have to complain of the obstacles that stand in the way of your education, you must admit that in comparison with other people you are in a very favorable position. For are not the great majority of people, those, namely, who either cultivate the soil or practice some industry, far worse off in this respect than you? How neglected most of them are even in the earliest years of their lives! How miserable the schools to which they are sent for a few short years! How soon are they snatched away from even this meagre instruction and chained to nothing but physical labor! Where can someone be found who will educate them further even on the days where, through a beneficial institution of Christianity, their labour is stilled? Where can they lay hands upon a book that offers the mind even the most basic nourishment? Among you, my friends, things are quite different, especially for those of you who are not obliged to devote most of your time to the instruction of others. How many opportunities to exercise correct thinking and to gather useful knowledge are offered by each of the sciences taught in this institution. And can even the poorest among you say that the lectures of his professors are the only means he has to cultivate his mind? Cannot everyone who earnestly wants to procure still other means for instructing himself on matters only touched upon during the professors' lectures? And if this is within your power, my friends, just consider how much you will have to answer for if you neglect to do it. Consider the stations that you will shortly occupy. It will be these stations that will give you an advantage over the vast majority of your fellow citizens, stations in which your behaviour shall be carefully observed and judged by many thousands. Whatever flaws may be found in you shall be eagerly seized upon by people as an excuse—they shall imitate your misdeeds, and indeed expand upon them. How pernicious shall be your influence on your contemporaries, then, if you are incapable of providing an example of wisdom, if time after time you betray ignorance of truths that you should know, if you yourself are still ensnared by prejudices that you should be working to eradicate. You will occupy stations that raise you to the position of teachers and leaders of your brothers. But in our texts, it is written: when the blind lead the blind, both shall fall in the ditch. How true this is! How illuminating! And yet, my friends, it is easier to imagine that one blind man leading another might not get into harm's way, than that a people could avoid its downfall when even its teachers and leaders are saddled with the most pernicious prejudices and have no insight. For the ditches into which a traveler may fall are few, but the *snares* that have been set for the well-being of a people, snares that would rob it of its rights and freedom and sink it into unhappiness, are without number. And if those who have been charged with teaching and ruling are not constantly on the lookout for every approaching danger so as to warn against it, then there is only one possible outcome: such an abandoned people must be in the saddest condition, its misery must grow with each passing day. How sadly has this been confirmed by the experience of the *most recent* times! Are not the countries in Europe whose leaders lag behind the others in learning the most unfortunate? Are they not the ones where the people are treated most severely? Do not their oppressors find it necessary to give only the appearance of legality to even the most shameful schemes they devise? Do they think it necessary even merely *to promise* that in the future the people shall be governed not according to their whim, but instead according to principles of justice? No—they do not have enough respect for such a people, since they know only too well that its teachers and leaders, broken by the recognition of their own ignorance, will never venture to advise them how to help themselves. My heart bleeds, my friends, when I am forced to state such a bitter truth. But may it bear fruit! May you finally become aware of your own worth! May you in noble indignation over the fact that they thus despise us form the firm resolution to save the honour of your people! May you today resolve to become wiser and therefore also more *awe-inspiring* leaders of your people than those alive now!

2. Whoever has resolved upon this, and resolved upon it for the right reasons, has no need for me to tell him *never to look upon the wisdom of other people as a threat to himself.* But as we are nevertheless often guilty of this failing, please allow me to say a few words about it. For if any point of view is apt to make the absurdity of such ways of thinking utterly obvious, it is the one from which we set out. If all misery on earth is merely the fruit of folly and ignorance, then, on the contrary, every discovery someone makes, every useful piece of knowledge he acquires, every step he takes that makes him wiser, is a benefit for all, something that helps not only himself, but all others besides. How stupid it would be to begrudge him this rare gift, provided by heaven for the benefit of all! How foolish to be upset because we are no longer the only wise men, that others begin to feel the need for wisdom, the need to cultivate their minds, that they indeed make such rapid progress that they bid fair soon to overtake us! It may well be that in so doing they will diminish our fame; but can this in any way alter the judgment that this is an auspicious development, and that we have reason to rejoice in it along with the rest of humanity? Perhaps our own fame is dearer to us than the good of mankind? But why should we desire fame? Why do we think it an advantage to have attracted the attention of the crowd and to have had it form a favourable opinion of us? If we are reasonable we know that our fame is beneficial only insofar as it puts us in a position to be useful to others. Hence if we are ignored simply because we are no longer the only ones who can serve the world with our wisdom, if we are ignored because others come along who are in a position to serve the world better and more vigorously, then there is no harm in the loss of our fame. Rather, it is right and fair that we are ignored when others attract more attention. We must think like the noble precursor of our Lord, who remarked that the latter's fame was beginning to darken his own. Thus it is fitting, he said, that He must increase but I must decrease [John 3, 30]. Let us suppress therefore all feelings of envy that would arise in us when we notice that others join us in striving for wisdom, and with great success! Let us shrink as from one of the most grievous sins against humanity before the thought of hindering others on the path of wisdom, or diverting them from it! Let us instead encourage everyone who enters into that path to tread it indefatigably. Let us look upon him as our friend, as someone working to accomplish the very things we

seek to. No single man will reach this goal, which can only be attained through the cooperation of all.

3. And for precisely this reason, my friends, it is most necessary that we do not keep the truth we just learned to ourselves. Rather we must seek to *spread it among the people* as far as lies within our power. Look upon this as the third duty that insight into this truth lays upon us. If we ourselves have seen that only ignorance and error are the ultimate causes of all evil, this is hardly the sort of truth one can keep quiet about, or which need not be spread—on the contrary, if it holds of any truth that we should (as our saviour said) proclaim it from the rooftops [Matthew 10, 27], it is this one. Every living thing must know that it is not God, the holy and all-merciful who is answerable for our tribulations, but only ourselves. Every living thing must know that evil does not stem from necessary and inalterable laws, but rather from something that is accidental, and can certainly be avoided, and some day certainly will be avoided. Every living thing should know this, be comforted by this news, and, with the prospect of a better future be able to bear the brutal present. Every living thing should hear that it is the irrationality, and nothing but the irrationality of humanity that has given rise to all evil, and not look for the cause of suffering in something that would be far worse, namely in mankind's evil nature. Every living thing should know where the cause of all evil lies, so that all may watch out for it and unite to fight against it. As much as we can, my friends, as far as our voices carry, we must seek to proclaim that ignorance is the mother of all ills.

But how shall we bring other men to believe us? How shall we convince them that what we say is true? From abstract arguments and general reasons we may expect little success. Mankind is best persuaded by means of examples, and especially by examples drawn from the sphere of their own experience. Thus we must point to experience, we must use it to demonstrate clearly that, with individuals as with entire *peoples*, the true cause of unhappiness always lies in some folly, sometimes the folly of those who are unhappy, sometimes of others. We must show through many examples how often people fall into the greatest misfortune simply because they were ignorant, because they lacked the most important knowledge about nature, because they knew nothing of the workings of their bodies, nor of the conditions required to maintain them in health, because they knew neither the laws nor the customs of the country, neither the duties nor the rights of a citizen, nor what to do if someone were to infringe upon their exercise of the latter. We must show from history as well as from the *most recent* experiences that the well-being of peoples is in direct proportion to their education and insight; that they become more happy the more care is taken to look after their instruction and education, and the wiser and more knowledgeable they become. And that, on the contrary, they sink ever deeper the more ignorance and superstition gain the upper hand. I cannot believe, my friends, that such proofs, drawn from experience itself, could leave anyone unconvinced.

4. Should we succeed, however, in making clear to others where the actual cause of their suffering lies, we may expect that they will resolve to remove it, especially if we provide an example for them by leading the way, if the zeal with which we strive for the knowledge of truth is not only great but noticeable and readily visible to other men. To lend this character to your zeal for learning is the *final duty* I will point out to you today. You must, my friends, *allow your inner striving after wisdom and rational thirst for knowledge to become visible to others so that it may encourage them.* For admittedly it is all too true that people find it far easier to resolve to become educated than actually to see it through. There are so many difficulties that get in the way of the development of our minds and the acquisition of useful knowledge, especially at the beginning: the path that leads to the temple of wisdom is at first so steep and unpleasant that most people grow tired after just a few steps, are deterred, and turn around. How important it is therefore to encourage those who are just starting on this path, to let them know that they are not alone on it, that others have struggled and still struggle against the same obstacles, but never allow themselves to become discouraged! How necessary it is for all who see themselves as travelers on this path and are not too distant from one another to join together so that, combining their powers, they make it easier for each other to overcome the obstacles in their way. How necessary this is when one wants to makes discoveries in fields of learning, especially in the field that is the most difficult of all, the only one in which right up to the present time human understanding has so far not been able to take a single sure step. How much more successful we would have been even in this science if people had not disdained to work together in a harmonious community. But people refuse to *work together* with others, because they themselves

want the fame of having discovered everything. They keep their distance from others because they do not wish the limits of their knowledge to be noticed; they are ashamed to ask someone else's opinion, because they want to appear not as one seeking the truth, but rather as one who is already in full possession of it. What folly, and doubly inexcusable in men who lay so many claims to culture and wisdom!

The true friend of wisdom is always very modest; he recognises and admits the limits of his knowledge before everyone; he hides from no one the fact that there are many things he does not know, and many others that he only assumes as probable. His thirst for knowledge is always apparent, everywhere he seeks to learn, and feels no shame in asking questions of even the most ignorant of men, provided only that he can hope to learn something from him. Precisely through this behaviour he gives the most evident proof that acquiring useful knowledge is more important to him than anything else; precisely through his behaviour he makes others desire to emulate him; precisely through this behaviour he encourages even the weakest, giving them the courage to become wiser. This behaviour, my friends, must also be yours, and not only at this time of your life, when it would indeed be unpardonable were you ashamed of learning and asking questions, but also for the rest of your lives. You must never abandon the thirst for knowledge and modesty; you must always want to learn, in order to make others want to do the same. In so doing you will not only promote the wisdom of others, but also perfect your own. For only he who never ceases to learn completes his education. For he learns as much as people here on earth can learn, and in this way is completely prepared when called by the Father to a better place in order to learn more. Amen.

On Ways and Means of Already Bringing about a Better Shape of Things at the Present Time

Read on the last Sunday after Pentecost in the year 1816 [November 3]

Luke 19, 41-44

> When he came in sight of the city, he wept over it and said, "If only you had known, on this great day, the way that leads to peace! But no; it is hidden from your sight. For a time will come upon you, when your enemies will set up siege-works against you; they will encircle you and hem you in at every point; they will bring you to the ground, you and your children within your walls, and not leave you one stone standing on another, because you did not recognise God's moment when it came."

Introduction

The passage from the gospel that I have just read, my friends, appears to contradict something that we recently attempted to convince ourselves was true. You will recall that recently we claimed that even in situations where the morals of a people have atrociously declined, it must still be possible, if not for any individual, at least for a group of several noble-minded citizens to bring this decline to a halt, and to bring about a rejuvenated better shape of things. And it was from the mouth of Jesus himself that we received this unequivocal assurance. But today he seems to tell us exactly the opposite. For does he not give us to understand in the text I have read that it would be impossible even for him, for Jesus himself, to save his beloved fatherland from the ruin towards which it was racing? O! unfortunate people! Thus we hear him call out, weeping over Jerusalem, O! You unfortunate people, if only you had known, or now wanted to know, what would save you! Just as if he had said: it would have been possible for me to lead you to salvation, if only you had acknowledged it! But—he continued—it was hidden from your sight, and so I can do nothing to save you. Or, in his own words, the day will come when your enemies surround you with walls, when they will encircle you and hem you in. And all of this, he said finally, you will suffer only because you did not recognise the day of your salvation. What do we hear here, my friends? Was Jesus, the all powerful, incapable of becoming the saviour of his fatherland? If he could not do it, then how could we? But if he could do it, and only chose not to because his fellow citizens had not met a condition that he had arbitrarily laid down, must we not lose faith in him? Heaven forbid that we should lose faith in our Lord! Let us instead take a closer look at the situation, and all will become clear. Admittedly, it would have been easy for our Lord to improve somewhat the condition of the Jewish state had he so wished, and thus to prolong its existence for centuries to come. But was not our Lord the emissary of God, sent to deal with the entire human race? Was he not supposed to become the teacher of a new religion that would rapidly spread among all peoples of the earth? Must he not have put this highest goal of his existence ahead of every other? So certainly he might have become the saviour of his nation, if only they, or at least their leaders, had, following his example, become wiser and better, and had themselves seen to the improvement of their institutions. Only this did not happen, indeed it was precisely the leaders who shamefully plotted to kill him, to kill the greatest benefactor of mankind! Must not this state, which had marked itself with such a shameful crime, suffer a punishment that would serve as a deterrent to others, namely, a rapid and ignominious ruin? Must not all the peoples of the earth see how God punishes those who called out sinfully: His blood be on us and our children [Matthew 27, 25]? Thus we cannot reasonably object to the example of our Lord, when he allowed his own state to fall to ruin. We can, however, perceive with astonishment how much power God has given to man—since it is clear that through his teaching Jesus became the saviour of hundreds of other states. And so the truth that we confirmed in our recent meeting through the combined testimony of the gospels, experience and reason still stands. Indeed it is to be hoped that it will become all the more evident once we have, in accordance with the principle we recently learned, treated in detail *the ways and means by which this better shape of things, whose creation is certainly possible, can be brought about among us, and indeed through you, my friends.* I feel the importance of the task I have set myself today, and beseech the spirit of the Lord for His heavenly illumination, without which no beneficial thoughts ever enter into our souls.

Discussion

Do not expect me, my friends, to incite you to rebellion, or to advise you violently to overturn the existing order, the sooner the better. No, this is so far from my mind that I must instead explicitly warn you against this mistake. For what good would be served by tearing down the present order when a better one has not yet been thought up, or, if a better one had been devised, had not been generally acknowledged? Could such new arrangements, instituted in a great hurry, could they turn out to be better than the previous ones? And if this were not the case, would our fellow citizens not be ever more opposed to any attempt to change things? So I know only three means, my friends, by which you can work to improve the present constitution of things. The first is the spreading of better concepts than those people now possess; the second: showing a rational and noble way of life through your own example; and the third: use of the influence that you may legitimately gain over the government and our country's legislation. These three means, as insignificant as they may seem, will be, if properly applied, fully sufficient to make our *entire* country more fortunate than any has ever been, and indeed, through our influence on neighboring peoples, gradually improve their lot as well.

1. Let us begin, my friends, by using the power we have to spread *better concepts* than the world has *hitherto* possessed. I do not mean better concepts of things that are of no importance, but rather concerning those things where error causes harm, and knowledge is beneficial. There are two kinds of such concepts: either they have to do with things that individuals need to know to advance their own happiness, or else they have to do with things that every citizen should know in order to contribute his own share to introducing a more appropriate constitution than we have at present.

a) For the same reasons I cited in our first gathering of the season in support of a similar claim, it is always possible for someone to bring something to light in either of these two areas, and indeed something well worth knowing, provided only that he does not shrink from taking thought. And if this is always possible, how much easier must it be in our country at the present time, where ignorance and error have, unfortunately, got the upper hand? Certainly, it requires little reflection to notice a number of greatly important truths of which people nevertheless remain entirely ignorant. Just to give proof of this through a couple of examples, how little the inhabitants of this country know what to do to maintain their bodies in good health! I shall pass over in silence that even the scholars among us, apart from those who belong to the medical profession, know little more about the constitution of the human body and the conditions required for its well-being than is apparent at first sight or through ordinary experience. Let us enter the workroom of the tradesman or the huts of the rustics: what offenses shall we not immediately find against the most fundamental rules of good health! Let us stay a little longer: what kinds of perverse principles shall come to our ears, what unsuitable behaviour shall we not see when illness begins to appear!

How much more deficient are the concepts of our contemporaries about the true nature of human happiness! Do not people believe in palaces as well as in huts that only wealth, only the possession of a great many earthly goods can make one truly happy? One can count on one's fingers the rare people who not only acknowledge with their mouths but actually inwardly believe and give proof throughout their lives of the conviction that riches not only are no means for assuring *happiness*, but are indeed not even compatible with true virtue, since wealth, no matter how legitimately it may be said to have been acquired, is and will remain theft, theft from one's fellow citizens sanctified by law, since it is only by greatly impoverishing others that you have been able to amass wealth yourself. Who knows the truth that it is not through pleasure, and least of all raw sensual pleasure, that a man attains the highest level of happiness possible here on earth, that instead self-respect, useful activity and an unclouded prospect of the future are the three requirements of a pleasant life? O, my friends, should it really be so difficult to make these and many other similar truths generally known? Shall not you yourselves be in a position to fill the entire country with these blessed truths within ten years, if today you resolve to make it happen? Just reflect on how many means you have at your disposal. Already most of you have been entrusted with the instruction, the first cultivation and education of tender, budding youth, often those of the most high-ranking families and houses. What an excellent opportunity you have here to implant the seeds of fruitful truths at this age, which is so receptive to all learning. And how many years will it be before your sphere of influence is no longer limited to a single family, but rather extends across the whole country, when you shall stand as men to whom civil society has freely entrusted its most important goods to administer at your own discretion, guided only by your conscience, men who are trusted and respected simply on account of their professions, and from whose mouths one expects to hear words of wisdom and instruction. In spirit, I travel the entire land, and look: in all of its regions I find you teaching, having earned the right to do so; I come across pulpits to which the faithful flock in order to hear from you what the word of God is, and how it should be understood; I see confessionals where you sit in order to give counsel and instruction to troubled sinners; I visit small schools, where I am overjoyed to hear how kindly your voice encourages the youth to set aside the prejudices of old and to venture to strive for perfection. But should I not expect still more, my friends, should I not expect that some among you have the gifts from God that will enable you to work as authors? Just think what can be accomplished when your words are addressed not just to one community but to the whole of humanity. Just think what you can do if these fortunate people, making the most of their God-given talents, make it the main aim of their lives to discover through silent reflection truths that bring relief to mankind, and having found them, to present them in the most illuminating, convincing and irrefutable way; when, finally, having repeatedly examined and improved what they have written at their desks, they entrust it to the press, through which it is multiplied to be read and re-read by hundreds of thousands and taken up with conviction? O! it is certain my friends that when you have so many ways—writings, oral instruction, public teaching and private conversation—to bear witness to the truth, human reason shall not be able to resist it! The power of truth is so great that it deeply moves, even if only one single man distinctly presents the reasons supporting it. But if many people unite to act as its champions, when they communicate the truth with firmness and courage, then whoever hears them cannot help but accept what he hears from all sides and with such decisive reasons.

b) Greater difficulty attaches, I must admit, to the spreading of truths that apply immediately to the improvement of existing arrangements. But even here far more can be done than many, out of fear, believe to be possible. If only a reasonable freedom of the press can be achieved, then one can freely look into the defects of the existing constitution of things, suggestions for a better constitution can be put forward and judged without reservations, and it will not be long before general agreement is reached on the basic lines of a constitution that, although indeed not faultless, is nevertheless complete enough to contain in itself the seeds of all further improvements. We and all of mankind shall be fortunate indeed once a better constitution has been thought up and generally acknowledged as such. For once it is generally acknowledged that a certain modification of existing institutions is undeniably for the better, then those who believe they will lose thereby shall resist in vain. For it is rightly said that the will of the entire people is the will of God himself. They must yield, and without the sword, with no loss of blood, there shall arise a state which, the first of its kind, shall never perish, since it is built upon the principles of Christianity.

2. In order to bring about this glorious success, my friends, we must do more than speak and write in favour of it; we must also act. And be not astonished when I tell you that the *most important thing* that we can contribute in order to bring about a better shape of things is *to serve as an example of a rational and noble way of life.* For it is in fact so. It should be looked upon as a settled truth that the happiness, if not of individuals, at least of entire peoples and states, stands in the closest relation to their moral perfection. It is therefore impossible to bring any people, still less the whole human race, to a higher degree of happiness if we have not first raised it to a higher level of virtue. But this can never succeed if we, who wish to lead the others, do not truly lead by our example. For our age does not so much need a description of virtuous behaviour as a proof that such virtue is humanly possible. Our age is not so unenlightened that it knows nothing of the duties people have. Rather, it doubts whether it is possible for someone to follow the precepts of virtue so fully and completely. And how can this pernicious doubt be

definitively set aside except by factual proof—when not just one man, but many in all regions of the country have realized this model of virtue? Not one man, I say, for, as I recently reminded you, this unbelieving age declares the virtue of a single individual to be an illusion. But when many provide the same example at the same time, when there are so many upright people that everywhere in the country everyone knows some of them not just through vague reports but from personally seeing and observing them, the doubt gradually dissolves. Then people begin to recognise with shame that it is indeed possible to live according to the principles teachers of virtue pronounce from their pulpits. Then some will venture, if somewhat bashfully, to do so themselves. Then they find that, contrary to their suspicions, it is not nearly as difficult as they had imagined. Then the approval of one's own conscience for a good deed is something known by one's own experience—this new and unaccustomed pleasure encourages repetition, and frequent repetition gives rise to skill, so that in the end it becomes a habit and indeed a need. Thus one arrives finally at the blessed conviction that the laws of virtue are only the laws of nature, that virtuous behaviour is for human beings the most natural and also the easiest. All of this you yourselves can bring about, my friends, if you dedicate yourselves to virtue, if you present to your fatherland the example in your own person of a rational and noble way of life it has lacked for so long. And should you fail to do this, then, to be frank, you may declaim and write as much as you like, but will accomplish nothing. The blessings of heaven will not support your attempts, for heaven, knowing the defects of your virtue, will lend you no help. Sooner or later it will become apparent to all that your way of life does not reflect your teaching. Your deeds will tear down what your words have built up. But I haven't said enough, for they shall destroy far more. And the higher the opinion that others had formed of you, the more complete their trust in your learning and your insight, the more destructive shall be the vexation people experience when the falsity of your virtue is exposed. But allow me to break away from these sad reflections, my friends. Let us instead cast another glance at the portrait of the effect you will produce if your virtue has earned you the respect of your age. For your example shall not only inspire others to strive to equal you in virtue. The reputation your virtue has earned you will also be of great service for many other salutary goals. A man who enjoys a well-founded reputation of unwavering uprightness, who is also wise and insightful, can do far more than one might have suspected given his station, his office; he stands out; he is, as the ancients said, as a king in his community A mere word from him does more than hundreds of oaths sworn by others. A reproach from his mouth does more to mark someone with shame than a conviction pronounced by an authority that is not respected. A word of approval from him releases even someone with grave accusations over his head from all suspicion. It befits him to do even bolder things. For he may venture to offer resistance to authority when it exceeds its bounds. And this leads me to the

3. final point that I will briefly touch upon, namely: *you can and should wisely exercise the influence you may legitimately acquire over the government and legislation of this country.* Every citizen has a certain influence on the government and laws of his country, though admittedly a very small one. Does he not have a say in the choice of many members of the government? With you, my friends, who shall occupy higher stations, this influence shall be far greater, especially among those to whom heaven shall entrust a government position, even an entire branch of government. May you all conscientiously do what your position will allow you in order to create better a shape of things! I know that someone who intends to introduce a new, beneficial law, and especially a beneficial change of the constitution itself shall almost always find the greatest obstacles in his way. But the good that you may accomplish even within the existing constitution and laws is already considerable! We should be called happy, my friends, if only the evils forbidden by our laws were to cease and the only good things were those sanctioned by our laws. Should I not demand at least this much of you? Who can prevent you from working within the laws of our country? If you hold back from introducing good measures that are sanctioned by our laws out of fear of losing the favour of some powerful man, is it not as clear as day that you have sacrificed the well being of humanity to your own self-interest? Let such things be far from you! Rather, I expect that when the occasion presents itself you shall find sufficient courage even to demand appropriate changes to existing institutions. And it is here above all that I place all my hopes upon you working together as one. For the proverb one may read over the door of that old tavern applies especially well here: when one man speaks, no one speaks. But as soon as

several, sometimes as few as two, stand up in defense of a good cause, as soon as the bold, yet true claim made by one person is seconded by another, who ventures to show his approval and give reasons in support of it, the timid, who so far have remained silent, summon up the courage to join in. Then the fools who were blinded by the number of opponents find the scales removed from their eyes, as the light of truth breaks upon them. But the enemies of the good are afraid and fall into confusion, because something has happened that they thought never would, namely, people have, to their own disadvantage, worked for the common good. They raise objections, but they are clearly refuted, and so must in the end, although unwillingly, give their assent to the good cause. What joy shall you then feel, my friends—for there is no more glorious prospect on earth than to see the triumph of good in the struggle with evil. And all of us shall share in this joy in the highest degree, if we resolve to do everything I have asked you to do today. Then it shall no longer be a case of a little good thriving here or there. Rather we, united, in all the regions of the country, working in so many different ways towards the common goal, we must succeed in this great undertaking to improve the entire country. And blessed be they, every one, who shall have contributed something! For, says the word of God, those who have guided their brothers on the true path shall shine above like stars for ever and ever [Daniel 12, 3] Amen.

On Correct Conduct towards Enemies of Enlightenment

Read on the Feast of the Epiphany, 1816 [January 6]

Matthew 2, 1-12

Jesus was born in Bethlehem in Judaea during the reign of Herod. After his birth astrologers from the east arrived in Jerusalem, asking, "Where is the child who is born to be the king of the Jews? We observed the rising of his star, and we have come to pay him homage." King Herod was greatly perturbed when he heard this; and so was the whole of Jerusalem. He called a meeting of the chief priests and lawyers of the Jewish people, and put before them the question: "Where is it that the Messiah is to be born?" "At Bethlehem in Judaea," they replied; and they referred him to the prophecy which reads: "Bethlehem in the land of Judah, you are far from least in the eyes of the rulers of Judah; for out of you shall come a leader to be the shepherd of my people Israel."

Herod next called the wise men to meet him in private, and ascertained from them the time when the star had appeared. He then sent them on to Bethlehem, and said, "Go and make a careful inquiry for the child. When you have found him, report to me, so that I may go myself and pay him homage."

They set out at the King's bidding; and the star which they had seen at its rising went ahead of them until it stopped above the place where the child lay. At the sight of the star they were overjoyed. Entering the house, they saw the child with Mary his mother, and bowed to the ground in homage to him; then they opened their treasures and offered him gifts: gold, frankincense, and myrrh. And being warned in a dream not to go back to Herod, they returned home another way.

Introduction

King Herod, who had such an important influence on the course of events whose memory we are celebrating today, to me represents one of the most repulsive examples of what becomes of a man whose spurious happiness and well-being owe everything to the ignorance of the masses. King Herod was one of those rulers who look upon their title not as a duty assigned to them for furthering the well-being of their people, but only as an opportunity to advance themselves, and who consequently know of no other use of their power than to secure and increase what they take to be their own happiness and comfort. With such a frame of mind, revealed all too plainly by his actions, he clearly owed his prosperity only to the foolishness and ignorance of the great masses. Nearly all people whose apparent happiness depends upon the ignorance of the rest find themselves intensely tempted to become enemies and opponents of any enlightenment of the human race. This also was the case with Herod—only no one ever sinned against enlightenment with more shocking cruelty and less success (indeed to his own great chastisement) than he. For as such men have a habit of sensing danger everywhere, even where none is present, Herod thought he saw in the child born in Bethlehem, who was actually heralded as the teacher and enlightener of mankind, an enemy and a rival for his throne. And as such men are usually evil enough to deem permissible anything they think necessary to avert danger to themselves, this disgraceful tyrant did not hesitate to issue an order that was—we like to believe in deference to other princes —the most outrageous cruelty that any king with similar intentions ever allowed himself. But just as the plans of those who seek to repress the progress of enlightenment or the good cause of mankind are generally thwarted by God's almighty hand, so too was Herod's cruelty unsuccessful. All that blood was spilled in vain; the child whom he begrudged the light of day was saved through God's providence, and that murderous attack would serve only to glorify the cause of Jesus. And finally, just as all who venture to harm the best of mankind for the sake of a single self-seeking advantage someday find their punishment, so too Herod found his in a most visible and frightening manner. It is well known that he, soon after this dastardly attempt to put out the light of the world, was condemned to wander in the shadows of death, and this through one of the most miserable of diseases that doctors had ever seen. Even his name has been so branded by the evangelist that as long as the gospels are read on earth, it shall serve as a byword for the most loathsome of princes. In our day, too, there are a great many men who, like Herod, base their happiness on the ignorance of others. It is very difficult, even for the wise—as the example of the wise men in our text shows— to deal appropriately with this class of people, to avoid on the one hand treating them unjustly, and on the other not to become oneself a traitor to the good cause of mankind. With this in mind, my friends, I intend to set out a few considerations *concerning appropriate conduct towards enemies of enlightenment.* May heaven's light show us in our difficult situation, just as it showed those wise men of the orient, what duty and prudence bid us to do.

Discussion

It is all too certain that even today, even in the most enlightened states, there are a great many men, indeed even entire professions and organisations, whose spurious happiness and well-being depends on the ignorance of the remaining citizens. Mark well that I speak not of their true happiness, but rather of what they suppose to be their happiness. For I in no way believe that it would be necessary for any class of people, or even for any single person, to be destroyed should our civil society take on a completely rational form. It will always be possible to find ways even for those who up to now have depended upon the ignorance of others to earn their keep in the future. Indeed, they themselves would gain from the change, since it would mean turning from an unnatural and shameful way of life to a natural and healthy one, from idleness or useless occupations to activities that are generally useful and therefore genuinely gratifying for them. But it is precisely this that they cannot grasp, as obvious as it is in itself. Because they tremble before the prospect of changing their way of life, to which they may someday be forced, and because they understand more or less clearly that they are able to continue their present way of life only on account of ignorance, they fear any enlightenment as a personal misfortune, and if they are bad enough, do everything in their power to hinder its spread.

1. This leads me to a truth that I especially recommend that you heed, my friends, namely, that *not all men who belong to this class are evil and enemies to all enlightenment.* The wise men in our text are thoroughly imbued with this truth; they live in the noble belief, as worthy for their own hearts as for all of mankind, that there may well be someone, even one occupying the station of a prince, who is not only good, but magnanimous enough to abdicate his inherited throne should a man appear who is more worthy to occupy it. They expected as much from Herod, when they received his hypocritical assurance that he too wished to see the dwelling of the child in order to pay homage to him; for this reason, they were in fact willing to show him the place where the child lived, once they had found it. Though they may have erred in this case—and let us learn from this example to go about our work carefully and not believe unconditionally every assurance of such people, nor their praise of enlightenment—it is also true on the other hand that we should not assume that everyone whose station or outer circumstances might lead us to suspect him to be an open or secret enemy of enlightenment really is one. We would be wrong, and sin most terribly against mankind, were we to believe this. Is it really impossible for a man to favor the best of the whole as well as his own advantage? Can one not be in favor of promoting enlightenment even when he knows that his comfort and reputation will suffer thereby? What if someone makes his own heart feel the necessity of looking upon and treating everyone as his equal? If he himself is disgusted by the idleness his position imposes on him, or by the worthlessness of the only engagement he is permitted? If he perhaps only remains in his post because for now he hopes to be able to do much good that would otherwise not be possible for him to do? Finally, do you really suppose that there are not a great many men who occupy inappropriate posts without being aware of it, and who consequently could not possibly bear ill will against enlightenment, since it has never occurred to them that enlightenment might someday prescribe an unwelcome change in their way of life? History and everyday experience give gratifying confirmation that there have been and still are men in every station who look favorably upon enlightenment even though their own advantage seems to demand something different. Let us therefore be very careful never to develop a general hatred for everyone without distinction in even the most pernicious of positions of society! Nothing

could be more unfair than to hate persons simply on account of their station, for there can be so many reasons why they entered the position, and so many causes that prevent them from leaving it. Finally, because people's ideas are so diverse, justice demands that we judge each according to his own level of knowledge.

2. This last remark reminds me of another truth, namely that *we should not assume that all the people who are opposed to the enlightenment of their fellow citizens are equally bad.* Rather, we should take a fair look at all that they might be able to adduce by way of a partial excuse. We must do this if we wish to follow the example of the one who was honored by the wise men of the east on this day. People often complained that he spent his time with tax gatherers, that is, with men whose station was rightly detested, and of which one could truly say that it owed its existence to the ignorance of the nation. They were, admittedly, men saddled with many grave faults. Nevertheless, Jesus did not overlook the good things that existed alongside these faults, and thought clearly of all that might be said to excuse their failings. For that reason alone he found it worthwhile to spend time with this class of people and to attempt to improve the morals of at least some of them. Every reader of the gospels knows how successful these attempts were, how many tax-collectors and sinners he reformed, how they gave back to the poor four times as much as they had unjustly collected, how a number of them indeed became friends and zealous spreaders of the word. And it is not just a virtue when we imitate our Lord in this fair judgment of others, rather it is a duty, since we in fact wrong others when we judge them without considering what might be said in partial excuse. For us, my friends, we who are more practiced in thinking, this obligation is doubly pressing, since it is easier for us to imagine ourselves in the circumstances and the entire situation of those we intend to judge. Let us never forget to do this, and we shall find that much can be said for many of those who do not advance enlightenment which, even it does not fully exonerate, at least excuses them. When we consider someone's upbringing, when we see that from early childhood he has been imbued with prejudices concerning the necessity of some social station or other, how through years of habituation this way of life has become a real need and indeed second nature to him, when we consider how shortsighted all of us are whenever it comes to recognizing truths that contradict the promptings

of our senses; how seldom it is the case that a man is clearly and fully aware of the damage caused by his opposition to the dissemination of better ideas; how easily he convinces himself that whatever good might be produced by enlightenment in the future is far outweighed by the incidental disorder caused by too rapid progress—when we consider all of this, it becomes clear that only a very few of the men who act as enemies of enlightenment are so truly evil as appears at first sight. We shall learn to see that what is involved is little more than an error of judgment, which merits punishment only insofar as it supports laziness or selfishness; and that for many such people moral and religious feelings are intermixed so that they believe themselves to be striving for the cause of virtue and religion when they fight for their station and their prosperity. Yet others we will find already more clearly aware of the injustice they do, but who have allowed—and this is indeed a fault—their force of habit and strength of passion to grow extremely strong. When we consider all this, and put ourselves in the place of such people, we will far sooner feel pity than anger towards them.

3. A raving madman deserves pity, but is madness therefore any less dangerous? Certainly not! This leads me to my third truth: people who are either demonstrably or even probably enemies of enlightenment *must always be looked upon as very dangerous people*, and we must be careful not to bring to their attention the promoters of enlightenment and the instruments they use. What a dangerous man for the cause of Christianity, that is, for the most effective of all institutions of enlightenment there has ever been and ever will be, was that single individual King Herod! How soon he would have nipped that excellent institution in the bud, had not providence intervened! And it was precisely those wise men of the east who gave him the alarm through their imprudent inquiry. How well this story teaches us of the great danger of pointing out the promoters of enlightenment and their instruments to people who are either certainly or probably hostile to enlightenment! There are also among us those who promote enlightenment, persons, namely, who take it upon themselves either to discover generally useful truths, or else to communicate them to others. They use different means and instruments towards this end: printed and handwritten texts as well as oral instruction, either public or private. Even sciences that hardly seem to allow any application to life can be an important, if remote, means to

promote enlightenment in that they train the understanding how to think correctly. The enemies of enlightenment are already all too aware of all of these, and are all too suspicious of them. In full consciousness of their evil intentions they sense danger everywhere and find even the most innocent of these activities threatening. So let us be careful not to make them aware of things that, fortunately, they have not yet thought about! Many things could lead us to do so. Often it is a matter of good-hearted trustfulness that knows no secrets, since one cannot even imagine how someone could be bad enough to misuse their confidences. More often still it is a matter of trying to gain more influence on a person one admires in order to earn praise and rewards. Often it is vanity that spurns doing good behind the scenes, and so comes out into the open where it is soon brought to an end. Let each of us happily renounce fame and shallow praise! Let us be satisfied when heaven helps us to do good, and let us demand no human rewards! Is it not a far more glorious reward than any prince can grant to know that one has done good? And if we do good expecting to win the approval of men, have we not, according to the Saviour's teaching, already received our reward? Away with such vain thoughts! Allow us, my friends, to do good in silence; in silence shall we thrive! Our Lord also avoided the castles and the dwellings of the powerful, because he wanted to teach the truth; he taught not in Jerusalem but in Galilee, except for his last days, when he intended to become a martyr for the truth. And he gave us to understand that we too should exercise such caution with his noteworthy saying: Cast not your pearls before swine, for they shall only trample them underfoot, and tear you to pieces! Amen.

On Correct Conduct towards Enemies of Enlightenment (conclusion)

Read on the first Sunday after Epiphany, 1816 [January 7]

Introduction

The subject we began to discuss yesterday and shall conclude today is one of those that one should never discuss before a mixed public—before an audience, that is, containing a lot of uneducated people. For with people who are uneducated and not practiced in thinking, it is well-nigh impossible to ensure that what one says is understood in its proper context, that nothing is misunderstood, or incorrectly applied. Fortunately, it is not necessary to speak of such matters before such people, for, not yet enlightened themselves, they have no calling to work to enlighten their fellow citizens. What end, therefore, would be served by instructing them on how to spread enlightenment and how to deal with its enemies? Things stand quite otherwise with you, my friends, that is, with those who will occupy higher stations, for you have a duty to promote enlightenment, that is, to seek useful truths, and appropriately communicate such truths to others. You could not possibly meet this obligation in the right way if you did not know how to behave when confronted with people who set out to prevent the enlightenment of the human race. You would be led astray in many ways. Fear, perhaps, or lethargy would lead you to remain silent when it was the right moment to make known a very important truth; again, failure to reflect, overeagerness, heat and passion may lead you to preach a truth in circumstances where it can only be perilous for you and perhaps also for your fellow men. Finally, it is very much to be feared that you will allow a very natural but nevertheless unchristian hatred against those who have shown themselves to be enemies of enlightenment to creep into your hearts, indeed that you will even gradually allow anger towards entire classes and stations to take root in you! In order to prevent these things, I think it my duty for once to speak in detail about *correct conduct towards enemies of enlightenment*, towards that group of people whose spurious happiness is based upon the ignorance of their fellow citizens. I asked you to take three things to heart. We must not believe that all people who belong to this class are in fact evil. We must also not even think that all of the people who oppose enlightenment are equally evil and despicable, but should rather give fair consideration to everything that might serve as a partial excuse. However, we must certainly look upon people who are proven or indeed probable enemies of enlightenment as dangerous, and take care not to draw their attention to the promoters of enlightenment or to the instruments they use in their work. Before continuing, let us read a passage from the word of God, which will show us the way to salutary thoughts.

Romans 13, 1-7

> Every person must submit to the supreme authorities. There is no authority but by act of God, and the existing authorities are instituted by him; consequently anyone who rebels against authority is resisting a divine institution, and those who so resist have themselves to thank for the punishment they will receive. For government, a terror to crime, has no terrors for good behaviour. You wish to have no fear of the authorities? Then continue to do right and you will have their approval, for they are God's agents working for your good. But if you are doing wrong, then you will have cause to fear them; it is not for nothing that they hold the power of the sword, for they are God's agents of punishment, for retribution on the offender. It is an obligation imposed not merely by fear of retribution but by conscience. That is also why you pay taxes. The authorities are in God's service and to these duties they devote their energies. Discharge your obligations to all men; pay tax and toll, reverence and respect, to those to whom they are due.

Discussion

The wisdom that the Apostle Paul showed in writing this passage of his epistle to the community of Rome deserves both admiration and imitation. The claims he makes here are all valid but, when carefully considered, only with certain exceptions and limitations. It is not universally true that all authorities are vested with force by God himself, that is, in perfect accord with the will or the commands of God. Still less is it true that only bad people and never the good need fear authorities, and that one must always and in all things obey, not simply to avoid punishment, but rather out of conscientiousness. How so, you ask? Does not the Apostle's own example show us that these claims admit of exceptions? Was it not the order of the very authorities he encouraged the Romans to obey, the order of the shameful Nero, to behead him? And when the other Apostles were forbidden by various courts to spread the gospel, was it not his habit to tell them: "one must obey God more than Man"? But the Apostle wisely said nothing of this in his epistle, since he was not sending it to a single individual, but rather to an entire community and indeed a community in Rome. Hence any mention of exceptions or limitations would have been dangerous. Here, with a people that had so much cause to be dissatisfied with their ruler, this could easily have unleashed rebellion. Let us therefore learn from the Apostle's wise behaviour still another precept we should follow.

1. *We should be wary of spreading even the most beneficial of truths among men who may take them as a pretext for all too severe revenge upon those who have hitherto profited from their ignorance.* For though I do not deny that every truth that deals with a subject important to humanity may usefully be communicated to certain people, and although I hold it to be the duty of anyone who knows such truths that are not yet known to others to ensure that they do not perish with them, but rather are bequeathed to posterity; yet I cannot but agree with those who call out that not every truth is suitable for everyone. Even the most useful of truths, brought forth at the wrong place and time, can be the cause of a great many ills. This happens most easily with truths the ignorance of which has provided a living, high standing, and power to certain individuals or indeed entire classes of them. That such people may not be culpable, having perhaps themselves been unaware that they profit from this universal ignorance, and that even those who deserve to be punished do not all merit the same punishment, and are rarely as numerous as appears at first glance—all this we saw yesterday. But it is all too certain that only very few people posses the insight and benevolence necessary to take this to heart and to embrace it. The overwhelming majority are rash in their judgments, violent in their passions, and their

thirst for vengeance will only be slaked with blood. If one were to explain quite clearly to a certain gathering that a given class of people was living entirely at their expense, fed and maintained through their ignorance; were one to show them that it is only their ignorance that provides such a comfortable living, so much wealth, and such wide-ranging, most shamefully abused power: what outrage would be expressed, every face red with shame, glowing hot with anger, furious with hunger for revenge; what curses would ring out, all now seeing as scoundrels those whom only minutes ago they raised almost to the level of gods! Would they not set upon them *en masse*, raging, and in a moment not only rob them of everything that they had amassed illegitimately and to the detriment of the whole, but also deny them the goods and rights that everyone may justly claim? Who among us, my friends, wishes to give the signal that unleashes such cruelty? Who would want to burden his conscience with the knowledge that he was, directly or indirectly, responsible for such atrocities? No, this is far from the minds of those who strive to imitate the one who came not to corrupt men, but to bring them blessings; who admonished two of his disciples so firmly, when they rashly wanted heaven to rain fire upon a city because it would not acknowledge their master, admonishing them for even making room in their minds for such thoughts, adding that they did not even know what kind of persons they would be if they harboured such thoughts! A follower of Jesus should never allow something to occur to him that has even the appearance of cruelty, violence and unkindness. According to his master's example, he must always show himself to be gentle of spirit and merciful; he must himself look after and speak in the defense of those who have drawn general hatred upon themselves and are in danger of being punished with unfair severity.

2. And we shall fulfill this duty all the more perfectly when we are convinced of a second truth. *While it is true that people whose good fortune has hitherto rested upon the ignorance of others admittedly have no right to demand that even after enlightenment we keep promises made under conditions of ignorance when keeping them would be detrimental to the whole, yet it is all the more certain that they are entitled to be provided for in a way that meets their present needs.* The pious wise men whose story we read yesterday did not think themselves obligated in any way to fulfill the promise they had made to King Herod once

it became clear that only through their ignorance had they been led to make it, not yet having discovered the king's evil intentions. And as the wise men decided, so too has sound human understanding judged at all times. Many scholars, operating with faulty concepts, were indeed at a loss to explain how someone could be justified in breaking any promise, even the most solemn, once it was shown that the promise was based on error, not to mention crime, and that fulfilling it would be overwhelmingly disadvantageous to the whole. It suffices that all people, thanks to their sound human understanding, see this and are convinced of its truth. Suppose that persons of some special rank are able to prove that they were promised certain privileges in the distant past, guaranteed in countless documents, and that this guarantee stretches indefinitely into the future. This does nothing to alter the fact that if we are generally convinced that the continued existence of this rank would be harmful, then these promises in no way prevent us from making appropriate changes. Appropriate changes, I say, that is, the kind which, along with many others, take account of the present needs of the people whose situations are to change. Suppose, for example, that certain artisans or craftsmen have thus far earned a living through work that was only desired and remunerated because of folly. When the increase of enlightenment in the land causes the demand for their work to disappear, is it not fair that the state teach the people who used to make their living through that work another way of providing for themselves? Is it not fair for society to be patient with these people, and, in case they are no longer capable of doing enough useful work, should it not even feed them free of charge? People, who have been raised in idleness and opulence through the defects of earlier customs, and who therefore now have a number of affected needs—should not any changes concerning such people at least leave them in a position to satisfy these needs? Obviously, this holds only insofar as their satisfaction is not disgraceful or illegal.

The less the great mass of people is likely to think on their own of this fair and necessary provision, the more it is our duty, my friends, to remind them of it. And certainly half of the people who now stubbornly oppose every change and seek to nip all enlightenment in the bud do so only because they cannot hope to be treated fairly if such changes are introduced. Let us therefore work to ensure that they are disabused of this doubt, and the sooner the better. Let us spread the truth that all citizens, even those who have hitherto lived off the ignorance and to the detriment of others, deserve to be provided for in a way commensurate with the needs they happen to have. And by doing so, we will speed up more than we think the introduction of a more rational order.

3. All the same I do not intend to raise too bold hopes in you, my friends. Many an inappropriate estate, and many ways of earning a living that we find reprehensible may well persist in unaltered form for as long as we live. But even should this turn out to be the case, we shall not become morose if we keep the following truth in mind: *Even though individuals, not to mention entire organizations and stations, who draw advantages from ignorance may put many obstacles in the path of enlightenment, their existence is nevertheless not entirely useless. Rather, God's providence knows how to use them, even against their will, as instruments that will help to bring about a better time.* Here we cannot but give heed to the example of Herod. For precisely through his attempt to remove in his childhood the greatest educator and enlightener of mankind from the world, he only served to exalt the cause of Jesus. It became all the more obvious that that child, alone among hundreds whose life could not be taken, stood under God's special protection. All the more credible became the story of those wise men who were supposed to have been called from the east by a star, in order to worship him. And as was the case here, so too with every estate and even with individual men, who seem pernicious: we will notice that they bring certain advantages to society without being aware of it or wanting to. The estate of rich people, whose existence one can genuinely say is founded on the ignorance of others: how much good do we nevertheless have to thank them for! On how low a level of culture would we find humanity today had the difference in wealth that makes for rich and poor never come to be, if at a time when people did not yet have higher motives, there had not been on the one hand poverty and wretchedness stimulating people to exert all their powers, to summon up all their intelligence for myriad experiments and researches, and on the other hand the wealth and luxury that was willing and able to reward these endeavors! Even were it the case that the rich really only rewarded the discoveries and inventions that flattered their vanity, or fed their luxury, or increased their power to defend themselves against their enemies, they still could not prevent what had been invented and discovered from being put to an-

other use; they could not prevent the spirit of invention, once awakened, from remaining active and from finally turning to the useful along with the merely pleasant. They will certainly never be able to forbid us completely and forever, once we have grown accustomed to it, from thinking and reflecting on everything, including the most appropriate constitution of a state. In this context it should sooner or later become obvious that these far too great differences in wealth are pernicious and that means exist to prevent them. But even when we cannot see clearly what use the continued existence of certain stations and ways of life might be, or where the damage they cause seems to outweigh any usefulness, let us console ourselves with the thought that God is infinitely wiser than we are, and frequently knows how to draw out the most beneficial results from things that seem harmful to us. Not, indeed, as if this thought should make us less determined in fighting against and eliminating what we judge by its visible effects to be harmful. No, only when despite all our efforts we are unable to remove the evil, only then may and should we console ourselves with the thought that the ruler of the world must have his reasons for not yet allowing our efforts to succeed, and that the evil against which we fruitlessly struggle must still be necessary as a means to bring about a greater good or to prevent worse evils. Let us thus comfort ourselves, when we are grieved that the enlightenment of the human race is proceeding so slowly, that we can do so little to encourage it, because others have closed our mouths, when we see with sadness that in all countries of Europe things seem to be regressing, how almost all writers ignominiously consent to advocate the oppression of mankind. God has permitted this to happen—there must be good in it. The Lord, said Job, did this, the name of the Lord be praised! Let us say with him: the name of the Lord be praised! Amen.

On Duties towards Unjust Authorities

Read on Palm Sunday in 1812 [March 22]

Matthew 26, 45-56

> Then he came to the disciples and said to them, "Still sleeping? Still taking your ease? The hour has come! The Son of Man is betrayed to sinful men. Up. Let us go forward; the traitor is upon us." While he was still speaking, Judas, one of the Twelve, appeared; with him was a great crowd armed with swords and cudgels, sent by the chief priests and the elders of the nation. The traitor gave them this sign: "The one I kiss is your man; seize him"; and stepping forward at once, he said, "Hail Rabbi!", and kissed him. Jesus replied, "Friend, do what you are here to do." They then came forward, seized Jesus, and held him fast. At that moment one of those with Jesus reached for his sword and drew it, and he struck at the High Priest's servant and cut off his ear. But Jesus said to him, "Put up your sword. All who take the sword die by the sword. Do you suppose that I cannot appeal to my Father, who would at once send to my aid more than twelve legions of angels? But how then could the scriptures be fulfilled, which say that this must be?" At the same time Jesus spoke to the crowd: "Do you take me for a bandit, that you have come out with swords and cudgels to arrest me? Day after day I sat preaching in the temple, and you did not lay hands on me. But this has all happened to fulfil what the prophets wrote." Then the disciples all deserted him and ran away.

Introduction

God's providence allowed Jesus of Nazareth to be placed in this relation to the authorities set over him so that his conduct could serve as a model for our own. It was not enough that the son of God, he who was the very image of the divine being, the reflection of God's glory, who took on human form and deigned to go about with men as if they were his equals—indeed, he wanted to be a servant among men. He chose to appear as a subordinate, recognized masters and authorities above him, and not only good and moderate, but also evil and unjust ones, who treated him with the most outrageous arrogance and the greatest cruelty. The evangelical text I have just read, my friends, brings a scene before our eyes in which the Son of God is summoned before his earthly authorities as a criminal. They carried swords and cudgels to be sure they could control him in case he resisted. They came with swords and spears, without thinking that they were coming after Him who is stronger than all armies; they did not remember that it was He who more than once had driven back the raging fury of an entire people with a single, almighty look; nor did they consider that for one who can work miracles, chains and bonds are the wrong means to force him to show due obedience to the magistrate. In order to make these foolish men remember these truths, and to make it quite obvious that he still did not have to obey if he did not want to, Jesus spoke just one word, and the armed band fell to the ground as if dead [John 18, 6]; with a wave of the hand, life and movement returned to their limbs. They picked themselves off the ground, and Peter attacked one of them; but He moves his finger and what had been done was undone. The soldier's ear that had been cut off was again safe and sound [Luke 22, 51]. Then he held out his benevolent hands, and willingly allowed them to bind him and take him to the judge. It is clear, my friends, truly clear that Jesus submitted to these unjust authorities not because he had to, but because he found it good and right—especially because in so doing he would serve as an example, showing us how to act in similar circumstances. For Jesus saw clearly that there would be a great many unjust masters and authorities among us; anyone who wanted to deny that it is thus even in *our day* would be lying out of contemptible fear of others, and truth would not be in him. Under these conditions people usually prefer to remain completely silent, and rarely does anyone raise in a public gathering the question of what is to be done, according to the principles of reason and Christianity, when one is confronted with unjust rulers and authorities. Granted, the fear of being misunderstood might be sufficient reason for never taking up this insidious question before a mixed public—but do I have any reason to fear this with the present gathering, my friends? Could it really be that young men who have been trained how to think, who indeed are instructed, at the behest of the state, in penetrating and scientific research, could it be that they are incapable of properly understanding and correctly applying clearly presented instruction on the topic I just mentioned? Would it really be more advisable to allow them to go out into the world having learned nothing about the subject? Is it really to be hoped that they will just happen to discover the principles that must be followed here on their own, without any guidance? No, the more trying the circumstances in fact are, the more necessary it becomes to educate people about them, and woe to the state that thinks it dangerous to teach the subjects of unjust authorities about the rights that God himself has granted them. Away, then with this doubt! With God's help, I will speak to you today, as free of fear of men as befits a servant of the Gospel, how we, *following the example of Jesus, should behave when confronted with unjust rulers and authorities.* May heaven see to it that the principles I shall set out today impress themselves deeply in your minds, my friends, and that you in turn shall spread them among others: then the human race will certainly suffer less than it does at present from the oppression of unjust authorities. May the blessings of the Highest help us in this!

Discussion

When we consider the example that Jesus gave us in his life and in his death, my friends, it becomes obvious first of all that:

1. *The wise man only decides to disobey the express commands of his superiors when the damage that would be caused by obedience is indisputably greater than that which would be caused by disobedience.* Jesus did not think it permissible to disobey in every case where he knew how to do better than the laws of his country prescribed. He anticipated the offense that others might take at his disobedience, and whenever he found that the latter was more significant, he obeyed the authorities. It was for this reason that he lived his life in accordance with the rules of the Old Testament, right down to the most trivial details, even though he saw quite well that the laws of Moses were not the most appropriate that

could be devised for the present time; it was for this reason that he also followed the new laws introduced by the then reigning civic authorities, namely the Romans, not only himself obeying but also teaching others to do the same. Give to Caesar that which is Caesar's, he said, and to God that which is God's [Matthew 22, 21], as if to say: do what is required to satisfy the secular as well as the religious authorities. It was also for this reason that we see him in today's text obeying the order of the magistrates, transmitted by their subordinates, namely, to appear before the court. He obeyed this order of the authorities, I say, even though he clearly foresaw that his obedience would mean death for him, death on the cross. Can there be a more instructive example, my friends, of how strictly we should obey, in duty, the secular as well as religious laws of our country? When the Son of God gave up his own life in order not to oppose the commands of the authorities, is it not already decided that all those who think themselves released from the obligation of obeying an existing law merely because it does not seem the most appropriate to them have fallen into a gross and most pernicious error? Is a single citizen, who may know nothing of the circumstances of the state, ever in a position to judge with complete certainty whether a law is suitable or not? Would not all laws be as good as absent if it were permissible for each to do as he thinks best, regardless of whether some law permitted or forbade it? For Sure! Must not every rational person pay heed in whatever he does or permits to the impression his example will make on others? Must he not leave many good deeds undone simply because they will be misunderstood by others, because others would see in them the excuse for myriad stupidities and offenses? The offense one commits by violating an existing law, the bad example others observe, believing to find in our disobedience a tacit permission for them to disobey, even though they have no equally strong reasons for doing so—do not these disadvantages often outweigh by far the good result we hope to attain through our disobedience? And what shall I say about people who violate the laws of the state not for the sake of the common good, but for their own selfish interest? Who allow themselves to use the most unlawful means to this end? Who resolve to lie and conceal, even going so far as to make false statements under oath in order to circumvent the authorities and avoid taxes they could easily afford to pay? Heinous behaviour this, which is nevertheless so common in our times that even the state looks upon it with such indifference that the worst punishment it metes out to one caught in such despicable fraud is a paltry fine, yet allows him to maintain in society the reputation of an honorable man! But if there are violations of the existing laws of the state motivated by shameful egoism that should be publicly punished, there are also *cases where it is not only allowed but even a duty to disobey the commands of one's superiors.* The example of Jesus establishes this beyond any doubt. He knew ahead of time that the authorities in his country would forbid the preaching of the gospel. Yet he expressly commanded his disciples to continue preaching. Go and spread the gospel, he said to them, among all peoples [Matthew 28, 19; Mark 13, 10]. You will indeed have to suffer many persecutions for this; governors, even kings will call you to account. But have no fear of men, who can only kill your body, but cannot harm your immortal soul. You should be much more afraid of him who can cast both body and soul into eternal ruin. You know well, my friends, how well the apostles followed this command of their teacher. The high council expressly ordered them to speak no longer of this Jesus. Yet they had the courage to reply with dry reason: judge for yourselves whether it is right to obey men more than God—a reply that should be a model for all who believe themselves caught in the sad necessity of disobeying their superiors. It cannot be denied that they are sometimes justified in taking this step. The reason is this: The ultimate ground upon which the duty to obey authorities rests is only the advantage humanity gains from obedience in general. Therefore it is readily comprehensible how this duty can fail to apply in certain cases. For if consideration of all circumstances indicates that the harm caused by disobedience, the offence it gives others, is to all appearance decisively outweighed by the evil that would result from obeying—then it certainly can and must be permissible to disobey. But may you never abuse this permission given by both reason and revelation, my friends! May you never forget, in the first place, that the wise man never resolves to take this sad step without the deepest reflection, indeed often thinks about what he should do for years on end. May you never forget, in the second place, that he never ventures to disobey laws of whose hidden purpose and connection with the whole, whose necessity and consequences he is in no position to judge. Thus, thirdly, he never deems himself justified in becoming a lawbreaker merely in order to gain material advantages for his fellow men—only a moral purpose, the widening of a beneficial sphere of influence can outweigh the disadvantages disobedience gives rise to. Nor does the wise man allow himself to violate a law when it is he himself who is most oppressed by it. For then he fears that his self-love portrays the measure in false colours, or at least he fears that his fellow men might suspect this of him; he is afraid that thousands of others might abuse his example, taking it to justify their own disobedience, which may be worlds apart from his. Thus he would rather suffer the most extreme abuse than resolve in such cases to set an example of disobedience. Thus a great many conditions, my friends, a great many conditions govern the permissibility of behaving contrary to an express command of legitimate authorities. And when all these conditions are met, it is the

2. *second* duty of the wise man, *to apply all means at his disposal to limit any offence the disobedience he sees as necessary might cause.* Here too our Lord set the best example. The laws of the Old Testament, already a heavy yoke, were made into an almost unbearable burden by the additions of the Pharisees. The effect was that those who could neither resolve to follow all these detailed prescriptions nor had the intelligence to make a prudent selection, found their consciences laboring under a heavy burden. On top of this, many of these customs obviously were harmful rather than conducive to virtue. For this reason, our Lord found it necessary to openly violate some of these, in order to show through his example that they absolutely deserved to be abolished. How easily his example might have caused offense, had he not shown on more than one occasion through his conduct and his teaching that he did not believe all the statutes of the Pharisees to be equally worthless. Did he himself not govern his conduct by many of them? Had he not often said to the people: practice and observe whatever they tell you, but not what they do. The apostles also followed the example of their leader. Although they recognized that it was absolutely necessary for them to behave contrary to all authorities, secular and ecclesiastical in one thing, that is, spreading the gospel, all their other conduct showed how important in their eyes was the duty to obey the existing commands of legitimate authorities. Who can fault them for even the slightest violation of the standing commands and laws of the various countries they visited? Did they not conduct themselves in all respects by the mores

and customs of where they happened to be, except in religious matters? Did they not impress upon their followers that every authority has been established by God, that it is a duty of conscience to obey not only the good but also the bad? In fact, my friends, if only all disobedience had been undertaken with such caution, there would be little grounds for complaint concerning the harm caused by it. But usually those who believed themselves to be compelled to resist authority have not hit upon the right method. They did so with heat and passion. Even if it were not the case that passion, rather than reasonable grounds, was the motive for disobeying their leaders, it had every appearance that it was. They broke more laws than was necessary; did not give sufficient proof of their conscientiousness in following all the other prescriptions, and people believed with great alarm that along with this or that law they wished at the same time to overturn a great many others, even civil order itself. The wise man is careful to avoid giving such offense. He takes care, first of all, to ensure that his law breaking becomes as little known as is possible without resorting to deceit or lies. He does this not in order to spare himself punishment, but principally because the harm that could come from his lawbreaking will be all the smaller, the smaller the circle that witnesses it. The wise man strives to show all who observe him that he is acting neither out of passion, nor rashly, but instead has only decided to break this law after long, careful deliberation. He acts with the greatest calm and composure, and makes known, as much as circumstances allow, the causes and motives that led to his decision. In order to avoid the objection that he perhaps goes too far in his law breaking, and wishes to bring down a number of beneficial laws along with the harmful one, he states clearly and unambiguously that it is only this or that single law that he permits himself to break, and that he honours and observes all the remaining commands of the authorities. And he does all this not only in words, but also, which is most important, shows it through his actions. In his acts he shows himself to be the most conscientious observer of all the remaining laws, not only the ones that are easy to follow, but also those that lay heavy burdens upon him—he follows them faithfully and exactly, and thereby shows in the clearest possible way that he has only broken a law because the common good required him to.

3. When we proceed in this manner, my friends, then surely we shall not only avoid giving great offense to our fellow citizens, but also edify them through our example. It is really not enough that we ourselves do what is right. As much as lies within our power, we must strive to enlighten our fellow citizens. Accordingly, it is a *third* duty of ours *to use the influence we have over our fellow citizens, whether it be great or small, to enlighten them, and to make the value of rational laws increasingly obvious to them. We must also put them in a position to tell the difference between rational and irrational laws, and to make them aware of the rights they possess with respect to the latter.* More than one of the speeches made by Jesus of Nazareth to the people, and preserved by the writers of the Holy Gospels clearly prove how hard he worked in this respect. The speech, noteworthy in so many other respects, in which he lays bare the hypocrisy of the Pharisees, must surely be in your living memory, my friends. Note how he tries in this excellent speech to awaken the reflection of the crowd; how he attempts wherever possible to open the eyes of the blind, so that they may see how shamefully they have been deceived. And who does not remember the way in which our Lord sharply contrasted on another occasion the decrees of the Pharisees and his own precepts, precisely in order to enable the great masses to tell the difference between reasonable and unreasonable laws? [Matthew 23] And did he not drop many hints about the inalienable rights a people possess in the face of irrational laws? Why else would he have drawn attention to the unreasonableness of so many pharisaical laws, if not to give them to understand that they possess a certain right to overturn them? O! Let this important example our Lord has given us be properly understood and imitated! No matter how much some people may be opposed to it, no matter what they may say about the impossibility and the highly distressing consequences of the enlightenment of the people, it is beyond a doubt that there is no more secure basis for the well being of a people than their enlightenment. By this I mean the appropriate development of the power of judgment in each individual citizen, as well as a certain stock of useful knowledge, especially healthy, correct concepts of everything having to do with virtue and happiness, attention directed towards the common best, direction and instruction in correctly judging whether something is beneficial or harmful for the common best; knowledge of the rights a people possess, and the ability to tell the difference

between wise and unwise measures; eagerness to follow the former and enmity and opposition directed towards the adoption of the latter. Enlightenment so understood, my friends can have nothing but the most blessed consequences, and it is certain that there is no better way to promote the happiness and well being of a people than by promoting such enlightenment to the full extent of one's powers. For setting aside for the moment all the other advantages it brings, what better means is there for preserving a people from tyranny and oppression? Even if a people have the wisest and best prince, even should he rule them with the most rational laws: if he does not see to their enlightenment, he has built something unstable. When he dies, what assurance do we have that his successor will be of like mind, that evil and vicious men will not sooner or later take control of the government, and abuse and oppress the ignorant masses, who cannot tell good from evil and who are duped by every pretence? Enlightenment alone is a secure protection against such tyrants, enlightenment alone makes it impossible for an alliance of evil-minded people to operate their nefarious schemes. They do not even attempt to foist their idiotic deceptions on an enlightened people since they would see right through them and reject their orders with scorn and derision. May you gather from this, my friends, what it is you have to do in order to do lasting, if unrecognised service to your fellow citizens. You must try to promote enlightenment. On every occasion that presents itself, you must try to spread more correct concepts of what is just, what unjust. You must strive to make people more attentive to the things that have to do with the common good; you must make clear to the ignorant the high value of wiser and more beneficial laws; you must try to make it clear to them that to violate a wise and beneficial law out of contemptible egotism is to sin grievously against one's fellow man, and indeed to dishonour and disgrace oneself. You must teach them how properly to tell the difference between reasonable and unreasonable laws. Finally, you must caution them against any rashness in judgment, and show them examples of laws that are often beneficial and necessary for the good of the whole even though not everyone can see their purpose.

4. From all this my *fourth* claim follows of itself, my friends: *The wise man always takes care to avoid stirring up rebellion, he spurns all violent means, and seeks to overturn an unreasonable law in no other way*

than by fostering the general conviction of its harmfulness. It cannot indeed be denied that even the Son of God has been accused of the crime of rabble rousing. This is an old trick of evil authorities, who seek to get rid of the well-intentioned citizens they hate by accusing them of stirring up the mob. But anyone not utterly ignorant of the gospels knows how little he deserved this reproach. So far was he from using such violent means to introduce what is good and fair, that he on many occasions wisely calmed rebellions that had begun against his will. Twice he fled when the masses, amazed by his greatness, sought to name him their king. And how impressively he rebuked his apostles in today's text when they sought to save him from his enemies by resorting to violence. Are not the words that he used on this occasion well worth taking to heart? All who take the sword, said he, will perish by the sword. Let us heed well the lesson that lies in these words, my friends, for it is both true and important. Whoever resorts to violent means in order to bring about some good, acts unwisely and causes far more evil than any good he accomplishes. Disastrous and unforeseeable are the evil consequences that revolution leaves in its wake. To say nothing of all other effects, mankind becomes savage when it lives through such conflicts. A people that has freed itself from burdensome laws by the dreadful means of rebellion is made savage through the terrifying scenes that are the inseparable companions of rebellion, and must afterwards rebuild its morals from the ground up. No, my friends, in order to make mankind better off, no one need murder anyone, especially not, as is usually the case in an uprising, people who are often completely innocent of the offences that have created the mob's thirst for vengeance. There is an easier, a more gentle means for overturning burdensome laws and for resisting the oppression of tyrannical authorities. And this means is—the general conviction of their injustice. When all citizens see that something is unjust, when the entire people speaks with one voice on the matter, who, my friends, will want to try to force it upon them? The villain may well command—no one obeys. Whom can he punish? He must punish everyone; and no one will lend him an arm to provide weapons for his fury and so to give power to his words. Thus he has to withdraw his commands, and resign himself to giving better ones. And all this happens without a single drop of blood being spilled. This, then, is the true method for warding off evil. Not by oneself resorting to evil, but rather through goodness, through gentleness and sound reasons. Thus befits it men to rebuke one another. Not with the sword, but rather through reason shall it be decided who is right. He who takes up the sword, whoever he may be, deserves to fulfil the prophecy made by our Jesus: he who takes the sword will perish by the sword. Amen.

On the Relations between the two Peoples of Bohemia

Read on the seventh Sunday after Pentecost, 1816 [July 21]

Introduction

It should be fair to assume of all Christians, my friends, that they know the true aim of their church. One can in fairness expect of a Christian that he know what Christ intended. Yet it is all too certain that one says something new and strange for thousands of our Christian contemporaries when one expresses the aim of Christianity in its fullness; when one says that the aim of Christianity is not to make us happy only in heaven, but rather also here on earth; that it is here on this earth that our Lord sought to found a kingdom of heaven; that he taught those who heed the teachings of his church not just how they should lead their own lives in order to become virtuous and to enjoy as much happiness as possible; but rather he also sought to gradually bring about beneficial changes in the civic institutions that have such a great influence on us; he sought to found states and kingdoms on earth that were so perfectly constituted, each living in such peaceful harmony with the others that one would be justified in saying there was really only one kingdom on earth, the true kingdom of God. To show that Jesus' plan really extended to our earthly happiness and particularly to the improvement of our institutions would, my friends, be a very easy matter indeed. We can adduce many passages from the scriptures from which this follows; and it follows directly from Jesus' whole way of thinking, and the spirit in which he went to work, that he would have extended the aims of Christendom as far as was possible. Indeed, even someone who knew nothing else about the great prophet of Nazareth than that he had once said "there will then be one flock, one shepherd" [John 10, 16-17] could already gather from this that the changes that this man [Acts 2, 22] wished to bring about concerned not only the inner life of men, but also their outer conditions, the constitutions under which they live. Yet the more certain this is, my friends, all the more is it clear how disapproving our lord Jesus is of the activities of all those who, instead of contributing what they can to the improvement of our institutions, do much more to cause their faults to become still greater and more glaring—a failing, not to say a sin, of which many in our fatherland are unfortunately guilty, although not always in the same way, and not always with the same clear awareness of the maliciousness of what they are doing. Here, above all, is to be numbered *the spirit of strife that has built up between the two peoples of this country over hundreds of years.* I was dismayed to learn, my friends, that even among you traces of this most pernicious hostility have occasionally been seen. It is apparent that even among you the Czechs and the Germans do not love each other as the citizens of one and the same country must if they do not wish to be the cause of their common downfall. It seems that your ideas concerning this topic are not yet sufficiently clarified. Permit me, therefore, to develop my opinions on these matters in more detail. It will be necessary first of all to give an honest account of the *causes* that give rise to the hostility between the Czechs and the Germans in our fatherland. Only then will it be possible to judge whether this hostility is fair and reasonable. And should the answer to this question turn out to be negative, it will be worth the trouble to think about means for controlling it. In view of their importance and scope, each of these three inquiries will require its own meeting. Now, my friends, if ever I need you to listen with an open mind to what I have to say, it will be during these talks. I know of no better way to call forth the frame of mind required here than to read for you what the apostle Paul wrote when he set out to promote peace and unity in a community into which the spirit of hostility had insinuated itself.

1 Corinthians 12, 12-27

> For Christ is like a single body with its many limbs and organs, which, many as they are, together make up one body. For indeed we were all brought into one body by baptism, in the one Spirit, whether we are Jews or Greeks, whether slaves or free men, and that one Holy Spirit was poured out for all of us to drink. A body is not one single organ, but many. Suppose the foot should say, 'Because I am not a hand, I do not belong to the body,' it does belong to the body none the less. Suppose the ear were to say 'I am not an eye, I do not belong to the body', it does still belong to the body. If the body were all eye, how could it hear? If the

body were all ear, how could it smell? But, in fact, God appointed each limb and organ to its own place in the body, as he chose. If the whole were one single organ, there would not be a body at all; in fact, however, there are many different organs, but one body. The eye cannot say to the hand, 'I do not need you'; nor the head to the feet 'I do not need you.' Quite the contrary: those organs of the body which seem to be more frail than others are indispensable, and those parts of the body which we regard as less honorable are treated with special honour. To our unseemly parts is given a more than ordinary seemliness, whereas our seemly parts need no adorning. But God has combined the various parts of the body, giving special honour to the humbler parts, so that there might be no sense of division in the body, but that all of its organs might feel the same concern for one another. If one organ suffers, they all suffer together. If one flourishes, they all rejoice together. Now you are Christ's body, and each of you a limb or organ of it.

Discussion

Nothing could show more clearly than this allegory of the human body how necessary it is for the members of any society to remain in harmony if the society is to flourish. You know quite well, my friends, how successfully this allegory was used by the Roman people in one of the most dangerous times of their existence (Menenius Agrippa in Livy, *Ab urba condita* II. 32). It must have enjoyed no less success when set forth by Paul. We might have suspected this already, even without the proof furnished by the joyful eulogy the Apostle gave in his next letter. So the Corinthians too became peaceful in spirit. In Christendom, Israelites and Hellenes learned to look upon and treat each other as brothers. Should I expect a similar success with you, my friends? Indeed, I have all the more right to this hope, for I speak not to a mixed public, but rather to a select group of educated youth, who know full well that their behaviour will be imitated by the entire people. For as the leaders go—so says the word of God—so too go the people. On the other hand, the reasons for the disunity that prevails among the two peoples in our country are not nearly as weighty as those fuelling the hatred between Jew and Heathen. This will become apparent when we consider the former in more detail and compare them with the latter. You yourselves may judge whether my enumeration either makes light of or entirely omits something.

1. I admit that in the first place the *difference of language* spoken by the two peoples of our country contains a natural cause, if not for mutual hatred, at least for shunning any more intimate contact or fusion. For however trivial it might seem at first glance to many that two different languages are used in our country, each of which is only understood and spoken with appropriate fluency by a certain part of the people, it is important in fact. And the history of mankind knows no example of a people where such a difference prevailed that did not to some degree engender a decline in community spirit. This is quite understandable.

a) For several languages among one and the same people already brings with it the disadvantage that *the image of the essential equality of all citizens is blurred by the difference in language.* The idea of equality is the foundation for all the public spirit that is to be met with in the members of one and the same society. The greater the equality that prevails or at least appears to prevail, the more successfully any differences that obtain between them can be put out of sight. The more easily one finds one's own fortunes in those of one's neighbor, the more heartily one sympathizes with the weal and woe of others, the more deeply people love one another, the more willing they are to stand up for one another. Each difference that strikes the senses does damage to the public spirit. The difference in language, no matter how unimportant the learned declare it to be, nevertheless remains a difference, and indeed one that cannot be hidden. And this difference counts for a good deal among ignorant people. Someone who speaks differently from them appears as a kind of fabulous creature from a strange land. They gawk at him, and don't know what to make of him. They do see someone who appears the same as themselves, and yet they doubt whether he is truly the same inside, since he emits completely different noises than they do. And though, perhaps, the strangeness and the strength of the impression are diminished through familiarity, [the sense of inequality] increases on another side. For once there are certain differences among people, nothing is more common than to ask: which party is the more worthy? Usually each thinks itself better than the other; and then this becomes the first conflict, the first disunity among them. The conflict embitters the spirit all the more the more difficult it is to recognize that the opposed party criticizes one's language out of ignorance, only because they are incapable of reproducing its powerful or soft sounds.

b) Another disadvantage that the difference in language brings with it is that *it strongly hinders—if it does not render impossible—mutual interaction.* Is there anyone who doesn't know how difficult it is to communicate one's thoughts to another when one can't use language, and is restricted to the small number of natural signs? And how feeble and unhelpful such interaction is! And so everyone deals only with those who understand and speak the same language. The result is that no matter how much outer unity the laws of the state produce between people who speak different languages, there is no inner unity. Yes, they call themselves members of one and the same community, but in fact they have nothing in common. They may live next to each other, but they do not live with each other, since they cannot even freely exchange their thoughts.

These, my friends, are the reasons a nation formed of people who speak different languages can offer by way of excuse when it is criticized for a lack of unity. We Bohemians could certainly offer these excuses. But let us not believe that they can justify us! Let us not believe that it is impossible to build a tightly bound community despite the difference in language, and to stand out for the high degree of our unity! The Christians of the first century could teach us better. People of the most varied tongues converted to the religion of Jesus Christ. And in what deep harmony they all lived together; what an active concern they showed for the sufferings and fates of each other, not caring at all which language they happened to speak—as is shown, to mention but one instance, by the fact that contributions for the poor of one region could be raised from all the regions where Christian communities existed.

2. The difference in language is, admittedly, not the only thing that hinders the advancement of unity among us. A second, far more important

factor is the *difference in the ways of thought, in the ideas, and in the degree of enlightenment that obtains between the two peoples of our country.* For it is obvious that at least now, if not always, the Czech and German inhabitants of our country differ significantly in the respects I have just mentioned. Each of the two has certain features in its ways of thought and its morals that deserve praise; each has features that deserve reproach. More striking still is the difference in the ideas and in the degree of enlightenment between the two parts. Indeed since I look to further peace, I need not worry about causing strife by expressing the truth here: the Czechs are less well educated than the Germans. There has been a good deal, indeed too much, dispute concerning the causes of all this, my friends. And all too often people have sought to explain it by appealing to certain inborn differences in the natural constitution of the two peoples that share our country. It seems to me—let me say this frankly—that every explanation of this kind is not only dangerous and unprovable, but also offensive and defamatory. I will never allow myself to be persuaded that entire families, not to mention entire peoples, are saddled by nature with certain defects that can in no way be separated from them. Rather, I believe that people become whatever they are through upbringing and environment, and that any people, were they put in favorable circumstances, would attain a degree of perfection completely equal to that of any other. In order to explain the differences that exist between our two peoples nothing more is needed than to consider the unequal fortunes that they experienced in earlier times and in part still experience, as well as to take into account the enormous inequalities that have existed for hundreds of years in the opportunities, means, and support available to the two groups for furthering their education. But however these important differences may have arisen, it is quite natural that they do damage to the spirit of community. For if differences that at bottom concern only the outer man (namely, language) are already disadvantageous to the spirit of community, all the more worrisome are those differences that belong to the soul itself, the innermost part of a person. What else but the harmony of minds brings forth all friendship and community? And must it not be true that there will be greater opportunities and motives for a society to consider itself a whole, if more of its members are already united through natural bonds? And further, does not every project to be undertaken by several people demand a certain uniformity of ideas and frame of mind? If one person is very enlightened while the other is full of gross superstition, can they really agree to undertake a project together and bring it to a successful conclusion? Don't most educated people find it shameful to make common cause with an uneducated person even in trivial affairs? But if nothing is to be undertaken in common, when people are even ashamed to work together, how can we speak of a spirit of community? But however true all this may be, I nevertheless claim that a single glance at the Christians of the first century must shame us through the obvious proof they give us how, despite all of these and greater obstacles, a spirit of community, unity and love could still exist. Indeed, were not the differences in ways of thought, in ideas and principles incomparably greater and more striking among the Christians of the first century than they are among us? Just consider how varied were the parts that made up that first Christian community! How many different corners of the earth were represented in that small flock! How little preparation they had! The turmoil in which the entirety of human thought then found itself! How many contradictory opinions were current even among the Jews, not to mention the Greeks and Romans, where things were still worse. These were opinions not just concerning things of little importance, but the most important of all: about God, the immortality of the soul, the true essence of virtue! And yet, my friends, and yet, as the Scriptures assure us, there was but one mind and one heart in that community, people lived in great harmony and love, and everyone regarded his property, small and large, as the common possession of all! Can we hear this without feeling ashamed? Have we advanced so little on the road to perfection in these eighteen centuries that we still lag behind them?

3. But you will no doubt object to me that I have not yet mentioned the most important reason for the discord and bitterness between the citizens of our country. You have in mind the *remembrance of events whose memory is so loathsome*, through which it came to be that in our country the German language holds sway together with the Czech, and which brought about as well the still continuing oppression and inequity that one part of the people inflicts on the other. As perilous as it is to touch upon this point, my friends, I was by no means of a mind to pass over it in silence. For what help would it be to us to try to hide from

ourselves and others the cancer that gnaws at us? Does a wound heal just because it is covered up? So let us confess it, let us always confess that it is truly the greatest misfortune of our people that its two parts did not come together from the beginning by free choice, but rather for the most part through external force, and that even today one part—to the detriment of the other—is all too privileged, and raised above them! It is understandable that the memory of the inequity and unfairness that were inflicted on the ancestors survives in the descendants, especially since the consequences live on and indeed new injustices are continually heaped upon the old. And that is truly happening here. Is it not the case that the German-born, and those who are connected with them, are privileged in a hundred important ways? Is it not the German language that is used in all learned communication in the country? And has not German been elevated to serve as the language of business in all public matters? Must this not, however little it can be criticized in and of itself, be most unwelcome to the other part of the people? When they are thus set back, must this not be bitterly felt? But still more: is it not the case that the great and high-ranking in the country, the rich and propertied, are all of them either German born or perhaps even foreigners, or else persons who, having long since abandoned the Czech language and customs, are counted among the Germans? Does not the entire Czech speaking part of the population live in a deplorable state of poverty and oppression? And—the most scandalous of all—have not their superiors always been either Germans, or persons who associate with them? Persons who, since they don't have the least ability to speak their language, are completely incapable of appreciating the appeals and complaints, the requests and petitions of the Czechs and the reasons with which they support them? People who have no heart for them, who do not consider them as equals, and consequently do not treat them in a fatherly way, but rather follow the example of that Egyptian taskmaster, and bleed them white? [Exodus 1, 8-13] Who can have lived in our country, or even traveled for a short time, without having to acknowledge the truth of what I am saying? So who can be surprised that there is almost no spirit of community in our people? That the Czechs and the Germans never cooperate willingly? That instead, they despise each other, avoid and hate one another? No, my friends, there is no need to wonder why this is so; it is natural and easy to explain, as it is with the origin of all evil in this world, how the aversion that rules between the two peoples of our country has come to be. But just because an evil comes to be in a way that is natural and easy to explain, must it also be inevitable? The example of the first Christians once again shows us the contrary. For if the Czech part of our people reproaches the German with unfairness and inequity, how much more cause for complaint had the descendants of Israel for the ill-treatment they received at the hands of the Greeks. But whoever adopted Christianity forgot the past, bore with patience the things in the present that could not be changed, and sought in the spirit of love to explain and to forgive everything by appealing to the circumstances of the time. Let this example not by given to us in vain, my friends! Let us renew it in our present situation, and show the world for a second time how, among the strongest temptations to discord and disunity, a realm of harmony and peace can emerge, and spread blessings over mankind. The preservation and rapid spread of Christianity happened only because of unity. And who knows how much good we can produce if we follow the words of the Apostle with the same zeal as those first Christians: Think of yourselves only as parts of one and the same body, and Christ the Lord as your head. Amen.

On the Relations between the two Peoples of Bohemia (continuation)

Read on the eighth Sunday after Pentecost, 1816 [July 28]

Ezra 4

When the enemies of Judah and Benjamin heard that the returned exiles were building a temple to the LORD the God of Israel, they approached Zerubbabel and Jeshua and the heads of families and said to them, 'Let us join you in building, for like you we seek your God, and we have been sacrificing to him ever since the days of Esarhaddon king of Assyria, who brought us here.' But Zerubbabel and Jeshua and the rest of the heads of families in Israel said to them: 'The house which we are building for our God is no concern of yours. We alone will build it for the LORD the God of Israel, as his majesty Cyrus king of Persia commanded us.' [...]

In the time of Artaxerxes king of Persia, with the agreement of Mithredath, Tabeel and all his colleagues wrote to him; the letter was written in Aramaic, and read aloud in Aramaic. Rehum the high commissioner and Shimshai the secretary wrote a letter to King Artaxerxes concerning Jerusalem in the following terms:

... the Jews who left you and came to these parts have reached Jerusalem and are rebuilding that wicked and rebellious city; they have surveyed the foundations and are completing the walls. Be it known to Your Majesty that, if their city is rebuilt and the walls are completed, they will pay neither general levy, nor poll-tax, nor land-tax, and in the end they will harm the monarchy. Now because we eat the king's salt and it is not right that we should witness the king's dishonour, therefore we are sent to inform Your Majesty, in order that search may be made in the annals of your predecessors. You will discover by searching through the annals that this has been a rebellious city, harmful to the monarchy and its provinces, and that sedition has long been rife within its walls. That is why the city was laid waste. We submit to Your Majesty that, if it is rebuilt and its walls are completed, the result will be that you will have no more footing in the province of Beyond-Euphrates.

The King sent this answer:

[...] The letter which you sent to me has now been read clearly in my presence. I have given orders and search has been made, and it has been found that the city in question has a long history of revolt against the monarchy, and that rebellion and sedition have been rife in it. Powerful kings have ruled in Jerusalem, exercising authority over the whole province of Beyond-Euphrates, and general-levy, poll-tax and land-tax have been paid to them. Therefore, issue orders that these men must desist. This city is not to be rebuilt until a decree to that effect is issued by me. See that you do not neglect your duty in this matter, lest more damage and harm be done to the monarchy.

When the text of the letter from King Artaxerxes was read before Rehum the high commissioner. Shimshai the secretary and their colleagues, they hurried to Jerusalem and forcibly compelled the Jews to stop work.

Introduction

The story I have just read to you, my friends, provides both matter and stimulus for many an instructive reflection. What makes it especially noteworthy for the inhabitants of our country is the unmistakable similarity between what we read here and what has come to pass in our own land, both in the past and in the present. Just as the population of our country is made up of two different peoples, so too the population of Palestine after the [Jews'] return from captivity in Babylon was composed to two markedly different parts, for certain heathen peoples had been moved into the emptied lands during the time of the captivity, and were now, along with the surviving children of Israel, supposed to make up a single whole. And just as we find in our case that the differences between the two parts gave rise to hostility and disunity that still endures, so too we see that this was the case back then. Just as with us one is favorably inclined towards one group and dislikes the other, so too our text shows this flaw to be present in those days. The Samaritans who used the phrase "we who eat the king's salt" in their letter to the king were seen by him as faithful subjects and he gave them orders to watch over the others, and even to use force to prevent them from carrying out plans that could be dangerous to the throne. It is easy to imagine, my friends, how shamefully they abused this authority! Quite likely the holy writer chose not to discuss the details of the offenses both sides allowed themselves to commit, in order that the memory of them would not lead to eternal mutual hatred. He was content simply to remark that the construction of the temple was stopped by force of arms and remained suspended until the second year of king Darius' reign. It goes without saying that the court would from then on look upon the Jews with suspicion, and would see any advance in their well-being or power, any increase in their knowledge, as a danger to the realm. As a consequence, instead of working towards these goals, they would do all they could to ensure the weakness and oppression of the Jews. And could not all of this have been avoided, my friends, had people been more tolerant? If the Samaritans' wish, which was certainly not ill-intentioned, had met with approval, and their desire to participate in the building of the temple had been joyously accepted instead of being rejected with offensive pride? Let us learn from this example the disastrous consequences that follow when citizens do not deal with each other in a tolerant way, but instead allow the spirit of hostility to break out among them! And if—as the apostle Paul so beautifully observes—everything that the spirit of God has recorded in the scriptures is there for our instruction [2 Timothy 3, 16]—we shall learn from this example how to act more intelligently in our own, similar circumstances. I by no means deny that among us there may be many temptations for strife. I myself spoke quite frankly about the causes that can lead to disunity among us in our last gathering. But although this *disunity* is entirely natural and explicable, I can *in no way see it to be fair or reasonable.* I now plan to speak in more detail about the reasons why I think this. I hope that you too will appreciate the weight of these reasons and, supported by them, will for the rest of your lives do everything you can to promote peace and unity among the different parts of our nation. Then the very thing that has up to now caused such problems for us, namely, the difference between the two parts, will become a true blessing, and a source of rare advantages.

Discussion

1. When we cast another glance at the causes of disunity we learned of in our most recent gathering, my friends, it becomes obvious that none of them is important or strong enough to fully justify this hatred. In showing this we give at the same time a first demonstration that the spirit of discord that reigns among the citizens of our country deserves reproof.

The citizens of our country avoid and hate one another simply on account of the fact that their respective groups have not learned the same *language*. It does not require a great many words to show that this difference in no way suffices to justify divisiveness and hatred. For even though it be true that speaking different languages makes closer everyday interaction more difficult, it in no way follows that it renders impossible the kind of community that should exist between the citizens of one and the same country. For this, daily consultations are not necessary, nor is it necessary that everyone should convey his opinions directly to others. Rather, it is convenient to rely upon intermediaries who, knowing both languages, are capable of communicating the opinions of both parties. It is even more obvious that the apparent deficiencies and imperfections of a language, the sounds that the untrained or insensitive ear finds repulsive, can never justify serious quarrels, still less bitterness and hatred. What is my neighbour supposed to do about the fact that from infancy he learned to refer to things with different sounds than I do, sounds that from lack of familiarity seem ugly to me? Would I not speak just as he does, if only I had learned his language? And if I find the sounds of the other tongue unattractive, is it not possible that he finds the sounds of my language no less so? Who is supposed to decide which of the two of us has more right to complain that his ears are offended? This much, however, is certain: if we are just patient for a little while, we will find ourselves growing accustomed to the sounds of the other language, and far from finding them repulsive, will in the end take pleasure in the new range of sounds whose laws we are already beginning to grasp.

Far more important, I admit, far more important is the difference in the *frame of mind*, in the ideas and attitudes that we find in the two peoples of our country. Yet that this difference too in no way justifies division or hatred, my friends, we can decide simply by noting that in these respects no less considerable differences are met with among the citizens of either group. Who would deny that some of the Germans living in our country differ from others, and some Czechs from others of their language community, to no less an extent than is generally thought to obtain between Germans and Czechs? If only people who were similar in every respect and who agreed on everything could act in a common cause, how could there be any community among the Germans, or among the Czechs? No, it is not every inequality in people's attitudes and ways of thought that makes a community impossible. As great and various as the differences between the Czechs and the Germans are, there are thousands of other subjects where they think with one mind. And truly, if only we were to use properly the principles that all agree on, we could undertake a great many things together. Yet we persist in underestimating ourselves: neither party believes that there is as much agreement as there really is, because we look at things through hateful eyes, and do not want to forget the unmerited advantages one group has gradually wrested from the other. But what has reason to say about such behaviour? It reproaches both parties. It finds those who have been handed the short end of the stick to be *unfair* because they wish to see their fellow citizens punished for wrongs committed not by them but by their forebears. It earnestly commands those who continue to commit injustice and thus give cause for righteous indignation to put an end to this oppression, and to make good use of their privileges and wealth in order to reconcile themselves with their fellow citizens through kindness and charity. Yet even if not everyone heeds these commands of reason, when there are many citizens of the privileged group whose behaviour is rightly found repugnant, are we thereby justified in hating the entire group? Are not the majority people of good will? Do they play even the tiniest role in the acts of oppression that individuals in their midst permit themselves to carry out? Are not they oppressed almost as severely by those same people as our Czechs are? How wrong, then, how wrong would be hatred in the heart of a Czech that was aimed at all Germans without exception!

2. Since we have, as I hope, seen through these reflections that no reason could possibly justify the hatred we find between the two peoples of our country, let us now consider just how *damaging and pernicious such hatred is.*

a) The first and most certain thing that must be mentioned is that *such hatred makes our own life miserable, and far from reconciling us with those we hate, rather prompts them to heap new injuries on us.* Even when one overlooks all consequences that the expression of hatred occasions, it is in itself a most bitter feeling. We cannot be cheerful, we cannot rejoice in any good fortune that comes our way, as long as fraternal hatred roils in our hearts. If we are right to call love the most blessed of feelings, and if he whose breast is filled with love for all of mankind has on earth a foretaste of heaven, then earth is already hell for him who hates even a single person, not to mention a whole people, especially a people with whom he is forced to live in the closest association, since they are his compatriots. Thus simply to avoid making our own life miserable, each of us should take pains to ensure that the seed of hatred of our fellow citizens is not allowed to sprout in his heart. But we can say much more than this, my friends. If one part of our people hates the other and—as naturally occurs when this is the case—this hate finds expression here and there through word and deed, will there not be further consequences of this? Even if we assume that such people will never be led by their hatred to do the sorts of things that would bring official punishment upon them, this would still not prevent those at whom this hatred is directed to hate them in turn. Does it not lie in the very nature of hatred that it is repaid in kind? But what consequences are to be expected from such mutual hatred? One side will try to harm the other as much as possible, and will convince themselves that this behaviour is not evil, but rather something they have every right to do. For each of them will say: since the other hates me and seeks my demise, the duty of self-preservation requires that I use every permissible means to render him incapable of hurting me. What a sad life this will be, my friends! What a repulsive sight, these people who use their strength only to destroy each other! How completely different things are where the spirit of love prevails, where everyone seeks joy and praise for having served and helped a great many of his neighbours!

b) But this reminds me of yet another reason that shows the harmfulness of hatred between citizens. *Countless generally beneficial projects that can only be undertaken with the help of love and unity must forever remain undone in a country where these virtues are not found.* Here I speak of something, my friends, that we, sadly, can hardly grasp in our fatherland. The centuries-old lack of unity has made it possible for us to forget completely what citizens may do for each other when they are united. Thus we expect that the government will solve all our problems, while we ourselves do nothing! We complain about so many things that annoy and torment us, we bemoan the fact that the government has done nothing to help, and it never occurs to us that it is in our power alone to solve these problems, if only we saw fit to stick together. Don't ask me to enumerate all the useful institutions that the citizens of a country can create on their own, or which they could compel even the most sluggish of governments to introduce, if only they would join together to insist upon it. I would never come to the end, if I were of a mind to begin such a list. A glance at the institutions that people have recently founded in neighboring countries should suffice to illustrate my point. Some further reflection will teach you that there are far more institutions, just as good as those tried so far, which might be created in the same way. But this can only happen, I admit, when an intelligent community spirit prevails, when all the citizens of the country see themselves as belonging to a cohesive whole, and understand that the advantage of all is also an advantage for each. But when there is division, when one side has no intention of uniting with the other for a mutually beneficial goal, since one side begrudges the other any advantage, when one would rather die than tolerate the other doing as well as it, when suggestions made by one side are rejected by the other with scorn, simply because the other side made them: then, admittedly, it is impossible for the citizens themselves to accomplish anything through their efforts. For they are powerless, not because of an oppressive government, but rather entirely through their own fault.

c) And this powerlessness is the occasion for a further evil, namely, that *the rulers now find in their hands the means for misusing their power, and are now able to look after their own enrichment instead of the well-*

being of the people. If there ever was any doubt, events of recent times have provided many noteworthy examples showing that those in positions of authority are only human, and thus fallible, and easy opportunities for malfeasance are just as dangerous for them as they are for us. In more than one country we have seen men who began with far better convictions gradually turning into genuine tyrants, as opportunity led them in that direction. And where are such opportunities, where is the temptation to evil greater, than among a people that lacks a spirit of unity, a people that lives in division and disunity? There everyone looks out only for himself. He cares not if his neighbour is oppressed, perhaps he even rejoices in it. There a government can quickly place the entire people under the most humiliating yoke of slavery, it can abuse them however it likes, simply by being cunning enough never to take on everyone at the same time, but rather to play one side off against the other. Such a people will never manage to deliberate together, still less to achieve unity and work together—for each side is deaf to the suggestions of the other. Here too the government can make many unfair demands, for it meets with no resistance at all, not even objections or reproof. And if a few isolated voices are heard complaining, they are never taken seriously, because those complaining do not speak to one another, and thus are never in agreement. With such a people, all too conscious of its powerlessness, fear prevails, and as a consequence sycophancy and the most degrading servility take root. Everyone is afraid that speaking a single word of truth would put him in the government's bad books, and bring upon him the severest persecutions and punishments, without advancing the commonweal in the slightest, because no others will add their voices to his. Thus he finds it easier to ingratiate himself by becoming a toady and a flatterer. Not only does he set himself, and the power entrusted to him on account of his position, as much as possible under the control of his superiors, he also works incessantly to extinguish the rights of the people, and finally to remove all memory of them. Among such a people a spirit of slander and false boasting prevails. Out of mutual hatred, each side tries to belittle the other and to make it look dangerous to the authorities. As we saw in our text, even the most innocent of activities can be depicted so as to appear suspicious, leading to its suppression. Is it any wonder, my friends, that all of this finally corrupts the people in positions of authority? Is it any wonder, when such people live in constant conflict, when they are so powerless, when they submit without resistance to all injuries and insults, when their judgments concerning the treatment they receive are so false and absurd, when they gladly abase themselves, and don't even seem to have anything more pressing to do than to complain to the authorities and thus cast suspicion on one another—is it any wonder that the rulers of such a people learn to despise them, and finally to believe that they in fact deserve no better than they get?

d) These, my friends, these are the most unfortunate consequences of such divisions within a people. But we suffer a still more important loss because of them. I have intentionally waited until the end to say a brief word about it. *Precisely because our people is composed of such heterogeneous parts, precisely because of this we may become, if only we can overcome the spirit of division, one of the most fortunate peoples of Europe.* For it is a noteworthy law of nature that in order to produce a whole that strikes us as perfect, a certain diversity among well-united parts is required. Just as the earth we stand on is only truly productive when it is composed of many different kinds of soil, so too the people that is nourished from this earth is only truly fortunate and perfect when it is made up of quite different parts. Families who choose spouses that too closely resemble themselves gradually lose their mental and physical vigour, while marriages between different people produce exceptionally able descendants who unite the virtues of the two without inheriting the faults. The most magnificent people of antiquity, the most gifted, the most admired by cultured peoples to this very day, the Greeks, were composed of the most diverse of parts: and who can doubt that this contributed mightily to their excellence? So who knows, my friends, what we ourselves would be or might become, if only we had used the differences between our two peoples (which were not brought together without God's concurrence) more wisely, as we are now beginning to do? Who knows what might become of us if instead of feeding hatred and division among ourselves, we offered our hands in friendship? If we spread the good features of each people to the whole, while gradually eliminating the bad? If we sought as far as possible to fuse the two peoples so thoroughly that in the end there would be only one? Who knows what true excellence might be reserved for this people not yet born, especially when so many other circumstances allow us to presume that we are not the most forgotten of God's children? What a fruitful land he has allotted us—but surely not just so that we who cultivate it might find our misfortunes all the more painful! Yet as long as we do not better ourselves, my friends, as long as we do not eliminate the spirit of division, things will only get worse, never better! May the words of our Lord not serve as a prophecy we fulfill, but instead as a warning to make us better: every kingdom divided against itself goes to ruin. [Luke 11, 17] Amen.

On the Relations between the two Peoples of Bohemia (conclusion)

Read on the ninth Sunday after Pentecost, 1816 [August 4]

Acts 6, 1-6

> During this period, when disciples were growing in number, there was disagreement between those of them who spoke Greek and those who spoke the language of the Jews. The former party complained that their widows were being overlooked in the daily distribution. So the Twelve called the whole body of the disciples together and said, "It would be a grave mistake for us to neglect the word of God in order to wait at table. Therefore, friends, look out seven men of good reputation from your number, men full of the Spirit and of wisdom, and we will appoint them to deal with these matters, while we devote ourselves to prayer and to the ministry of the Word." The proposal proved acceptable to the whole body. They elected Stephen, a man full of faith and of the Holy Spirit, Philip, Prochorus, Nicanor, Timon, Parmenas, and Nicolas of Antioch, a former convert to Judaism. These they presented to the apostles, who prayed and laid their hands on them.

Discussion

It was in our last gathering, my friends, that we became acquainted with a truth that brings shame upon every inhabitant of our land, namely, that the Christians of the first century lived with each other in greater harmony and love than we do, even though they had far greater cause for disunity and hostility. The text I have just read may, however, show that that harmony was not without its interruptions, that some disagreements arose even in the first Christian community that existed in Jerusalem—disagreements which, however, were quickly resolved through wisdom. To the Christians of heathen origin it seemed that less generosity was shown to their poor than to the poor Christians of Jewish descent. It matters not whether this was really the case or merely imagined; it is enough that it provided the occasion for complaint, which, expressed with the frankness of the time, soon reached the ears of the Apostles themselves. The wisdom of their demeanor in such an unpleasant situation is wonderful indeed, my friends! First, they did not put off dealing with the matter, knowing well that a division of the spirit that had only recently come into existence would be easier to heal than a split resembling an old wound. No sooner had they heard reports of the evil than they took the steps necessary to cure it. It was suspected, whether rightly or wrongly, that the distribution of money to the poor was not entirely fair, that, even if the cause was not partiality towards their fellow Jews, they had not always given to the poor on the basis of correct judgment of the needs of the people. At the time they were still inclined to lay the blame for this on the many and varied activities that the apostolic vocation brought with it. Given a little more time, this thought would have developed into the wish that the Apostles agree to divide their duties, and put the business of looking after the poor in other, less busy, hands. Yet the apostles wisely anticipated the development of this desire. They summoned the community and announced that they wanted to be relieved of the duty of caring for the poor. This was an unequivocal proof that they had not held this job in order to look after their own interests, but rather only because there was no one else who could have done it in their place. But—and mark this well—they themselves did not choose the people who would occupy the office in the future; rather, they extended to the whole community the right to choose. Thus it was that they showed in the best way that it was in no way a matter of continuing to exercise influence on the society through the appointed people; thus they showed that their hearts were free from any of that vanity that rules those who want the final say on all sorts of matters only because it will appear that they are the source of everything. Thus their example puts to shame and rebukes all those who hold power in the world, who claim for themselves the right to appoint officials, often even in cases where they don't even know the person who is to be appointed. The far wiser actions of the Apostles caused the community in Jerusalem for their part to do what was fitting, since they now saw how honestly the dispute was being handled. All seven officials were chosen from among the heathens. Such a touching example of magnanimity shown to the heathens by the Jews: how could it have failed to reach its intended aim, how could the party that thought itself excluded not immediately be reconciled, and how could it have failed to convince them that they had been wrong to complain about people who could behave so nobly? O! If only the *disputes* that divide the citizens of our country could be *settled as happily*, my friends! They could be! But we must recognize the necessary *means* with the wisdom the Apostles displayed in their time, and we must be willing to lay down on the altar of patriotism the *concessions* that must be offered by both sides, with the same magnanimity that we saw in the party of the Jews! Let us reflect honestly, my friends, and before God, about what is to be done. This reflection is the subject that we previously set down for today's gathering.

Discussion

If we want to succeed in our battle against the hostility that prevails between the two peoples of our country, and establish unity and harmony, my friends, then we should be most concerned with doing everything we can to remove the causes that have produced and still sustain this hostility.

1. The investigations we presented in our second last gathering indicate that the greatest obstacle standing in the way of unity in our fatherland is the *difference in language*. If someone could remove this obstacle, if he could bring it about that all the inhabitants of our entire country spoke a single language, he would be the greatest benefactor of our people. Just so, if anyone could bring it about that everyone in the entire world spoke the same language, he would have to be the greatest benefactor of the whole human race. But as confidently as we may state that one day—after many millennia, I mean—this will indeed happen; and as much effort as the wise leaders of the Catholic Church have put into making this happen, and as much as we owe them thanks for making the number of languages and dialects spoken in Europe, as well as the extent to which they differ, much smaller than it otherwise would have been; as much as experience clearly teaches us that the number of languages spoken on earth becomes smaller with every passing century: nevertheless, the happy day when just one language shall prevail in our country is by no means close at hand. We must therefore be all the more ready to use

whatever means we can to make sure our linguistic differences cause as little harm as possible. The first is that we must *properly explain the difference in language to the as yet uneducated part of our people—the Czechs as well as the Germans.* We must explain to the ignorant how it came to be that different languages are spoken around the world; we must show them that it is purely a matter of convention whether one speaks of things in one way or the other, that because of the isolation of different peoples they must have hit upon the most diverse ways of designating their ideas; that the *differences in language that have thus come about are by far the least important differences* that can obtain between people; that it is therefore the greatest foolishness to believe a man to be better or worse than us simply because he expresses himself in a language different from ours; that it is purely a matter of habit that we find some sounds more pleasing or more melodious than others; and that nothing is more natural than that everyone finds the sounds of his mother tongue the most pleasing of all. So much, my friends, for the completely uneducated part of our people. As for the educated part, we must ask them in addition to either completely set aside the dispute over which of the two languages is intrinsically more worthy, or at least confront it with the greatest possible composure and moderation. It is in any case a pointless dispute, since no matter how it is decided, it will have no impact whatsoever on people's lives. Since no one invented his own language it should really not matter to either side whether their language or the other prevails in the dispute, yet people generally still get mightily exercised over the issue, and those who in the end are asked to concede that their language is less refined feel gravely injured. Consequently, my friends, every reasonable man should set himself the rule never to speak ill of a language within the hearing of those who revere it as their mother tongue, unless he is certain that he is speaking to people who have risen above all doubt about the truth I just spoke of. But all of this can prevent only the quarrels among you that arise from linguistic differences. The differences themselves have not yet been removed. But you should know that you can do a great deal to remove or at least reduce these differences, far more than the enemies of our well-being would like. Listen, and I shall tell you how! Those of you whom God has called to care for the souls of our people, shall also be entrusted with the administration of education in all regions of our country. Provided you do not shrink from expending some effort for this great aim, this very position will almost always allow you to provide the tender youths pouring into your schools who are only able to speak one of the languages, with an effortless introduction to the other. Almost never will you find that the authorities or the parents oppose your intentions. Children and their parents will instead be most grateful for the opportunity to learn something truly useful in your school. And provided you use appropriate methods of instruction, not instructing them through explicit exercises, you will be astounded by the fast progress your students make. In less than a year a boy, who began not knowing a single word of his neighbors' language, can employ it to express his thoughts readily and comprehensibly. What a great, immeasurably great benefit, especially for all the Czech inhabitants of our country! If he has acquired the German language, he can travel throughout the land, and everywhere find people he can communicate with; all the sources of learning created by his German neighbors are now open to him as well; he can gain an appropriate knowledge of all the laws that affect him; he is able to seek justice before any court; he can speak with authorities whose sovereignty is acknowledged by the lowliest up to the most prominent citizens. But it is also a great advantage for a German inhabitant, as well as for the whole country, when he learns the language of his Czech countrymen. Now he needs no interpreter to speak with any Czech; now he finds they no longer hate but instead love him; now he too learns to love a people of whose sound, healthy judgment, warm-heartedness and many other unrecognized virtues he now—thanks to his knowledge of their language–sees new proofs every day. And—do I even need to point out something so obvious, my friends? — one of the most holy duties of every German whom fate elevates to a position of authority over Czechs is to learn the language of his subordinates. For without understanding their language it is hardly possible to fulfill the duties of our post, and harder still to gain the love and trust of our subordinates! Without this, we must seem like paid enforcers to them, and indeed could not be more. For every good shepherd (as Jesus held) must have a voice that his sheep recognize [John 10, 4]. As arduous as it may be, this must happen, if even the most humble in our land are ever to be helped. But how? Do we not know many other languages, languages that concern us far less? Do we not learn the languages of the French, the Italians, the English, with great application and at great expense? Do we not strive to attain such perfection in this as to earn from them what is in truth equivocal praise, namely, that we speak their language like a native? Who would guess that we, who are so keen to learn foreign tongues show so little diligence in learning the other language of our own country? So little diligence, I say? I should rather say that we neglect it completely, yay, that we even—and this is almost unbelievable—are ashamed of speaking it! O, my friends, let us strive to cure our fellow citizens of this foolishness, which makes foreigners look upon us with such contempt! Instead of the mostly useless learning of foreign languages, let us aim at mastery of the two languages of our country. Let each of us encourage every fellow citizen he knows to do the same.

2. The more successful we are in this, the more Germans we enable to learn Czech, and the more Czechs to learn German, the more we shall diminish or even remove the second obstacle to unity in our fatherland, namely, *the differences in ways of thought*, ideas and attitudes prevailing between the Czech and German inhabitants of our country. It is no wonder that people who, despite living so close to one another, cannot understand each other's language diverge greatly from one another in their ways of thought, ideas and attitudes. For they lack the most important means of assimilation, namely, *social intercourse*. It is the mutual exchange of opinions that occurs in frequent contact, listening to the reasons for these opinions, and the counterarguments that can be raised against them, it is seeing different behaviour more often, and the often habitual but no less effective imitation of it that gives this interaction the force of assimilation. The more often and the more easily the citizens of one and the same country are able to interact, the more they become alike in their ways of thought and customs. In addition, people who can speak the same language can maintain a kind of interaction even when separated by great distance, since they are able to communicate their views to others by means of written essays. Add to this that people who speak the same language generally obtain their ideas and knowledge from the same sources, since the same book that one has read with profit and praised to the other can also be read by him and used as a guide. They will accordingly be instructed by one teacher, and hence be of one mind. How then could unity and community fail to prevail among them? But perhaps hearing this, you will yourselves recall, my

friends, that there is a way to communicate the ideas and attitudes of one part of the people to those who have not yet learned their language well enough. This is translating into the other language the writings that are most widely read by one group and have the greatest influence on their education, in order to make them accessible to the others. It brings me great joy to be able to say that in this gathering there are some who have already thought of this salutary activity, and indeed have already set to work on it. May heaven see to it that this small beginning has a truly blessed success, and that in each year more co-operators, generously supported, will be added! May no vanity or love of fame spoil the purity of your aims, and cause conflict and division or pernicious mistakes! May heaven protect you, so that certain evil men, who are enemies to all good, may never find an opportunity to portray the most innocent and peaceful undertaking in a light that makes it appear dangerous to the peace of the state, so that it may be suppressed with force by the authorities!

3. The activity of writing is also the best way to fight against the third obstacle to unity among us. I mean the *status* of the German inhabitants of our land in relation to the more ancient inhabitants *which gives rise to such bitterness*, a status that existed in the past, and in part still exists. That this situation might be removed, even just the parts that endure in the present, my friends, is something rather to be wished than realistically to be expected, especially since carrying out such a change, even if the state were in favor of it, would encounter other great difficulties. So there are really no other means available for instilling unity among the citizens of our country in spite of this inequality, really no other means in our power than *spreading ideas in the country that make the necessity of common spirit ever more obvious, and the emergence of excellent individuals from each of the two peoples whose merits will make their entire peoples worthy of the other's love.* O, that each of us might only do everything in our power to further this twofold goal! Everyone upon whom God has bestowed the higher gifts, and who feels himself suited to be a writer for his people, can be sure that he cannot use his God-given talents better than to produce writings that promote unity in our country, writings that make ever more clear to our people the important truth that the division that has existed up to now, this lack of unity that shows itself in so many ways, harms no one more than themselves, and brings more

joy to their oppressors than anyone else. But also those upon whom God has not bestowed the outstanding talents that allow one to succeed as a writer, or those whose circumstances hinder the pursuit of this activity, should not neglect to do whatever they can for this noble goal. Whoever he may be, whatever position he may occupy in life, will he not find numerous opportunities to speak with his fellow citizens about what is best for all? Are there not daily gatherings where we exchange views on events affecting the common good? How many opportunities here to correct the distorted judgments of our fellow citizens; to acquaint them with the advantages that unity brings and how much good they themselves could bring about, if only they would seriously stick together! But I have still greater hopes for the second means I mentioned. For it is human nature for someone to love or hate an entire class, even an entire people, for the sake of one worthy or unworthy individual among them. Thus each one of us can, if only we are willing, contribute a great deal to the reconciliation of the two peoples of our country by making ourselves paragons of excellence among our own people and especially by making ourselves worthy of love to the others. May each Czech among us seek on every occasion heaven presents him with to show love and goodness to the Germans; may each of the Germans here do the same for the Czechs; I am certain that if only the small group assembled here were to follow this rule, which is so easy and which brings immediate rewards, then in fewer than two decades all the hatred between the two peoples of our country must fade away and disappear! This is all the more certain to happen if you all also conscientiously apply the other means I spoke of today. Do so, my friends! Let us not show ourselves to be obstinate in the face of the present, beneficial demands like that group of Jews of the time of Jesus, who wrung the bitter complaint from him that he had striven in vain to show them the path of redemption: that he had striven in vain to gather them like a hen gathers her chicks! [Matthew 23, 27] O, a shameful downfall was the punishment of this obstinacy—a warning to all later peoples! Let us learn better than those people "what leads to our salvation" [Luke 19, 42], so that we may come to stand among the peoples who seek to rise again after the pillars of tyranny collapse! God, who looks with love to the well-being of peoples, will stand by us too in the struggle for freedom that is our lot! Amen.

On Conduct towards the Jewish Nation

Read on the Feast of the Presentation of our Lady at the Temple, 1809 [Nov. 21]

Luke 2, 22-35

> Then, after their purification had been completed in accordance with the Law of Moses, they brought him up to Jerusalem to present him to the Lord (as prescribed in the law of the Lord: "Every first-born male shall be deemed to belong to the Lord."), and also to make the offering as stated in the law: "A pair of turtle doves or two young pigeons." There was at that time in Jerusalem a man called Simeon. This man was upright and devout, one who watched and waited for the restoration of Israel, and the Holy Spirit was upon him. It had been disclosed to him by the Holy Spirit that he would not see death until he had seen the Lord's Messiah. Guided by the Spirit he came into the temple; and when the parents brought in the child Jesus to do for him what was customary under the Law, he took him in his arms, praised God, and said: "Lord, now lettest thou thy servant depart in peace, according to thy word: For mine eyes have seen thy salvation, which thou hast prepared before the face of all people; light to lighten the Gentiles, and the glory of thy people Israel." The child's father and mother were full of wonder at what was being said about him. Simeon blessed them and said to Mary his mother, "This child is destined to be a sign which men reject; and you too shall be pierced to the heart. Many in Israel will stand or fall because of him, and thus the secret thoughts of many will be laid bare."

Introduction

Great expectations were these, my friends, expressed by this pious old man in our Gospel concerning the child Jesus. He would later serve as the saviour of all peoples, the light of the heathens and the glory of his own people, the people of Israel. That these hopes were no empty delusions, that they were based on solid foundations, and that they were completely correct—this has been gloriously settled by the best judge of all, success itself. The weak child that Simeon then held in his arms grew up to be the great man, the only one among all mortals who in this way understood and carried out the infinite resolution to sacrifice himself in order to save and bless the entire human race. This weak child grew up to be a man who through his understanding of life set up a light of wisdom whose beneficial rays then spread throughout the world. We too, my friends, are witness to the fact that also our country has been illuminated by his light; we too, if only we want to, belong among the number of those blessed through his death. Simeon therefore prophesied of this child with good reason that he would serve as the saviour of all peoples, and be the light of the heathens. And knowing this, was it unfair of him to flatter himself with the third hope that this child would become the glory of his people, the people of Israel? Who would not have thought that the well-deserved fame that Jesus would enjoy among all peoples would not redound to the credit of his own people? Is it not fair for us to honour the people that brought forth the saviour of the entire human race? Is it not fair for us to esteem the nation that counts among its members the most perfect of all mortals, the Son of God become man? But it is, unfortunately, only too obvious that up to the present moment exactly the opposite is the case. Israel's scattered descendants not only enjoy no reputation among us, but are instead in almost every country treated with contempt and oppressed and abused in the most unbearable ways. Nor is it just the rabble of Christianity that allows itself to abuse them in this way: even persons who may lay claim to education, and whom in every other respect one must accord both insight and uprightness, give vent to the most bizarre ideas on this subject. How often one hears them without a second thought and in all seriousness claim that the Jews, every last one of them, are deceitful and evil! How contemptuously they are treated, the individual members of this nation, for no other reason than that they are Jews! But no matter how common this behaviour is, and that it has gone on for centuries, it is nevertheless anything but right, and anything but pleasing to our God, the God of both Christians and Jews. May I then be permitted to raise my weak voice to help to put an end to this hateful abuse? I will first *set out the correct point of view from which we should judge the condition of the Jewish nation and our usual behaviour towards them. Afterwards, I shall draw certain conclusions concerning how we should behave.* If, my friends, you allow the truth that you shall hear in this hour to work upon you, the result cannot but be that many thousands of people will be able to enjoy a much more gentle fate than they have had to endure up to now. But in order to bring about such happy success, I need your help, O sublime Son of God! You who certainly do not want to see us treat with such contempt the people among whom you found it worthy to live.

Discussion

1. Whoever reflects with an unprejudiced mind upon *the true characteristics of the people of Israel and the generally predominant behaviour of Christians towards them,* will admit several things, my friends. This people—he will admit—has many considerable failings; but—he will add—these failings are a natural consequence of the hard fate it has suffered; for—he will further remark—these failings by no means lie in the very nature of this people, as is shown by the many virtues and merits it has displayed, partly in the past, but also in the present; and it is utterly pointless—he will finally remind us— to attempt justifying the ill-treatment of this people by claiming it to be destined for them by God's providence. We want now to convince ourselves more firmly of each of these points.

a. *That Israel's scattered descendants, as they now find themselves, have many significant failings*—this, my friends, can indeed not be denied. As painful as it is to the true friend of mankind when he must attribute not only to a single man but also to an entire nation—that is, to the majority of many thousands of people— certain offenses and failings, the love of truth obliges him to admit that the majority of the Israelites have the detestable failing of avarice. One finds among the majority of them a love of money which is commonly implanted already in tender youth and grows and becomes more deeply rooted with increasing age—but not in order to use it, rather merely to accumulate and hoard it. The friend of humanity observes with sorrow how this avarice, especially when other circumstances contribute, brings in its wake a far more detestable vice, namely, unscrupulous cheating in trade and traffic. For sad experience teaches us that only a few among this people have the honesty not immediately to take advantage of every occasion where money can be got through fraud or other means. It saddens the friend of humanity when he so often finds such low thinking among the lower classes of this people, so that one cannot even awaken the natural desire for honour among them. For one sees clearly that a common Jew cannot bring himself to desire the good opinion of others; provided only that he profits, we can say or think whatever we wish of him, he shall not blush before any curses. This utter lack of for a sense of honour extends even to their posture, and in ways distressing to every observer is displayed in many gradations, from a complete lack of adornment to the most extreme uncleanliness. With deep sadness, finally, the friend of humanity observes the extreme ignorance and the bristling superstition that reigns among the majority of this people. For the poor classes of this people not only do without knowledge that aids the comfort and advancement in life, one also finds no trace whatsoever of definite and correct ideas of the true nature of virtue, of God, and of the life hereafter—instead of which, one finds the most ridiculous and harmful ideas firmly rooted.

b. Yet as true and undeniable as all this may be, my friends, I have no hesitation in claiming that *all of these various and great flaws of the people of Israel are merely the natural consequences of the hard fate it has had to suffer for so many centuries.* Consider for yourselves the reasons that I will briefly adduce to prove my claim, and I hope you shall reach the same conclusion. For no one can deny that it has been a hard fate, an unprecedented fate that the scattered descendants of Israel have had to suffer in all the countries where they have been dispersed, ever since the unfortunate destruction of their state, that is, already for more than seventeen hundred years. It is not difficult to understand how such an unparalleled harsh fate that has endured for so long could have reduced the character of this nation to the degraded state in which we now find it. The Jews were prevented from employment in any of the crafts and were restricted to commerce alone. But is it not precisely this kind of employment that gives the greatest opportunities and the strongest inducement for the love of money and avarice? This hated people was forced on the one hand to pay such high levies and taxes, and on the other denied all means of raising the required sums by honest means, so that almost nothing else remained but to cheat, to raise the money by cunning and trickery of all kinds—in order to give it back to us! Is it any wonder when men who have learned through necessity in this way to cheat would continue to do so, even when no longer forced? People have always thought themselves justified, indeed they saw it as a sign of zeal for Jesus most agreeable to God to hate the Jews with their entire being—the unfortunate children and grandchildren of those depraved people who had cried out the dreadful "crucify him!"—and, when they are weak and defenseless, to let them feel their contempt and ridicule. These poor unfortunate people learned from experience that it didn't matter whether they behaved well or ill, that they would be hated and held in contempt in either case even by upright citizens, simply because they were Jews. What is more natural than that they in the end lost heart, and abandoned all attempts to secure a better reputation, that they lost the desire for honour and in the end almost gave themselves over to the despicable behaviour that everyone already held them guilty of? And when the most extreme poverty and want is heaped on top of this indifference to honour, should it be hard to grasp why uncleanliness should have become so common among the lowest classes of this people? People were so cruel that they would not allow the Israelites into our schools; they had forced the majority of them into such a wretched condition that they no longer had the desire or the means to support their own teachers; in such circumstances, how could it fail to happen that ignorance and its constant companion, superstition, more and more came to prevail? Why do we sit and wonder why the people of Israel have so many faults, when we ourselves have implanted them? Why do we seek the causes for these flaws in the most improbable way, in some I know not what kind of special nature this people is supposed to possess, when everything is sufficiently explained by our behaviour towards them?

c. That the former kind of explanation is not only completely arbitrary but also contradicts the truth, my friends, is shown clearly by the fact that *Israel's people had so many advantages and virtues in former times and indeed also at present*, virtues that no truly corrupt nature could produce. For every unbiased observer must admit that even today, even in the wretched condition in which they have languished these seventeen hundred years, the character of the Israelites still has many excellent advantages, which show their intrinsic capacity for greater perfection just as a glimmer betrays a jewel, even when it is covered with dust and grime. Moderation in the enjoyment of sensual pleasures, assiduity and persistence in pursuing the goals once chosen, grateful remembrance of charitable deeds they have received—these, my friends, are beautiful and admirable virtues, through which the people of Israel are particularly distinguished even to this day. And let us not think that the ignorance and superstition that we find among this people is the product of a natural incapacity of the understanding—on the contrary, it is astounding how many proofs this people gives of its wit and clear judgment. Let us just return to ancient times, when this people could still lay claim to its independence, and stood at the peak of its greatness: there we see no trace of the failings that now brand it. Rather, we see quite the opposite: numerous shining virtues and high distinctions. In the days of David or Solomon this people, of which we now have such a low opinion, was an object of attention and admiration throughout the Orient. It was a magnanimous people, a generous people, which did not even possess the idea of avarice, which was just beginning to learn about trade; it was a faithful people, whose word was sacred and who punished perjury by eradicating an entire tribe; it was a courageous people, that set a high value on its honour. Far from contemptible dirtiness, it loved instead the highest cleanliness, the finest manners, and in public buildings, in their temples, the greatest magnificence and excellence. Of all peoples that of Israel was then the most enlightened, that which had the most correct concepts of the true essence of virtue, of God, and of the condition of men in another life; people came from far away lands to learn high wisdom in the city of Zion. Indeed, the remnants of its learning and some songs of its holy poets are still counted among the greatest masterworks of their kind. A people, my friends, that once stood at such a high level of perfection demonstrably has the inner capacity for the best things. And if its present condition is contemptible, the cause can only lie in its outer circumstances, in the harsh treatment at our hands it has had to suffer for so many centuries.

d. But perhaps we seek to excuse this treatment, my friends, by saying that *it was planned by God's providence*. God, we say, had long ago spoken through his prophets, saying he would punish the people that had rejected his Holy one. Do we then not simply carry out God's will when we treat the Jews in this way? *A futile excuse*, my friends! For if it were valid, then it would also excuse the behaviour of the Jews who had unjustly condemned Jesus to death—for this too was planned by God's providence, it too was foretold by the holy prophets. Everything that happens lies within the scope of God's plans, and without God's concordance nothing happens. Nevertheless, everything that men do against the clear voice of their conscience is evil, and shall be punished by God. He lets us know quite clearly through our conscience that we should never oppress anyone, still less an entire people, and by so doing engender vice. If we do so anyway, we do something evil, and shall be punished by God —even if He clearly foretold that things would happen in this way. He in no way commanded us with this prophecy; rather, He told us, through the apostle Paul, to revere the people from whom came—at least in body—the one who is at the same time the highly praised God in eternity. And can we mention the example our Jesus gave on the cross, still praying for those who had murdered him? Can we still doubt whether He would have preferred hard blows or a sympathetic, friendly treatment of his former fellow citizens, whom he loved so tenderly, for whom—foreseeing the imminent demise of their state—he could cry the bitterest of tears? O, certainly it was not just that downfall but also what would come after, the centuries-long oppression of his countrymen, which he already foresaw—this was why those tears flowed. You Christians think you honour Him through this oppression, and it embittered his death!

2. Yet we do not want merely to be moved by idle feelings, my friends; rather, we want to see whether we ourselves can do something to put an end to such great abuses. We already made known our intention to draw from these general truths *certain consequences concerning our own behaviour.* To this end, we shall seek to answer the following three questions: what can we do now, immediately? What at least mediately? Finally, what will we be able to do in the future to improve the condition of the Israelites?

a. Already *at present*, and indeed *immediately* and *through our own efforts* we can do a good deal to improve the situation of the Jews. Admittedly, at the moment we are too weak to bring about changes of great scope, involving this entire people. Yet we can have a beneficial effect on individuals, we can spare them a good deal of suffering and do much to improve their condition. Let us look upon as one of our most sacred duties, my friends, to use these opportunities to our utmost! The greater the injustice that our fellow Christians inflict on this people, the more incumbent it is upon us to notice this injustice, and, by opposing it, do whatever lies in our power to put things right. Far be it from us ever to join others in employing that tone of contempt and mockery people so often permit themselves to use against the Jews. On the contrary we shall use every occasion when we speak to them to show that we are not in the grip of this general prejudice; we will attempt to show them in every way we can that we do not hold them in contempt simply because of their birth, simply because they are Jews, that we do not automatically expect to find them guilty of dishonesty or some other vice—they shall see that the opinion we have of them depends upon their behaviour alone. Through our humane treatment all the better members of this people shall be encouraged, shall take heart and feel drawn towards us; he shall not see in our every word and glance the reproach that he is only a Jew, he shall be able in an instant to forget the deep divisions between him and us, and we shall speak together as one man to another. When a suitable opportunity presents itself for the misguided to learn from those who know better, when we can make it obvious to him that it is himself that he most harms though fraud and deception, when we can cast some spark of truth in his soul, let us do it with piety. If we can help a poor, oppressed person, the fact that he does not share our faith in no way prevents us from lending him our support. Perhaps he will not venture to talk to us about it—why, then we shall do it of our own accord, thinking all the while that so much remains to be done to make up for the wrongs we have heaped upon this people for seventeen hundred years!

b. But we can do still more for the good cause, my friends, for what we ourselves do not have the power to do can yet be accomplished *through the strength of others*, when we seek to spread the views that we endorse more and more to others. As long as people do not see the faults of a certain way of behaving, how can we expect them to change for the better? To this day only the tiniest number of Christians are clearly and vividly convinced that their behaviour towards the Israelites is unjust and sinful; only the tiniest number believe that the command to love one's fellow man extends to Jews as well as to Christians; most are still foolish enough that they think it an offense against the faith, and believe they detect concealed freethinking, when one seeks to extend to the Jews the same civil rights that Christians have, and to demand that both be treated the same. Even should powerful people now want to introduce such a sudden change by legislation, they would encounter the greatest resistance. So you see, my friends, it is first of all most important —that this beneficial change be spread quite generally in the minds of Christians, that better concepts are first spread among the people before the complete restoration of the suppressed rights of the Israelites can be contemplated. So let us make good use of every occasion where we can do something to foster the dissemination of better concepts! Each of us has such opportunities, some of us more than others. Will not the example we set through our own behaviour towards the oppressed Jews already make a most splendid impression on the Christians who observe it? It shall convince them far better than mere words that their opposite behaviour is sinful. Should conversation happen to turn to such topics, let us prove with solid reasons that we owe the Israelites better treatment; let us rigorously refute all objections and contrary prejudices, and clearly show their nullity. But let us especially shine a light on the harmful consequences that our harsh treatment of the people of Israel produces, in that it is precisely the cause why this people so unanimously clings to its old religion, and does not take the small step from the immature religion of their ancestors to the mature religion of Christendom. This would have happened long ago, were it not for the fact that, on the one hand, the extreme ignorance and abundant superstition in which this people—through no fault of its own—found itself, kept it from recognizing the palpable errors of its present beliefs, and on the other hand the hatred that it bore towards its oppressors, the Christians, which they took in with their mother's milk, so blinded them that they could not see the obvious advantages of our faith.

c. And this now leads me to the answer to the third question: what will we have to do for the well being of Israel *afterwards*, once our influence has perhaps become more significant? Our strength, my friends, increases with every passing year; and as weak as we may still be in this hour, many of us shall find ourselves in a few years' time in a position of influence from which many things are possible—perhaps it will be through writings that we work upon the thoughts of many thousands; perhaps it shall be by taking part in the government of the country that we shall be able to affect entire peoples—but when it happens, my friends, let us work wisely towards the complete restoration of the wounded rights of the people of Israel! Wisely, I say—let us not demand things that, given the opinions and prejudices that may still prevail in our country, are not feasible; let us not move too suddenly nor too violently, for this as a rule does not succeed and in the end only makes the evils worse. Let us only insist upon, let us work towards ensuring that better educational institutions are provided for the people of Israel, that better care is taken to ensure their enlightenment and the cultivation of their minds, that better prospects are offered to them, that they not be restricted to commerce, but indeed encouraged to work in other fields, and that the taxes they are obliged to pay be reduced! Only in this way, my friends, shall we gradually remove the great wrong we have inflicted upon this people; only in this way shall we wipe out the stain that the unchristian treatment of this people has left on the history of Christendom. Then this nation shall be raised from the dirt, shall leave its blindness behind and take up in friendship the religion of Jesus, as is their right, and that blessed time that Jesus rejoiced over shall finally be near: when there shall be but one flock, and one shepherd! Amen

On the Mission and Dignity of Womanhood

Read on the Feast of the Ascension of Mary, 1810 [August 15]

Introduction

If we count the annual feast days our church has dedicated to the memory of certain of her renowned members, we cannot fail to notice that nearly equal numbers of them are dedicated to members of the female and to the male sex. More important still, the feast days of a certain woman, the esteemed mother of our Lord Jesus Christ, are celebrated with more solemnity than those of all the rest of God's saints. I conclude from this that the Catholic–Christian Church has always maintained and manifested special attention and respect for the half of humankind we call the female sex. The concepts of the mission and dignity of woman which the Christian Church confesses and has spread wherever it gained a foothold are entirely different from those which were common to nearly the whole earth before the introduction of Christianity. In our days it almost seems as if the views of the mission and dignity of women that Christianity has established are more and more pushed into the dark and marked for oblivion. The vile heathen opinion is revived that the female is essentially inferior to the male in dignity and importance, that woman is given to man for no higher purpose than sensual pleasure, that a woman has no special rights or entitlements and no higher duty than to live for the carnal appetites of the male sex. How can such an unworthy opinion fail to have the most detrimental consequences? Can boys and men who incline to such an opinion treat women with the respect that is rightfully theirs? Can they fulfill the most important obligations they have toward individuals of the other sex, whether of sons to their mothers, of husbands to their wives, or, more broadly, toward acquaintances and contemporaries? And should women themselves be unfortunate enough to adopt such debased ideas of their own dignity, and thus cannot even imagine their own high mission, how can we expect them to fulfill it? From this you can see, my friends, how necessary it is to stress again the *more authentic concepts of the mission and dignity of women*, and impress them especially upon young men, for they, more than others, are in danger in more than one way of sinning against womankind. Therefore let nothing stand in the way of my speaking today about this subject! The biblical text that our church asks us to read to the faithful on this day will serve us as an introduction to our discussion.

Luke 10, 38-42

> While they were on their way Jesus came to a village where a woman named Martha made him welcome in her home. She had a sister, Mary, who seated herself at the Lord's feet and stayed there listening to his words. Now Martha was distracted by her many tasks, so she came to him and said, "Lord, do you not care that my sister has left me to get on with the work by myself? Tell her to come and lend a hand." But the Lord answered, "Martha, Martha, you are fretting and fussing about so many things when only one thing is needed. The part that Mary has chosen is best; and it shall not be taken away from her."

Discussion

This gospel, my friends, is a striking proof of the attention and esteem Jesus had for women. It is a woman whose house the great prophet found worthy to enter. Now demonstrations of respect toward women are often nothing but hidden sensuality, but no one who knows Jesus' character will suppose that this was the reason why he preferred the presence of these noble sisters to the company of others. In the present case his own conduct is proof of this: He enters the house of Martha in order to teach. How very much does Jesus' behaviour contrast with what is common in our day, where we have accepted the foolish notion that women are not capable of being taught serious subjects, were the only instruction they receive concerns useless elocution skills and ruinous arts of vanity and coquetry! Jesus thought of woman with more dignity. He sternly reprimanded Martha for being too worried about gratifying the senses of her guest, while he praised Mary for choosing the best part, preferring the education of her mind to concerning herself with her guest's material satisfaction. If we consider the thought that Jesus here expresses in the context of what he frequently said about women, we can construct the following view of their mission and dignity. [. . .]

1. To begin with, nothing is more certain than Jesus' conviction that *the female sex is equal to the male in all important respects, or that both sexes have the same capacity for the three goals—wisdom, virtue and happiness, and that they therefore enjoy the same rights on earth.* We have already seen that Jesus thought women, and not only men, capable of serious and exalted knowledge: he entered the house of a woman to convey his sublime messianic teaching and, after all, had among his companions not only male, but also female disciples. Indeed, does not the well known incident of the Samaritan woman at the well of Sychar [John 4, 6-42] prove that he must have thought women more adept than men at grasping with lively appreciation a hidden truth and spreading it among the people? It follows at once that he attributed to womankind the same predisposition towards virtue and happiness. Or did he ever make a distinction in this matter? Did he not admit both sexes into Christianity? Did he not promise both of them the same immortality and reward? Did he not promise that in heaven whatever distinction still prevails here will be removed and complete equality introduced? But it is also clear that it was his will that those who are completely equal in the other world should treat each other in the present world as equally as at all possible and should grant each other the same rights and privileges. It would be better for you, O you oppressed womankind, if in our principles, customs, habits and civic institutions we acted in harmony with the precepts of Jesus. Then you would not be barred from all serious learning and higher knowledge that men now keep only for themselves; then no one would fancy that everything possible was done for your education as long as you are given some useless elocution training and are taught skills of a sort that entertain fools and annoy the wise; then we would not read in acclaimed writings that there can be no virtue in the female sex, that here all apparent virtue is only weakness, instinct or the effect of vanity; then men would not seize all rights and claims to earthly goods; then you would not be the afflicted part and without protection, whose lamentation no one hears, destined to live in pain and merely to serve the lust of others; then you would not tremble all days of your youth for fear that some evil fellow might fall on you in a weak and unarmed moment and rob you of all your happiness, then

go unpunished while bringing upon your head the ridicule and derision of the whole town; nor would you have to fear being neglected in old age, after giving life and education to many a good citizen. If habit has not rendered you entirely insensible to all these follies and crimes of our sex—if you feel the great injustice that to the present day one half of humanity has visited upon the other: then I beseech you to oppose this nonsense by spreading the truth that womankind has the same capacity for wisdom, virtue and happiness as men and for that very reason should have nearly the same rights and entitlements.

2. I said nearly the same rights and entitlements, for as long as they reside on this earth an exact equality between the two sexes is of course never present and never desirable. The difference that nature herself has introduced leads to certain distinctions in mutual rights and duties: but this should not be exaggerated. Rather, attending to the teachings of Jesus, we should never forget that *this difference is only temporary and aims at the mutual furtherance of virtue and happiness of the two sexes as well as the reproduction of our species*. In the view of Jesus, and in the judgment of common reason, the reproduction of the human species is the final cause why the wise creator has introduced the difference between the sexes. But procreation is not the only purpose: without doubt this difference was also to bring about certain social arrangements that should promote virtue and happiness not only of the man, but also the woman. But—I now come to what is perhaps the cruelest aberration to which humanity was led by passion—almost everywhere on Earth the male sex has been able to arrange the marital institution in such a way that their wildest carnal appetites were given their widest range, with little regard for the happiness of women and the advancement of virtue of both sexes. In most states man was allowed to have as many wives as he wanted, provided that he was rich and powerful enough. Where polygamy was not allowed only men, but not women, were given the right to choose. Without even asking if she wanted him as her companion and master, the man could buy his wife from her father. Afterwards he was free for the most dubious of reasons to desert her. If he violated marital fidelity, he was mildly chastised when for the same offence she was cruelly punished. One could truly say that before the appearance of Christianity the distinction between the sexes served the pleasure of men, but for womankind was nothing but unspeakable misery and dis-

tress. How much this was improved through Christianity, and how much more improvement would occur if only we listened more carefully to the teaching of Jesus! Jesus explicitly forbade polygamy, and happily it has been eliminated in all countries that can rejoice in the presence of Christianity. As well, the woman can no longer be forced to enter into wedlock; rather, marriage is a free contract requiring the agreement of both sides, and this contract lasts for a lifetime. There can be no arbitrary cancellation, and all divorces that serve only the voluptuous urges of the husband and impair the happiness of the wife have been completely abolished. In brief, in the spirit of Jesus the matrimonial estate must be so arranged that the difference between the sexes does not merely serve the lust of the male, but also raises the wife's joy of living; it must serve to develop in the wife as well as the husband the highest virtues.

3. Yet, as much as Christianity insists that both sexes should derive equal benefits from God's provisions for the procreation of the human race, it was nonetheless the will of Jesus that *for the sake of good order the husband should be the head of the matrimonial household, and the wife should be viewed as his first and most important helpmate and friend.* From the very beginning of the Christian Church this has been their doctrine and custom. And the apostle Paul does not hesitate to use this analogy: the husband is the master of the wife as Christ is the head of the church; and just as the church must obey Christ, so also should the wife be subject to the husband in all things. But, you men: treat your wives with the same love that Christ had for his church, he, who sacrificed his life for it. If we consider this carefully, my friends, we cannot find a wiser arrangement. For their must always be a leader in any society no matter how small; and in a marriage, too, there would be innumerable arguments, fights and divisions if it were not determined, from the outset, which of the two members was to give in to the other. [...] That Jesus determined man to be the master shows his deep knowledge of human nature. If we carefully consider the specific character of the two sexes, if we take into account the man's urge to dominate, his stubbornness, his more vivid sense of power and if, on the other hand, we consider the more gentle disposition of the woman, her patience, her frequent infirmities that make it impossible for her to run the household, her moodiness, we can clearly see that the wife will frequently resist the domination of the husband, but also that the man would in no way

allow her to rule over him. It was with wisdom that Jesus allotted the final say to the man. But if he declared him to be the master, he did not confer any right to him other than the right himself to determine in an altercation that does not allow a compromise which in his best judgment would be the outcome that would most benefit the well being of both. He is not the master in order to serve his own advantage rather than his wife's; he is not to view himself as the object of the association, but as a means to preserve its harmony. [...]

4. I need not even say how happy married couples would be if they had Jesus' principle in mind when choosing and living with their spouse. Jesus left yet a fourth instruction pertaining to womankind, which especially concerns our sex, whether we are youths or men: *the male sex is to accord the female special respect and protection because of the burdens they bear, because of their delicacy, and their merits.* In particular, sons should love their mothers above all others. There are clear indications in the story of Jesus' life that he himself treated women with special respect. We noted earlier his special affection and respect for the sisters Mary and Martha and that among his followers he accepted many virtuous women. Can there be yet stronger proof than that it was these same pious women who were the first to be cheered by his presence after his glorious resurrection? [John 20, 11- 18] But we should not believe that he gave his special respect only to a few especially deserving persons, respecting only their virtue and not their womanhood. Let us simply remind ourselves what he did on the path of his execution when he was lamented and bewailed by all the more sensitive inhabitants of Jerusalem. He addressed only the women and did not think them unworthy to receive a word of consolation and warning. You daughters of Jerusalem, he cried, do not weep over me, but weep for yourselves, and for your children. For if they do these things in a green tree, what shall be done in the dry? [Luke 23, 28-31] ... But he demanded especially from sons to hold in their hearts the most tender love for their mothers, more for them than their fathers. The example he set for us in this, when even hanging on the cross he did not deny his tenderest love and care to his good mother, is too well known to bear repeating [John 19, 26-27]. Every one of Jesus' demands is perfectly justified and grounded in sound reason. Plainly, women are weaker in bodily strength; is it not therefore just that they should be protected by the stronger sex? In their nature, the

female sex is subject to special dangers and afflictions that are unknown to the male. Is it not therefore the latter's duty to pay special attention to the former in order to protect them from those dangers and nurse them in their afflictions? Women make their own special important contributions to humanity, unlike anything men have to offer. We owe them the continuation and education of all humanity. Nothing follows more naturally than that we should take every opportunity to show womankind our special respect, our tenderest care and our fullest protection. But does this happen in our day? I claim that at present there is no trace of true respect for womankind. For the superficial tributes distributed most freely by the most unworthy of our sex, the thousand trifles in which women are allowed to make their choice and the abject subjugation to women to which some men lower themselves: this is not true and rational respect but is a mere effect of sensuality existing side by side with the most brutal violations of women's rights. True and rational respect for womankind would manifest itself in an entirely different way. We would have to remove from our dealings with women everything that demeans them, everything that leads to the thought that woman has no higher destiny than to satisfy our desires; we would no longer allow ourselves vulgar jokes and suggestive remarks; we would do nothing that might arouse desires in us that would demean the dignity of women, but we would also avoid everything that would awaken a woman's sensuality; and we must as well take note of the weakness of women and treat it with respectful care. This, my friends, is the respect for womankind I would like to see promoted through your example. But especially, those among you fortunate enough still to have the mother that gave birth to you and educated you: may you never forget with what difficulties you were carried in her womb for nine long months, how her least negligence would already have brought your life to an end at that time, with how much care you were tended in the early years of your childhood, how many sleepless nights, how much sorrow, how much fear, how many tears you cost your mother, and only her! Consider this: your heart must be without all feeling if the most tender love for your mother does not grow in your breast. For nothing on earth is in every respect more worthy of grateful human love than one's mother. For whoever does not love his mother, says the word of God, is damned by the Lord. Amen.

Part II

On Rights, Civil Disobedience, and Resistance to Authority

On the Right of the Clergy to obtain their Livelihood from Persons not of their Faith (selections)

Preface

For many years England has been engaged in a dispute that has captured the attention not only of all Europe, but of the educated public in all parts of the world. It concerns the question whether the Protestant clergy in almost wholly Catholic Ireland have a well founded right for continuing to obtain emoluments that were established in earlier days—by ways and means still well remembered. Nothing is more understandable than that all participants conduct this dispute with great passion—and who in the entire island kingdom is not connected to it either directly or more remotely? The question cannot be answered affirmatively without destroying the hope nourished by millions to be finally released from what they feel to be a crying injustice. It cannot be answered negatively without changing the holdings of the richest families in the country and frustrating the expectations and preferment of many hundreds. This lies so clear before everyone's eyes that even the most myopic cannot miss it. But this question assumes far greater importance if one only thinks of more remote effects and of the influence of a decision for one or the other side upon a hundred other issues that have already been raised or will be raised once such a decision has been made. For the inhabitants of other countries, whether they profess the Protestant or the Catholic or some non-Christian religion are not wholly disinterested observers of this dispute. They cannot but ask themselves what rights they should grant or deny persons in their surroundings based on the opinions they profess. I shall not dwell on the fact that in quite a few countries there exist conditions very similar, only to a lesser degree, to those now disputed in England and Ireland, for example when Jews contribute to the maintenance of the Christian clergy, etc.

There is little hope that, where such interests are at play, a majority of participants will be able to engage in a calm consideration of all reasonable grounds on both sides of the dispute. Nonetheless, we must never despair that truth will in the end triumph. Indeed, all who are in the least able to help truth obtain its victory by putting the grounds on which it rests into brighter light have a deep obligation to do so. To contribute to this end was the innocent purpose we had in mind when penning this essay.

§. 1.

The problem we want to address in this essay has to do with the question whether or not something is a right. It is necessary, therefore, to begin with a closer determination of what is meant by this. For surely, much darkness still surrounds this concept even if in recent times much has been done to elucidate it. If we set aside the non-essential meanings this word has in common discourse and focus only on the concept used by legal scholars or jurists, it is obvious that they make a clear distinction between what is a *right* and what is *ethical*. Suppose a jurist was to claim that the Protestant clergy in Ireland have a well-founded *right* to continue receiving the emoluments they now receive *de facto* from the Catholic inhabitants of the country. He would not thereby assert that the conduct of this clergy, were they in fact to enforce this law and collect the tax, perhaps even with the use of force, should be termed ethically good. He could leave the latter an open question or even insist that under the current conditions in Ireland, where a great many inhabitants languish in the most abject misery, humane duty demands that one not make the poor even poorer. Despite all this he could insist that these clergymen have a right, a perfect right, to collect their tithes. Thus to say of an action that it is based on a right in the contemporary juridical sense is no praise and no declaration that it is irreproachable. If a jurist allows that the Anglican clergy have a right to collect those tithes, he does not impose a duty on the clergy, but on the Irishmen. But what duty? Not, surely, the duty to hand over these tithes even if the clergy do not demand them. Nor does he forbid every attempt to dissuade the clergy through peaceful submissions. Rather, the only duty he imposes, if the clergy insist on payment, is to obey them and not forcibly to thwart the collection of these funds. And this holds generally: whenever a jurist calls an action *rightful*, he imposes a duty on the rest of humanity not, indeed, to insist on this action, but not to thwart it if the entitled person wants to perform it.

But does this give us the entire concept we associate with this word? Suppose for the moment that nothing but what I just explicitly stated is required to make an action rightful. Suppose, in other words, that an action fails to be rightful only if it in fact imposes a duty on some other persons to oppose it by force. Now, where opposition is not an available option, it cannot be a duty either. Hence, an action of ours would be right or not depending on the accidental circumstance whether the people in the area have enough power successfully to oppose it. Suppose somebody lives on an island with only one or a few other persons and that he is much stronger than all of them. Then all resistance against him would be in vain, and indeed, by enraging him would make their condition much worse. In these circumstances the duty of prudence would doubtless demand that one suffer in patience whatever this overpowering person wants or does. Hence this man could do whatever he wanted, no matter how outrageous and in other circumstances deserving of the harshest penalties, and yet those around him would have the duty to submit. Would you then say that everything this strongman undertakes is right and that in the circumstances he would not even be able to commit a crime that deserves to be called a violation of rights? Surely, this would very much misinterpret the use of this word. It is undeniable, rather, that by the *rightfulness* or *unrightfulness* of our actions we think of certain properties that belong to their *inner* essence and are entirely detached from the circumstance whether at this time there is more or less power of resistance. It follows that a certain ingredient is missing from the explanation we gave above, and it is not difficult to guess what that is. For we say that an action is *unrightful* if its inner character is such that there would be a duty forcibly to oppose it if a sufficiently large number of people were present and willing to protect the victims of such a deed. By contrast, we call an action *rightful* if it may not be forcibly prevented even if a sufficient number of persons were present and willing to do this.

This, I believe, is the concept that these days we have begun to connect with *rightness* when it is taken in its *juridical* sense. I cannot deny, however, that the *definitions* found in the common textbooks occasionally deviate from this. Yet everyone assumes, as we have done as well, that relations having to do with rights apply only to *humans*, that is, only to rational beings (perhaps even only to rational and sensate beings). Inanimate objects and animals have no rights and can violate no rights; only humans have rights and can violate them. Everyone maintains, if not in their definitions, then in the conclusions they draw from them, that persons acting within their rights may not be forcibly thwarted and, moreover, that force can be used against those who violate the rules of justice. There are two circumstances that more than anything encouraged me in my belief that the explication I have sketched does not depart very much from the truth. The first is that the concept I introduce is highly important and worth investigating. Even if it were not to be designated by the word "right", some different name would have to be found for it. Secondly, the concept I have introduced clearly explains all cases where it is beyond doubt that an action is to be characterized as rightful or unrightful.

§. 2.

I cannot develop this any further at this point but leave it to the reader to give it more thought. I cannot refrain, however, from remarking on the connection my definition establishes between the principles of *right* and those of *ethics*. It is well known that there is a lot of controversy about this, and that the connection between the two is represented in very different ways. Some even claim that the theory of rights and ethics can oppose each other and that the first sanctions many an action that the latter forbids. But if by a rightful action we understand nothing other than an action that others should allow even when they have enough power and assistance forcibly to prevent it, then it is obvious that rightfulness is in no way inconsistent with ethics. Rather, the principles of right in their totality can be proved only *on the basis* of ethics, for we can claim to have a *right* to a certain action only if ethics can prove that it is the *duty* of those around us not forcibly to interfere with this action no matter how much power they have at their command. In the presentation of jurisprudence it has been an error of the schools usually to formulate the supreme rule needed to determine the rightfulness of an action in the form of an *imperative* (Always act in such a way, etc.) or in the form of a *permission* (You are permitted etc.). These forms are out of place here, for if an action is found to be right, it follows in no way that it is permissible and even less that it is obligatory. Rather, what is at issue here is merely the duty of *other* persons, namely, those around us, not to use force to prevent us from doing so, even if they realize that the action is unethical, and even if other methods, e.g. peaceful persuasion, have been unsuccessful.

§. 3.

It is even more important for our present concern to take note of the *relation* between what is *right* and the *law of the state*.

According to our definition, a rightfully established state is one that ought not to be overthrown by the citizenry (perhaps with the aid of others) even if this were possible. There can be no argument that such a state is entitled to introduce laws that bestow rights upon some persons (rights that would not exist without these laws) and corresponding obligations upon others. Thus, for example, in most states only the rightfully established public authority determines the rate of interest a creditor can demand from a debtor. This alone establishes the right of the former to demand from the latter the payment of a certain interest (depending on the rate in force at that place) and to invoke legal remedies if he defaults. One must not, however, go so far as to claim that that the only source of *all* rights (and the corresponding obligations) is the state through its laws, so that there would be no rights whatever in the raw state of nature. Conversely we should not believe that everything laid down by a rightfully constituted state at once establishes a right. Even a rightfully established lawgiver can in certain cases introduce laws that are not rightful. It should be noted, however, that citizens are not at once excused from obeying a law if its unrightfulness becomes known. On the contrary, only in exceptional and rare cases is it permissible to disobey laws of this kind as long as they are in force. It is, however, permissible and even a duty to state openly that we consider a law to be improper whenever we discover that it is less conducive to the common welfare than some other arrangement that could take its place. We should, and indeed must, call such a law unrightful if it bestows advantages upon some citizens only by removing far more important benefits from others. We should, and indeed must, call a law *deleterious* if we find that it leads to damage and disadvantage of a substantial proportion of the citizens. We should, and indeed must, frankly declare such a law to be unrightful and the rights it bestows on certain citizens merely fictitious. These citizens should not in conscience make use of such a law if its consequences are obviously so deleterious that it should be resisted, provided only that enough force and good will can be summoned to make this resistance a likely success. It is easy enough to persuade oneself of the truth of these general propositions. But I must confess that it is most difficult to apply them to individual cases. It requires much thought and a consideration of *all* circumstances before one can declare in good conscience that a given a law deserves to be censored as unrightful. We are well advised in case of doubt to judge too leniently rather than too harshly. It is better, if we are to assess an institution, to pronounce it inappropriate, unjust or deleterious than to declare it unrightful. Suppose we do not want to go so far as to say that in the given case circumstances allow and even demand that we attempt forcible resistance, and suppose that we are satisfied to urge a retraction of the law through speech and reasonable argumentation: then it does not make a great deal of difference whether we call it unrightful or merely detrimental and deleterious. There are, however, some cases where there can be no doubt that the strongest word must be used. These are cases where we must say without reservation that what is here decreed is unrightful and binds no one if it were not for might here being stronger than right. Hence, if one does not peacefully submit, nothing remains but to wish that all those who still suffer under the pressure of such an unrightful law should obtain the authority, the sooner the better, to free themselves from degrading coercion through powerful counterforce, or that others who are not immediately injured take up the cause of these victims from sympathy or moral conviction.

§. 4.

There can be no doubt that a law must be considered unrightful if it can be shown to be detrimental not only to the mundane well-being, but even the morality of the citizens. This holds, for example, for a law that creates an irresistible temptation to coarse debauchery or that encourages idleness and indolence, or perhaps just pride and arrogance, particularly if there is every reason to expect that by revoking this law and introducing well-defined, useful and tested institutions, sin and vice can be curbed and virtue improved. In such a case it is virtue itself that hands us weapons and demands that we should shrink from no earthly sacrifice, even of our life, to have such a law repealed. Only our powerlessness, only the clearest conviction that any resistance we would allow ourselves would be fruitless and might even increase the evil: only such conditions can exonerate us if we comply at times with that law. Meanwhile we denounce this law with the power of speech as loudly and strongly as we possibly can and should not cease to enlighten our fellow citizens about it.

§. 5.

Since I thus suppose that cases where insubordination is permissible can sometimes occur, it is necessary to describe their nature. There are only three types, or rather levels or degrees of permissible insubordination against rightful authority.

The first degree occurs when we simply refuse to carry out the demands of an unrightful law, without further transgressing existing laws, and do not even evade the undeserved penalties the authorities bring to bear on offenders. This is the kind of opposition that the Apostles of the Lord and all the first preachers of the Gospel permitted themselves. They continued to preach the Gospel against the prohibition of their governments and willingly bore the punishments imposed on them.

Take the case where the authorities want to forbid us to spread among the people beneficial truths that we have somehow discovered. This is one of the most obvious cases where it is not only permissible, but even a duty, to resist the prohibition by continuing to teach the truths that we have discovered.

It is a second and somewhat higher degree of insubordination if we also seek to elude the penalties imposed on us, especially those that would hinder further public-spirited activities by taking steps that are *additional* transgressions of existing decrees. These steps, however, must never essentially harm others.

For this behaviour, too, we can cite examples from Scripture. Who does not recall what St. Paul reports of himself in 2 Corinthians 11.32?[1] And why should we not be allowed to transgress an otherwise appropriate law, decreed by man and not by God, if this alone gives us the freedom to lead a life willingly dedicated to nothing but the public good? It is understood that no one is essentially harmed by this action, and that the only possible detriment is that, as a transgression, it sets a bad example. But this is diminished by the clear purpose of the action and far outweighed by the service to humanity it enables us to perform.

[1]When I was in Damascus, the commissioner of King Aretas kept the city under observation so as to have me arrested; and I was let down in a basket, through a window in the wall, and so escaped his clutches.

But can we go even further? Can it be permissible to sacrifice not only one's own life but that of other persons, indeed innocent persons, to preserve the right? Can it be permissible to inform the authorities, even legitimately established authorities, that their use of force will be met with counterforce although it can be foreseen that blood will flow and that persons who are the instruments of their power will sacrifice their lives and other innocent persons will suffer the greatest adversity? He whose destiny it was to become the most exalted paragon of all virtue, a shining example especially of gentleness and charity, never used this means to carry out his grand plan which embraced all of humanity and seems to have forbidden his disciples and followers to use such methods.[2] The Apostles of the Lord, when any of the secular authorities in whose domains preached the Gospel attempted to seize their persons, never attempted a defense that would endanger the life of even a single person. As far as I know all later missionaries followed this beautiful example. But should it be absolutely prohibited to repel force through counterforce? This is indeed the faith and conduct of an admirable group of Christians, who think it unworthy of a Christian to spill blood in defending themselves against a wholly illegitimate authority and even more so against a legitimate authority that commands unrightful action only in a particular case.

Still, this view is not likely to be correct. For, surely, there are conditions that force us to choose one of two things: either we must patiently allow ourselves to be tortured and murdered as well as all others who no longer wish to obey a law that is a detriment to virtue—or else we must defend ourselves and by courageously repulsing the aggressors discourage further attacks, shedding some blood to prevent the loss of much more. If we can confidently expect that armed resistance, and it alone, will save humanity from much greater distress, then it is not only permissible but must be a duty, however heartbreaking, to prevent a greater evil by introducing a lesser one. But how much circumspection is needed to determine that such conditions in fact obtain! With how much care must every possible means of a peaceful settlement first be explored! With how much forbearance must one proceed in such a case!

[2]Matthew 26,51: One of those with Jesus reached for his sword and drew it, and he struck at the High Priest's servant and cut off his ear. But Jesus said to him, "Put up your sword. All who take the sword die by the sword."

How loudly and repeatedly must it not be declared that the revolt is not against the authorities themselves, but only against a single unrightful decree of theirs! That one will gladly obey all other prescriptions and will put down arms at once if secure assurances are given that the abhorrent institution will be removed! How sad if in the end the force of resistance, earlier thought to be sufficient, is found to be too weak, and if after so much sacrifice and bloodshed the only result is the return of the old abuse and vice rearing its head more impudently! Finally, how dreadful if the dangerous force you have assembled merely to curb a certain abuse becomes stronger than you intended and in its impudence no longer submits to rational guidance and along with the evil tears down much that is good because there is no one who can master the forces that have been unleashed and no one can foresee how much evil they will wreak, nor where it will end.

§. 6.

But enough discussion of a point that has no necessary connection with our problem, to whose solution we can now directly progress. Hence let us first articulate and prove the following proposition.

> Any contract between the teachers or ministers of a religion and the faithful must be considered invalid under the law and indeed wholly unrightful, if it stipulates that the latter as well as their heirs and descendants will be compelled by main force to pay in perpetuity certain taxes to the former even if they have changed their religious convictions while the clergy maintained theirs. Such a contract conveys upon that clergy not a true but only an apparent title to these emoluments. This means that they may not in good conscience make use of such a contract if a change of beliefs in fact occurs.

There is a simple proof for this important proposition. It rests upon a truth that I am not to the first to articulate and that has been unanimously endorsed by all teachers of morality and law, as follows: a contract has no validity if one or the other party promises or demands something that is in itself evil or forbidden. I mean by this a stipulation—possibly prompted by evil intentions or convictions—that will bring forth evil because of unchanging impulses and dispositions of human nature and not because of circumstances arising later and unforeseeable when the contract was drawn up. A government informed of the existence of such a contract, far from being obliged to lend its authority to its enforcement, must at once declare it void and, depending on circumstances, must punish one or the other, or perhaps even both of the contracting parties. Common sense demands this! If the opposite took place, if the state itself were to support contracts of this kind, then it would promote the perpetration of evil, which no one, whoever they are, is permitted to do. Whoever you are: if you are called upon to arbitrate a dispute between two parties or even to aid one against the other and you become aware that you are to defend a claim based on nothing but a contract that the party now trying to enforce could see to be unrightful when it was first entered into: never find in favor of that party and by no means actively support their unrightful demand. And if ever so many promises, ever so solemn declarations and oaths are offered in evidence, and if the party that insists on fulfillment of the contract can prove beyond doubt that their side has precisely delivered what was promised, and if they can show that in expectation of payment they made various arrangements that result in grave damage now that the promised sum is not delivered—none of this should move you to lend assistance to the party that started the abuse so that they can carry it to completion. Rather, you must respond to the villain that the damage he now suffers is only a deserved punishment he has brought upon himself.

In this manner, I say, each individual must act; and should not the state as a society that commands ever so much more force than any individual have even greater obligations? Should not the state be obliged to forbid any and all contracts that are immoral by their very nature, to bring to light all those that were secretly contracted and to punish them in a way that will deter others? Any attempt by the government of such a state to conceal this duty must be in vain. It is preserved and continues even if it is not acknowledged. Nothing changes even if centuries have passed without any thought of compliance or if the legislative authorities of the state have spurned their duty to the point that they promised a part of their citizenry that such transgressions will never be punished, but rather protected. Did I say that none of this makes any difference?

Rather, I should say this: when reason finally awakens and legislative intelligence comes to recognize its previous error, it has an even greater obligation to remove the evil it has tolerated and supported far too long. A government supervises the whole and can order any measure it deems necessary for the advancement of the common good. It will therefore be able to find ways and means even in the most complicated cases to soften or eliminate the damage to individual citizens resulting from the sudden annulment of such contracts (provided this damage may not be viewed as just punishment). The more obvious this is the less can there be a reason for the government to disassociate itself from this duty.

If, therefore, it can clearly and distinctly be shown from premises whose truth is irresistibly obvious to common sense that a contract such as the one described above between parish and clergy is in itself evil and impermissible since it can only result in harm, given the unchanging impulses and dispositions of human nature: then it is already determined that no state on earth has the power to declare such a contract valid and to bestow upon persons who benefit from it an actual right resulting from it.

§. 8.

To compel participation in religious ceremonies is iniquitous, as is enforced religious instruction. Acts of devotion are devoid of all inner worth and salutary effect if they issue not from our own free decision and a kind of moral urge but, in conflict with our own conscience, are performed merely to keep others from abusing us. This is so true that any positive religion that taught the opposite and thus permitted devotees to force dissenters to perform such acts would thereby reveal itself as a false religion. For how could it justify such a procedure? Not, surely, by claiming that these sacred ceremonies have a supernatural grace that will bless even a person who performs them with antipathy. Is it possible that a true divine revelation should teach such a thing? Can God tie his mercy and blessings to actions that are in themselves immoral? Can He permit, nay even command, something that is in itself evil? You may not as you please or on a whim assume that God has spoken; such an assumption must be based on reasons that are convincing and afford complete certainty. Careful thought will teach you that you are never and nowhere justified in making such an assumption unless the doctrine presented as God's revelation requires things from you that your own reason shows to have beneficial and salutary consequences. Where the opposite is the case you are in no way justified in assuming that God has spoken, even if the most extraordinary apparitions are presented to your senses and you are at a complete loss to explain why God should have made this possible, and even if they are claimed to be omens, signs through which He wants to show that you should to do something you clearly see to be evil and harmful to the parish.

§. 19.

This has been a brief survey of the consequences of a contract that will oblige a parish to continue paying tributes to their clergy even after a change of religious convictions no longer allows them to employ that clergy's services. Since these consequences are grounded in nature and concern not merely the loss of external goods but the moral conscience of persons it follows that even a single one of these would be sufficient to conclude that such a contract is in itself impermissible. No matter how solemnly it was introduced, it can have no validity and can ground no right. We already know that it would be in vain to plead that the state itself knew of this contract, approved it, and promised to protect it. None of this changes in the least the pernicious consequences and indeed only magnifies some of them. The state failed when it permitted the conclusion of this contract and promised to protect and uphold it. But it would add a new error to the old one if it agreed to support the clergy in their illegal demands now that a case thought merely possible in the contract has actually arrived. The only obligation that can arise from this earlier error is to admit all the more loudly and frankly that a mistake has been made. It is the state that must then provide for the clergy whose trouble resulted in part from its error. One must not object that such a procedure would increase the state's expenditures and that every one will pay to remedy an error committed by only a few, if this cost is equally borne by the totality of all citizens (which seems the most reasonable option). It is of course true that *any* error committed by the government has certain negative consequences, sometimes for one or the other part of society, sometimes for the whole. If, in the first case, the damage is in fact of a kind that its distribution over the whole is not impossible, and if it can be carried out in a way that does not too deeply offend anyone, then we should consider this a truly fortunate thing. It would be folly not to make use of so important a benefit that a civic constitution affords us.

§. 20.

The case we proposed to investigate in §6 has now been discussed at great length. This makes it possible to be much more brief in all other cases that can here occur. The next is likely that of a clergy which, after suffering the misfortune of losing the confidence of a parish that adopted different views, continues to request the previous tributes *without being able to appeal to a contract between the two parties*. The reasons we have given why such demands have no force in law even in the case where a contract about them exists may be disputed, even ridiculed, but cannot be refuted. On the contrary, the more impartially they are considered and examined the more incontestable they will be found. It stands to reason that there is even less of a foundation for a right of this kind if there is no contract at all. For then the few, albeit insufficient, reasons fall away that the clergy can use to deduce the rightfulness of their demand from the *promise of the parish* contained in the contract. Without that, what could they possibly advance as a foundation for their right? "That they want to live? That the defection of their parish was not to due to their own laxness? That this defection was a kind of perjury for whose punishment the parish deserves to support their former clergy as well as the new one?"

This, in brief, is the sum total of reasons that have been and could have been advanced in such cases. But we already know the nature of these reasons.

It cannot possibly be maintained that a person commits a sin, specifically the sin of perjury, when he forsakes a faith to which he had adhered. It would be even more unjust to accuse a whole parish of acting against their conscience if they give up previous religious opinions, especially if it is unclear what special advantages induced them to take such a step. We can claim with much greater confidence, nay certainty, that the clergy is to blame if a whole parish casts aside the doctrine they preach and converts either to a better or even a worse one. If the former: what obstinacy if a whole commune recognizes what is better and only their teachers are cursed with a blindness that does not recognize the better choice! But if the second: must not the clergy be guilty of negligence if not only individual members, but the whole parish is so poorly instructed that they desert the truth and convert to error? If there is a question of punishment then it is certainly not the parish that deserves it but their spiritual teachers.

Of course I do not want to imply that one should leave them to starve to death. Such a clergy must be given an opportunity to earn their subsistence. It is properly the state that should assume this responsibility. But if it does not do its duty, then I would demand of the parish, in grateful recognition of services received earlier, to see to it that not a single member of this clergy is in need. I said that none of them should be *in need*. But what reason could there be to do more than this? What reason could there be to provide without subtraction all levies they had been granted when they still worked for the parish? Was it perhaps precisely the excessiveness of these levies that caused them to become negligent in the performance of their duties and to degenerate? Finally, what reason could there be to pay levies not only to those who occupied offices when the parish defected, but even to those who most illicitly took over their positions after their death?

§. 22.

It leaps to the eye that claims are even less justified if advanced by a clergy who were of a faith different from that of their parish when first brought in and were imposed by force and not because the parish had asked for them. It is well known that precisely this is the case in Ireland for the majority of her unfortunate inhabitants. The injustice that was imposed is so enormous and obvious that one must doubt that those defending this practice believe in their hearts that they advocate the cause of truth and justice. Surely no one will be misled by the absurd excuse that forcing these religious teachers upon a parish contributes to the latter's spiritual welfare. More apparent plausibility attaches to the claim that if this measure had not been taken and persistently enforced, then the true faith, that is, the faith which in the opinion of the imposed clergy is the true one, would soon vanish from the entire country. But I ask you: even if it were indeed so, would you be justified in applying such unrightful means for the preservation of the true faith? Can one do any evil deed to realize an end that one takes to be good? But in any case things are not as you imagine or perhaps only pretend. There is a different, more reliable method for preserving your religion in the country and indeed to win more adherents, provided only that it is the true faith. Do you want to know what it is? It is the exact opposite of what you are doing. It is this: send teachers to the handful who still observe the true faith and let them live modestly from the offerings of their own co-religionists. Let them be men of exceptional ability who do not force themselves upon those who do not want to hear them but are more than willing to provide instruction to all who so wish—and who will prove the truth of their teaching not only in words, but through their deeds.

I should not have to point out that the injustice is the more offensive the larger the emoluments that this clergy obtains, and the poorer the people from whom they are extorted. If only part of what eyewitnesses tell us is true, if those tithes are extorted from people who live in the most abject misery, of whom hundreds die every year of starvation, while the Protestant bishops luxuriously consume the extorted abundance in another country, O! then I ask if the cruelties for which a *Christian* clergy is responsible cannot be compared to the most atrocious horrors that history reports of any *heathen priestly regime*, not excepting the horrors of human sacrifice? For these human sacrifices take the lives of only a few who, if they were adults, could console themselves in dying that they were expiating angry gods through their death. The priest sacrificed them not for his own pleasure, but from a sense of duty, however erroneous, by believing that he had to obey the strict will of the deity. For my part I find the deed that you, preachers of the gospel, here commit more abhorrent.

§ . 23.

But I shall try to persuade myself that I am considering the issue from a wrong point of view; for it is all too difficult for me to believe that Christian priests conduct themselves in ways more evil than heathens. Every time I have examined the issue I have come to the same conclusion, namely, that the same legal argument which the Protestant clergy of Ireland cites to justify their conduct could have been, and may still be, used by all other priesthoods, e.g. the Catholic or the Jewish, or even the heathen, should they find themselves in similar circumstances. Thus one can boldly claim:

> If the Protestant clergy in Ireland have a well founded right to demand a tithe from the Catholic inhabitants of that country, then all those who once converted from paganism or Judaism to the Christian faith had no right, merely because they changed their religion, from then on to withhold the taxes they used to pay to their previous priestly class. Indeed, there can be no other method of reparation than to reinstate those expired positions and offices of the Jewish as well as the pagan religions and to compensate persons who wish to take on these offices (if indeed they can be found) in the amounts their ancestors had once been pledged.

The inference is absurd but not because of any of the many differences between Christian and pagan priesthoods, but merely because the assumption is absurd that a clergy of whatever kind should have such a right. I do of course not wish to deny the many and important virtues that elevate the Christian clergy above those others. But I challenge anyone to name a single distinction from which such a right could possibly be derived. Surely the fact that the Protestant clergy consider themselves the preachers of the one and only purified doctrine cannot establish a right of this kind, for this must be an article of faith of all other priesthoods as well. As well, we have shown above that this circumstance, even if it is allowed to be true, in no way implies a justification for these demands. Or do you think that among the *positive doctrines* of your faith there can be found a proposition on which this right can be based? *A priori*, I must deny you permission to deduce from such positive doctrines of a religion conclusions that *contravene reason*. There is no sign from which you can infer that God has spoken, that He has revealed a doctrine which he wants you to believe and accept if this doctrine contravenes reason. What doctrine did you want to cite for this purpose? You abide by Scripture. Well then, which passage gives you the right to demand taxes from a parish whom you do not teach and who do not wish to be taught by you? Scripture tells you, as far as I know, that you should accept without blushing only what is offered to the satisfaction of your basic needs, provided you have satisfied the spiritual needs of your parish in the time you could have used to earn your livelihood. "And into whatsoever city ye enter, and they receive you, eat such things as are set before you. For the laborer is worthy of his hire" [Luke 10, 7–8].

Scripture nowhere allows that you should be entitled to collect, if necessary by force, certain contributions from those you have instructed, that you should be allowed to collect even from those who have rejected your teachings, that you should be permitted to live in idleness while those whom you allow to feed you starve to death: indeed in all these matters Scripture prescribes the exact opposite. Scripture demands that you not impose your presence upon a parish that no longer wants to hear your instruction, but to seek others who are more receptive to your teaching. "And whosoever shall not receive you, nor hear your words: when you depart out of that house or city, shake the dust of it off your feet" [Matthew 10, 14]. Elsewhere Scripture says in plain terms and without exempting anyone from this command: "Let it be your ambition to keep calm and to work with your hands" [1 Thessalonians 4, 11], and "If any would not work, neither should he eat" [2 Thessalonians 3, 10], and "But they that will be rich fall into temptation and a snare, and into many foolish and hurtful lusts, which drown men in distraction and perdition. For the love of money is the root of all evil" [1 Timothy 6, 9].

But if you perhaps want to imitate the order of the Old Testament and what we are told of those days, then I must remind you that the founder of Christianity demanded greater perfection from his adherents. As well, our civic constitutions differ significantly from the state of the Israelites so that there is no way that the clerical estate could still be granted the same rights that were allowed to the tribe of Levi.

§ . 24.

Let us see, if it should still be thought necessary, how the alleged right that we here dispute should be judged according to the principles of the Catholic Church. The Protestant side has always been inclined to object that the clergy of the Catholic Church unduly elevate their own dignity and importance, that they pride themselves on their divine ordination and a mass of privileges that were bestowed on them by the supernatural grace of God and on rights that flow from them. If indeed there is some truth at the bottom of these accusations, must one not fear that, if even the Protestant clergy have arrogated to themselves an alleged right to tax persons that don't share their beliefs, that this will have happened even more often and in more cruel ways on the part of the Catholic clergy? I need not concern myself at this point with investigating whether there is confirmation in history for this concern. For the purpose of this discussion it suffices to show that in the *doctrines* that must be considered Catholic because *all* (at least now living) Catholics unanimously subscribe to them, there is not the least trace of a claim supporting that alleged right and that, on the contrary, the Catholic Church has always propounded doctrines, argued with great generality, that explicitly opposed such a right. It is very easy to prove this.

From which of the many doctrines that exist in the Catholic Church could one correctly deduce such a right? Perhaps from the doctrine that ascribes divine ordination to the clergy? But does the Catholic Church not also claim that the state of marriage was instituted by God? And could this mean anything other than that they are estates well pleasing to God, as He announced in His own revelation? Does it follow from the fact that the clerical estate is good and beneficial that any and all, even impermissible, methods can be used to preserve it? Would it not precisely be the case that if they were granted that alleged privilege, its use would necessarily make them so hated and would cause such calamities that they deserve to be, and no doubt soon would be, stamped out by force?

Or should a right of this kind follow from those *higher ordinations* that the members of this estate have received, or from the *supernatural grace* for whose administration God has elected them? But no matter how important and of immense value, according to Catholic doctrine, the acts of grace may be that we receive through the office of the priest, or the grace that God bestows on him when he is ordained: the designation "*supernatural*" does not describe the always mysterious and for us inscrutable way in which we receive God's grace, but merely indicates that their presence is known to us only *through revelation*. Concerning the *conditions* that govern the dispensation of divine grace we must not forget that we can expect sacramental consequences only from acts that have a *natural power of edification*. For example according to the explicit doctrine of the Catholic Church the holy sacrament of baptism of a young child cannot be legitimately performed unless the child's parents or guardians declare that they themselves desire the child's acceptance into the pale of the Catholic Church, and look upon this action as one that places a stronger obligation on them—namely, to educate the child in the way appropriate for a future Christian. Thus here too, even if the child is not edified by this event, others are. If this holds in general, then it would be the greatest absurdity if one wanted to derive from the supernatural grace that the clergy have received and are directed to dispense, their entitlement to force themselves upon the parish and thus inevitably become odious to them. The exact opposite is the case: the Catholic minister must establish sensitive relations to his parish because he must make it possible for every one of its members in time to develop trust and love for him, strong enough to ask for his counsel in the most intimate matters close to their hearts. It is for this reason that a Catholic minister must carefully avoid all actions that could awaken the suspicion of selfishness or in any way deprive him of the parish's trust. One may admit all of this and yet remind me that the Catholic priest, made haughty through the delusion of higher rank, enforced by the doctrine that the sacrament of holy orders has impressed an indelible mark upon his soul, believes that he would compromise his spiritual dignity if he earned his livelihood through any activity other than his clerical work. Hence if his parishioners change their faith he will feel pressed to apply to them for the cost of his sustenance at least until his death. Such opinions, even if they have been announced by some clerics of the Catholic Church I must declare to be malicious prejudices, entirely opposed to the spirit of our religion. Did St. Paul, the great world apostle, think that he imperiled his dignity in the least when, appearing in the luxurious city of Corinth, he earned through the work of his hands what he needed for his sustenance? Should it indeed dishonour you if you earn what you need for your sustenance through work in the common interest? And is it not more dishonorable if you spend your days in idleness while you still have force of mind or body to produce something useful?

No! These surely are not concepts for which we can blame the Catholic Church. Her canonists have always announced a severe doctrine that states the exact opposite. "The cleric," they say, "is never and nowhere allowed to request payment for his instruction or his religious ceremonies. Based on the word of Jesus *Freely you have received, freely give* [St. Matthew 10, 8] all dispensing of spiritual goods for the purpose of secular advantage is declared a damnable crime, a crime that shamefully desecrates the most holy and deserves the most severe punishment which the violator shall not escape" [Acts 8, 20 ff.]. "Only he who has no other income," they say, "is permitted to accept gifts to satisfy his needs from the parish he serves. But these gifts are not his property, but are to be considered and treated as a *common good*, a good intended for moral purposes on which especially the poor and needy have a most indelible claim, and of which he may take only as much as necessity requires." The moral teachers of the Catholic Church know nothing whatever of a right to extract by force contributions from those who do not voluntarily support their religious instructor and even less of a right to tax even those who have not received our instruction or do not want it. They have no other counsel for a cleric who suffers the misfortune of losing the confidence of his parish than to leave it and seek out another. They are so far removed from granting him the right to use force in such a case that even when clerics that belong to another confession confiscate by force what was actually meant for him they make it his duty not to leave his parish in their hour of need, but to suffer and die with them. But I say too little when I merely say that this is the *teaching* of the Catholic Church; I can say with joy that it is also the practice! In the very country where the Protestant clergy gives the just mentioned shocking example of violence, the Catholic clergy conscientiously carries out what we just described as honorable conduct in such a case. O! that they should always and everywhere have acted in the same spirit! But one can see that the *doctrine* of the church is in no way to be blamed if Catholic clerics have somewhere acted or still act in violation of the concepts we have established above.

The *doctrine* of the Catholic Church entirely agrees with what I have claimed and derived from principles of reason in this discussion. For Catholics I have said nothing new in these pages.

§ . 25.

It is possible that my readers concur with everything I have said so far, and yet when they are to *apply it* to an actual case occurring in civil society they will find themselves not only embarrassed, but the most divergent opinions will come to the fore. This is due to the *disarrayed relations* we encounter everywhere in our civil constitutions. It is due in particular to the various ways in which the laws of the state allow property to be acquired and lost. It is due, finally to the close connection between different members of the state, which causes every change in the prosperity of one part to have a number of repercussions for the condition of many others. Obviously I cannot on this occasion enumerate all the institutions that lead to this disarray and still less can I evaluate their propriety or impropriety. Least of all am I in a position to indicate the various and most appropriate initiatives a wise government should undertake if it wants to put an end to the abuses under discussion. I will allow myself only a few very general suggestions on this topic at the end of this essay.

§ . 27.

Yet another change is brought about with respect to rights if the original parties who were rightly or wrongly charged with the maintenance of a cleric are allowed to *transfer this obligation to others* who are willing who take it on if they are compensated. Such a case occurs when someone transfers the annual tithe owed to a cleric by letting him have a piece of real estate at a price lower in proportion to the amount owed. One can see how contracts of this kind, if the state leaves them to the discretion of the citizens, must in time result in extremely confusing situations, so that in the end, even with the best intentions, it becomes impossible to balance everything in such a way that no one has been harmed. Determining a *single* payment equivalent to a recurring annual contribution is always a matter of great uncertainty for the simple reason that neither the value of the money nor the interest rate are wholly invariable. But in the special case when the obligation consists in sustaining the cleric it is entirely impossible even approximately to determine the monetary value. For if it is true that maintaining a cleric cannot be the duty of a parish under all conditions and for all time, but only to the extent and for a time in which clergy and parish remain in good harmony: who can predict in a given case how enduring this obligation will be? Who can look into the future and can tell us if the clergy or the parish will not sooner or later change their concepts to such an extent that they must part ways? Therefore, a properly constituted state, which does not allow citizens to engage in enterprises that can only lead to duplicity and disputes, will not permit contracts allowing whole communities or even only some of their members to transfer to others their obligation to maintain a cleric. For, in addition to the impossibility just mentioned of correctly estimating the burden that one part takes upon itself, such contracts create a mass of other grievances. Consider the most admissible case, namely, where the persons to whom the liability for the annual contributions has been transferred themselves belong to the parish and have therefore contributed all along, but now must raise a larger sum: does this arrangement not upset the attractive condition of equality within the parish? Will the clergy not soon find themselves more dependent upon these few? What will happen if they change their confession? What trouble! After their secession, do we want the obligation to pay to return to those that had it all originally? But have they not already made a single large payment in hopes of being forever relieved of his obligation?

It is obvious that the difficulty is even greater if those who assumed the obligation were already apostates when they made the contract. Will they be trustworthy in paying these tributes? Even if they think, to begin with, that they were not unrightfully treated because they were compensated once and for all, will they not believe, later on, when many conditions have changed, that they were defrauded? Could this not actually be the case? But what is more, could it not seem to be so even if it is not? And finally, if it has been determined that these tributes must be paid forever, the descendants will think of their obligation as a burden, no matter how great the profit their ancestors were able to gather when they made the contract—in my opinion they are not entirely wrong in this. For if we look at the matter carefully, we find that there can indeed be good deeds important enough to create in the heart of the beneficiary a gratitude that is, as we say, *eternal*. But can any good deed be momentous enough to bind someone to a gratitude that is supposed to endure among his descendants indefinitely into the future, and to be demonstrated through physical services and sacrifices to certain other persons, perhaps the descendants of the benefactor? Consider the point of all gratitude: it consists for the most part in encouraging further charitable acts. If it is so enormously stretched out, then the means far exceed the boundaries of the end, and the happiness of the whole would diminish rather than increase. Thus even acts of charity cannot be the foundation of a division among men that obliges some of them to offer up goods to others who are then entitled to demand these offerings; obviously there can be no act of any other kind that leads to such an effect. Or could benefits granted for purely selfish reasons in return for services to be rendered have higher value than those granted in love, which are thus *charitable acts*? Hence every contract that places burdens not only on us but also on our descendants and heirs to all eternity with someone who grants us a certain benefit but incurs a liability only as an individual—every such contract is unrightful and a true sin against humanity. This is so even if our profit is very high and even if we could have no descendants at all unless we entered into this bargain. A wise civic constitution will not allow citizens to conclude contracts of this kind, and those that already exist must be declared invalid and measures must be taken to replace unrightful conditions with equitable ones.

§. 28.

The matter is of course quite different if, for an annual contribution or tribute, a benefit is offered that does not accrue only once, but is also continual or at least is renewed annually. Contracts of this kind need not be evil, but they cannot be permitted in the special case when the maintenance of a clergy is at issue, for the reasons that have been given. One should also carefully consider whether the perpetual advantage one contracting party claims to grant the other in the end does not rest upon some prejudice or owe its apparent existence to certain ill-conceived institutions. Not quietly to pass over a point of very great importance: of this kind is the mere granting of *permission to till a piece of land* when construed as something that entitles someone to an annual tribute (called ground-rent and the like) for all time. You can say what you want, but you will never be able to prove a natural right of this kind. For even your own toil in bringing the land into production could add at most an entitlement to a rent for a certain number of years. But prejudices that are thousands of years old, spread over the whole earth, and indissolubly tied to the interests of the privileged classes are not easily abandoned by these classes. And do not all who read these pages more or less belong to these privileged classes?

§. 30.

But if such steps, though repugnant to reason, have already been taken, if more than one unrightful condition has been introduced and has existed and been admired for centuries as a holy and inviolable institution: then it is indeed difficult to say what has to be done gradually to pass over from this perverse world into another where people are more happy.

This much is certain: the current sad condition in which our kind finds itself even in the best organized states can be genuinely improved only through *education*. We must begin with true enlightenment, with the dissemination of correct concepts about the true nature of human happiness, the conditions and methods for achieving it, and our rights and obligations. And it must be well understood that, to make this progress possible, not only our lower classes, but most especially the privileged ones need instruction in this point and must be drawn away from certain pernicious prejudices that still infect them. We must at long last openly tell and unmistakably point out to these classes what their duty is, their eternally imperative duty and obligation. Not only this, we must create in them a living and strong conviction, we must make them understand that they in fact *lose nothing* by carrying out these their duties. A voluntary abandonment and renunciation of all the *apparent* rights and privileges they have claimed up to now will not hinder their enjoyment of the highest happiness we can achieve on earth. On the contrary, they will be more sensitive to every genuine and natural joy and will be much less susceptible to the pain, suffering and accidents of life.

Once this has been accomplished we may suppose that the majority of the people and the majority of privileged citizens will recognize and willingly try to apply measures suitable to usher in better conditions. And then it will not be difficult to persuade everyone that in proportion as circumstances are confused nothing more can be done than the following: Citizens whose every effort produces only the barest minimum of what they need to lead and enjoy their lives must always and everywhere receive preferential treatment. By contrast, citizens who own one hundred or one thousand times as much than anyone would have if all earthly goods of the country were equally distributed, must always and everywhere be considered to have been favoured much too much by the imperfect constitution of the state, and their affluence must be seen as the direct or remote cause of the poverty of those others. Only by reducing the income of the rich, and in no other way, can the penury of the poor be relieved to the advantage of both sides. But the question is how this is to be done. Almsgiving and poorboxes are indeed the favourite, but certainly also the worst, method for this purpose. Every state that employs this method not only in exceptional cases but in the ordinary course of things only displays its own disgrace and admits that the privileged part of the citizenry and the government that is in league with them think they have done their whole duty if they merely save the poor from starving to death and keep them from taking up arms in desperation. The first and most important thing is, on the one hand, to relieve them of all unrightful taxes and tributes that up to now they had to pay to the state itself or some of their fellow citizens and, on the other hand to increase the wages for their work in such a way that gradually they are put in the position to acquire through their industry a few amenities that improve their lives. If the changes introduced for the purpose initially do nothing other than divest some of the citizens of the abundance they enjoy, then we must view this not as a harmful, but as a salutary effect. If, however, some of these initiatives cause citizens who do not own very much to lose some of their property or even if the loss suffered by the rich is too severe or too unevenly distributed, then the state must intervene to compensate for these damages. If necessary, the state can use a method that is always available and always legal, namely, to take money from the public treasury to provide adequate compensations for those damages. The public treasury itself will be able to meet these obligations if the countrywide tax that is proportional to everyone's annual income is raised as required by the increased expenditures.

Part III

Ethics and Philosophy of Religion

Selections from the *Treatise of the Science of Religion*

Part I: *On the Concept of Religion, on Different Kinds of Religion and our Obligations with Respect to Religion*

§. 10.

An inquiry that must precede all the others

If it holds for all teaching that one must strive to engender conviction in the claims put forward, it obviously is all the more incumbent upon me to do so when giving instruction in the most perfect religion, that is, when I present the science of religion. I must strive to produce a conviction that will not only prove impervious to all present doubt, but which we can expect not to be overturned, nor even shaken, during the entire lifetime of my listeners. I cannot possibly accomplish this if the assumptions I use in my proofs, that is, the propositions I accept as *premises* in my arguments, are not all *certain* and *undeniable*. For the degree of probability of the conclusion of an argument is never higher, but usually somewhat lower, than the degree of probability of its weakest premise.

Now there is scarcely a *single truth* that has not been doubted or indeed contested by some *individual scholar*. Already among the *Greeks* there was a numerous sect of philosophers, the *skeptics* (i.e. *doubters*), who made it their business to find plausible objections to even the most obvious of truths, and to point out alleged contradictions in them, thus rendering them unreliable and doubtful. Thus, for instance, they denied the possibility of motion, the existence of a physical world, the existence of other thinking beings beside themselves, and some of them even their *own* existence.

1. But the worst is that the danger of falling into a kind of *scepticism* is real for *everyone*, at least for the educated, if no preventive measures have been taken; I will say that there is *scarcely a single truth* that an *educated* person could not feel *tempted* to doubt at least once in his life. Such temptation can arise:

a) *when a truth goes against one of our passions.* For it happens only all too frequently that people begin to doubt a truth simply because it gets in the way of some passionate desire that arose in them. And the more people are used to taking thought, the easier it is to convince themselves by seeking out apparent objections that what they had always taken to be true is in fact false.

b) *when we learn that this opinion has been doubted and disputed by many others.*

c) when reflection and comparison appear to reveal *a contradiction between the given proposition and other propositions we hold to be true.*

d) when we have undertaken to *discover the grounds of this proposition,* and have unfortunately been unsuccessful in our search. For then the suspicion arises in us that the proposition in fact *has* no ground; and we are all the more inclined to suppose this to be so, the more examples have made us aware of the fact that many a belief to which the great masses confidently adhere has turned out upon closer inspection to be false and groundless.

In order to prevent such scepticism as much as lies in my power, I will in what follows not assume anything to be certain and settled if it can in any way be made doubtful, unless I have previously provided a proof for it. I will go so far as to imagine that I have before me an audience that is at least sometimes *in a mood* to believe that nothing is certain. And I ask myself: what is the *first thing* I can convince people in such a condition is true?

Clearly, it cannot be a truth that requires for its proof the *assumption* of one or *more others*. It must instead be a truth that is *certain in and of itself*, in that its *negation contradicts itself*. The only truth of this sort is that *there are truths*, as shall be shown in greater detail in the next section.

§. 11.

There are Truths

1. Everyone will find it obvious that there are several, or at least *one*, truth as soon as he has properly grasped the meaning I attach to this claim. In particular, I must remind you that I take the word *truth* here in its *objective* sense, according to which any proposition is called a

truth if it asserts that something is the way it is, regardless of whether or not this proposition is actually recognised and expressed by anyone. Thus we distinguish between *truths as such* and truths that are *thought* and *recognised* by someone. We do not yet wish to claim that there are truths of the latter sort, i.e. *recognised* truths or *cognitions*, for this claim actually presupposes several things, namely:

a) That there are truths as such; and

b) That there is a being who judges.

Only if these two things are assumed can the question be posed whether (all or at least some) of the judgments of this being are true.

2. That there are several objective truths, or at least one, can be shown without any other presuppositions. For the opposite proposition, i.e. the claim that absolutely nothing is true, is self-refuting. For if nothing was true, it would also be false to say that nothing is true. With the help of this simple inference, even the worst skeptic can convince himself that there is at least one objective truth.

§. 12.

There are several, and indeed infinitely many truths

1. It is certain from what has been said that there is at least *one* truth. Should someone now raise the doubt whether there are *several* truths, I would attempt to convince him that there are in the following manner.

2. I can designate the one truth whose existence the skeptic grants me with the formula A is B (whatever it may say). I now claim that alongside this truth there is at least *one* further truth. For whoever supposed the contrary would have to advance as a truth the claim that *apart from the truth* A is B, *there is no other*. This claim is, however, clearly different from the claim A is B and thus, if true, would constitute a *second* truth. It is therefore not true that there is only *one* truth; rather, there must be at least two.

3. Similarly, it can be shown that there must be more than two truths. For whatever the two truths whose existence someone is willing to concede

may say, they can be designated by the formulas A is B and C is D. Just as before, it can be shown that *the two truths* A is B and C is D *cannot be the only ones*. For, if this were so, the contrary claim, namely, that *nothing is true apart from the truths that* A is B and C is D, would constitute a *new*, *third* truth.

4. Anyone can see that this kind of inference can be repeated *ad infinitum*, and that consequently there must be infinitely many truths.

§. 13.

We humans are in a position to know truths, and actually do know some

1. Should the preceding considerations suffice to bring the skeptic to avow that there must be truths, and indeed infinitely many of them, I attempt to bring him further to accept that he has the ability to know at least some of these truths.

2. Plainly, the only way for me to do this is to bring him to form some judgment or other, for should he in fact form no judgment whatever, it must needs follow that he knows no truth, for every cognition presupposes a judgment.

3. Should I bring him in one way or another to make even a single judgment, no matter what it may say, he will in so doing ascribe to himself the ability to recognise truths, for he holds this judgment to be true at least at the time when he expresses it.

4. The skeptic may now admit that he cannot withstand the impulse to form judgments, but perhaps he doubts whether these judgments have truth in them. Should he understand this to mean merely that not all of his judgments are true, we need not dispute this in the least, as we shall soon see. But the skeptic means that perhaps *not a single one* of his judgments is true. But this is absurd, for the assumption that all of our judgments are false is self-refuting, it being itself one of these judgments. I believe that whoever ventured to claim this would have to admit to himself that not all judgments are false, and that consequently truth lies in several or at least in a single one.

We could then show in a manner similar to that used in §12 that he in fact recognises *several* truths, indeed (over time) an indeterminate number of them.

§. 14.

We do, indeed, sometimes err in our judgments; but under certain conditions we can be more or less assured that we do not err

Even if the preceding made it perfectly clear that not all of our judgments are false, it is equally certain that we err only too frequently—for how often do we not claim the opposite of what we maintained before, and now hold to be true what formerly passed for false, or false what we formerly thought to be true. In such cases we must either have been mistaken earlier, or else at the present time. But should we not trust even a single one of our judgments because we err sometimes? Then we would once again fall victim to the self-contradictory claim that all our judgments are false. We must therefore make some sort of selection, and fully aware of our fallibility in certain matters, shall then be able to trust some of our judgments with complete confidence. It is a matter of the greatest importance that we learn the rules that govern rational choice in this matter. Here, however, I can only present a few of these rules, and will say that if we observe these conditions we can be *more or less assured* that we do nor err in making a particular judgment.

1. *When a judgment impresses itself upon us irresistibly*, as for example the judgment that two straight lines cannot enclose a space, and we cannot possibly think otherwise, then we may trust it completely. For if we were not willing to trust even *such* judgments, we should obviously be all the less able to trust *others* that do not force themselves upon us so irresistibly, that is, we would have to believe that we recognise no truth at all, which amounts to the contradiction pointed out above.

2. *Judgments that merely express a present perception (i.e. a sensation or idea) in us*, without attempting to assign a cause to it, that is, *pure judgments of perception*, are completely certain. Judgments like "I have the idea of a *red colour*"—where I do not mean to claim that some red

object or other actually stands before me—may serve as examples. For such judgments impress themselves upon us irresistibly.

3. Judgments in which we allow ourselves to *pronounce on the cause of a perception we have had*—in which we assert, for example, that the very object that brought about the sensation A in us was also the cause of the sensation B—in brief, *judgments of experience* in the narrow sense of the term, are as such only probable. However, when we have already experienced the two sensations or ideas A and B on a great many occasions *simultaneously*, but never the one without the other, the probability of the judgment that the object that brings about perception A is also the cause of perception B becomes so great that we can consider it a complete *certainty*. An example of such a judgment of experience would be: the stove warms me. That which I *see* of the stove = A; the *warmth* I *feel* = B; the stove itself is the object I designate as the cause of the perception A, and insofar as I now say: *The stove warms me*, I assert that the same object (stove) which is cause of the sensations of *colour, shape* and the like (A) is also the cause of the sensation of warmth (B).

4. Judgments all the elements of which are pure concepts, and which can accordingly be called *conceptual judgments* or *judgments from concepts*, though they are more commonly called judgments *a priori*, attain a very high degree of probability when they are *confirmed by a large number of experiences* (independently of any other reasons), that is, when we have many experiences which occur precisely as they would *have to* were the conceptual judgment true, and which could have been completely different if it were *not* true. Examples are the laws governing the collision of elastic bodies, those governing the reflection of light, and the like.

5. *A judgment that is derived by means of a very easy and brief inference from another very secure judgment is itself quite certain*, e.g. the judgment that this rock, were I to let it go, would fall.

6. A judgment that *must be derived by means of a long series of inferences* can also be quite certain when *one* or *more* of the following conditions are met: a) we have followed the series of inferences *repeatedly*; b) especially *at different times*; c) when we have arrived at the

judgment in more ways than one; d) when we have allowed our chain of inferences to be verified *by several other people*. Thus the judgment that a sum of a large numbers of addends has been done correctly will attain a high degree of probability when we have figured it several times, in different ways, etc.

7. Judgments upon which almost all people agree, and which on this account I call *general judgments of common sense*, are to be considered nearly *infallible* when the following three conditions are met: a) when the judgments concern matters that can be decided using *reason* alone or else *experiences* that everyone can and does have; not however when experiments or researches are necessary that only a few men have performed or can perform. b) when it is not a matter of *complete indifference* for a person whether his judgment on this issue goes one way or the opposite. c) when the judgment is not one that is formulated to *flatter our sensuality*, but rather one that denigrates it. Examples of judgments that possess all these properties are the following: *lying is a sin, gratitude is a duty*, and hundreds of other such *judgments of duty*. By contrast, an example of a judgment that would not be reliable even were it to be universally embraced is that the rising and setting of the sun results from its east to west motion—for this judgment meets none of the three above conditions. I prove that a general judgment of *common sense* that meets the above conditions has the greatest reliability as follows: if the matter can be judged simply by *reasoning* (without special experiences or experiments), then every one is *able* to adjudge it. If it the matter is *not indifferent*, everyone will find it *worthwhile* to ponder it. Finally, when everyone concurs in a judgment that *doesn't flatter* their sensuality but rather denigrates it, then there is hardly any reason that explains this agreement other than that the *force of truth* itself has compelled this concordant acknowledgment. I attempt to adhere to the rules I have set out here in each of the judgments I put forth in these lectures, and to estimate the degree of certainty of each of them. You shall find, I hope, that those of my claims that must be accepted in order to find convincing the proof set out here for the truth and divinity of catholic Christianity are fully reliable, and this indeed for the most part because they belong to the deliverances of common sense as just described. In some cases, I shall especially establish this.

§. 15.
Human beings are capable of being virtuous and happy

In order to arrive at the concept of religion in a way that at the same time indicates the reality of this concept, i.e. that it really has an object, that there in fact is something as thus defined, we must begin with a brief consideration of human nature.

1. We human beings have the ability to sense that our own *condition* is either *pleasant* or *unpleasant*; in other words, we can *feel* pleasure and pain. If we state this in the *singular* rather than the *plural* (which can be done here without loss of generality), it reads as follows: "I (a being who judges) have the capacity to have pleasant or unpleasant sensations," and this is an immediate consequence of the simple perceptual judgment: "I feel pleasure/pain," which, according to §14, 1 and 5 is indubitable. This capacity to find one's condition either pleasant or unpleasant we call *sensibility*, or (less accurately) the *faculty of feeling*. We human beings have, therefore, sensibility.

2. Around us we find beings to whom we must attribute a similar sensibility (capacity to feel pleasure and pain) due either to their *thoroughgoing* or at least *multifarious similarity* to us, namely, men and animals. This is an *empirical judgment*, and is accordingly only *probable*, though here the probability is so high that no reasonable person doubts in earnest whether men and animals that surround him are really alive and sensate. (It is debatable whether Descartes, who, on account of some preconceived opinions, declared animals to be automata, really persuaded himself that they were no more than that.)

3. We have the capacity to bring about *a variety of changes in and outside of ourselves*, e.g. to move our limbs in various ways, and thus to change all sorts of outer objects. We arrive at this *judgment of experience* in the same way that we learn that this or that outer object has certain powers (i.e. capacities to act). As we learn, for example, that the *magnet* draws iron to itself, so too we learn that *our own hand* holds the magnet, that we can move this hand in this way or that, and so on. Here we *ourselves* are the object that is observed. Effects that we ourselves bring about consciously we call *actions*. Thus we have the ability to *act*.

4. Many of our acts also affect our own condition, and bring about either pleasant or unpleasant feelings in us.

5. But not only in ourselves: our actions can also affect *other* sensate beings in our environs, men and animals, altering their condition and generating in them sometimes pleasant, sometimes unpleasant feelings.

6. In many cases we can know in advance, with greater or lesser probability, what influence a certain act will have either on ourselves or on others.

7. When we have *performed* a certain action several times, or when we have *seen* it performed by beings similar to us, e.g. human beings, we infer with more or less certainty that we are also *now* in a position to perform it. Thus, for example, I believe that I am now capable of reciting Gellert's fable of the rhinoceros, or of tearing up this promissory note, and the like.

8. When we form an idea of a certain change from which we expect pleasant consequences for ourselves, this idea brings about in us a certain something that we call a *desire* or a *longing:* we wish, desire, or long for this change. The ability to wish, to desire, or to long for something we call the *faculty of desire*; in certain contexts we also speak of a *drive* or an *inclination*, etc. And as the collection of all that is pleasant is called *bliss* or *happiness*, we also call the *general ability to wish* the *desire for happiness.* Thus we human beings have a desire for happiness, and all our *other* urges are expressions of this.

9. When we think that it may be possible for us to perform an action that will produce a change that we *wish*, we also wish the performance of *this* action, we long to perform it.

10. On the basis of a *principle* of which we may not be distinctly conscious, we judge certain actions we think *possible* to be *obligatory*. This concept of *obligation* is one of the most noteworthy of all that occur in human knowledge. It appears to be an utterly *simple concept*, one that can neither be defined nor analysed. Instead of saying that someone *should* do something, we also say it is his *duty*, his obligation, and so on. Admittedly each of these words is associated with different secondary

concepts. However, we can disregard these here, and pay attention only to what they all designate in common. To *have to do* something, to be *obligated* to do something, to be *obliged* to do it, etc., we thus consider the same. The ability of our faculty of cognition to recognise such *obligations* or *duties* has been called *practical reason*, since judgments in which we express an obligation or a duty are called *practical*, all others being called *theoretical*. Practical judgments, i.e. those that express an *obligation*, are occasionally also called *moral laws, laws, demands, commands, imperatives, even categorical imperatives of practical reason*. When speaking more precisely, we distinguish between judgments that treat of *single cases* and those that are *general*. Only the latter are called *laws* or *moral laws*. The collection of all moral laws is also sometimes called *the moral law*, where "law" is understood collectively. In another sense, however, we understand by "the moral law" or "the highest moral law" only a single proposition, from which all others can be objectively derived, that is, as consequences from their ground.

11. It sometimes happens that *two or more actions appear possible to us*, that is, it seems to us that we are capable of acting either this way or that. In such cases we consider the various *consequences* these actions would bring, and measure them as well against the moral laws. Should it turn out that one of these actions, *A*, has especially *pleasant consequences for us*, while another, *B*, *appears to be in conformity with the moral law, we feel from this moment on with the greatest distinctness that it is possible for us to will either one of these actions*. The concept of *willing* should not be confused with that of *wishing* (no. 8) For it by no means follows from the fact that we *wish* something that we *will* it. The *capacity to will* is called simply the *will*, or the *faculty or power of willing*. And the peculiar circumstance that it is possible for us to will either one of two actions is called *freedom*. Instead of saying we can will one of two actions, we usually say that *we can choose*. Thus freedom can also be defined as an *ability to choose*. But it should not be forgotten that *willing* something and *making that thing happen* are not exactly the same—the latter is just a very common, but occasionally unrealised *effect* of the former. If, for example, I *will* to burn this paper, then presumably I will succeed in burning it. But I might also find my hand suddenly paralyzed, or it might just happen that the paper is made of *asbestos*, and so cannot be burned, etc. Accordingly, we can never

say with complete certainty that one of these two actions will be possible for us; however we can say that it will be possible for us *to will either one*. For this reason, when we set out to express practical propositions accurately, the *obligation* governs not the *action itself*, the production of an outer result, but instead only the *willing* of this result; that is, we do not say: "You should *do* this or that" but rather "You should *will* this or that."

12. When we will an action that we should will, that is when we will an action we recognise to be our duty, this determination of the will is called a *good, morally good, or a moral will.* A being whose *ruling* will is to do what it should is called *good, morally good, moral, virtuous*, or indeed *holy*. And the quality responsible for this is called the *goodness, moral goodness, morality, virtue*, or *holiness* of the being. When on the contrary we will an action that our drive for happiness urges upon us against the demands of our reason, we call this determination of the will a *bad, morally bad, immoral*, or *sinful* will. A being whose ruling will is to perform actions forbidden by reason is called *bad, morally bad, immoral, sinful or depraved*, and this quality *badness, moral badness, immorality, sinfulness or depravity*. Precisely because we recognise a moral law and have a drive for happiness, we are *capable of being either virtuous or depraved.* Often a being is called an *ethical* or *moral* being simply when it is capable of being either *virtuous* or *depraved*, and is thus capable of acting either *ethically* or *unethically*, *morally* or *immorally*. Evidently, one here takes the expression "ethical or moral being" in a *wider* sense, understanding by it a being that at least can be *ethical* or *moral*, though in fact it may not be. In this case one opposes *ethical* or *moral* beings to those that are *not free*, that is *physical* or *merely natural beings*, e.g. animals. We do well to remark here that an act of will of a rational being is called *morally good* when it *accords* with the moral law, even when no opposing wish of the drive for happiness, and thus no *freedom* in the sense explained above, is present. Thus, for example, all the actions of God are called *holy*, even though no drive for happiness and no freedom of the kind that consists in the ability to do the opposite is to be met with in Him.

13. When we act *freely*, that is, when we decide to will one of two actions, *one commanded* by our reason, the *other wished* by our drive

for happiness, then no determining *ground* can be present. For anyone arguing that a *ground* was present which in one case determined us to *fulfill our duty* and in another to violate it, that is, to *perform the action our drive for happiness wishes*, would have to seek this ground in the circumstance that in one case the command of reason, and in the other the *wish of the drive for happiness*, was stronger. But closer consideration shows that these two things are not homogeneous, i.e. cannot be *measured* with the same units, and consequently one cannot say that one is stronger or weaker than the other. A *wish* is no part of a *judgment*, a judgment no part of a wish. The famous *principle of sufficient reason* (*principium causalitatis*)—namely, *everything that happens has a ground*—is thus not universally true, and really should be expressed only as follows: *always seek a ground*, look to see if one is present, and if so, *what* it is.

14. There is, however, a *manner of speaking* according to which when we choose to do our *duty*, *the duty was the motive for our act of will*, and when on the contrary we choose what we *wish*, our *drive for happiness was the motive*. Here, therefore, one must take the word "motive" to mean a *ground* not in the *strict* but rather in an *improper* sense, as a *condition* or *partial ground* (a *conditio sine qua non*). The acts of free beings indeed occur *without grounds*, but they presuppose as *partial grounds* or *conditions* (*conditio sine qua non*) a) *the existence of an acting being* (where there is no acting being, there can be no free action) b) the *property of freedom* in this being, which in its turn presupposes α) a *knowledge of the moral law* (or practical reason) and β) *a drive towards happiness*; finally c) at least a *motive* improperly so-called, i.e. the representation of two actions both of which appear *possible* to the being, one of which its drive for happiness *wishes*, the other of which its practical reason recognises that it should will. Only *morality* (in the sense explained in No. 12), not *freedom* (the kind of freedom *people* have) is a *true perfection* of a being. This freedom stems from the presence of both a *drive for happiness* and of *reason*, and the circumstance that the two are sometimes in a so-called conflict (i.e. demand conflicting ways of acting). The existence of a *drive for happiness* (certain needs) and still more the conflict between the wishes of this drive and the demands of reason are of themselves imperfections. Only *relatively* speaking, i.e. in comparison with still more imperfect beings, such as those that lack all

sensation, or possess no reason, is moral *freedom* an *advantage*; in comparison with God, and considered in and of itself, it is an imperfection; and the closer a man comes to perfection, the less frequent becomes the conflict between the wishes of his drive for happiness and the demands of his reason, the more frequently he acts *virtuously* without actually having acted freely.

Note: I must not neglect to remind you at the end of this § that what is said here concerning the *freedom* of the human will is merely *my* view of the matter, which can be mistaken, without affecting the other things that have been said. Since according to this view it is supposed that a human act of will (a free one at least) has no *determining* ground at all, it has been given the name of *indeterminism*. Opposed to this view is *determinism*, which maintains that there is a determining ground for every act of will. Whichever opinion may be correct, human common sense has decided infallibly that the human will has a property that we call by the name of *freedom*, and that using this freedom we sometimes act in a morally good, sometimes in a morally bad way, and that morally good actions deserve reward, morally bad actions punishment.

§. 16.

Many of the concepts and opinions people hold have an influence on their virtue as well as on their happiness

1. No matter which opinion one holds concerning human freedom, one must consider as something undeniably demonstrated by experience that we humans follow the demands of our reason all the more often and more reliably, and thus become all the more virtuous:

a) the more *readily*, as well as *accurately* and *vividly*, we recognise our duties. For if it never even occurs to us what our duty is, it is impossible for us to fulfill it;

b) the *less frequently* the wishes of our drive for happiness *contradict* our reason. For only when such a contradiction appears is it possible for us to deviate from our duty; finally

c) the *weaker* and the more *moderate* the wishes of our drive for happiness are even in the case of such a contradiction. For then we may expect with more confidence that these wishes will not drive the idea of our duty out of our consciousness. And only as long as this hasn't happened is it possible for us to obey it.

2. After these preliminaries it is easy to show that we have a great many concepts and opinions[1] that profoundly influence sometimes our virtue, sometimes our happiness, and sometimes both. It should be remarked, however, that I am not speaking here of the influence that such beliefs *accidentally* have, but rather of the sort of influence that is grounded in human nature, and that therefore is quite *general*. Any mathematical or physical truth can cause harm accidentally if, for example, it induces us to perform an experiment that goes wrong; but this is not the effect of a universally active ground rooted in human nature.

3. Such a general influence on our *virtue* is exercised by:

a) the concepts that we form of our duties and obligations. It can only be highly advantageous for our virtue when we recognise all of our duties exactly, vividly and easily; it must have a very damaging influence on our virtue if we remain ignorant of many of our duties, or have but an obscure, uncertain and hard-won knowledge of them—for how would it then be possible for us to fulfill each of our duties as we should?

b) Furthermore, *our concepts of the effects upon ourselves of fulfilling or failing to fulfill our duties* have a considerable influence on our virtue. It can have nothing but beneficial effects on our virtue if we are convinced that almost every good deed will sooner or later be rewarded by the natural course of events, and that each vice brings its own punishment; that beyond this there is a just God, who sees to it that no good or bad action, however trivial, remains without its due reward. The opinions that every fulfillment of duty is onerous, that virtue, at least here on earth, always leads to unhappiness, that the vicious, at least down

[1]We remark here once and for all that the word "opinion" is taken here and in all similar cases in its widest sense, namely as designating any proposition that someone accepts as true, thus every judgment that he forms, regardless of whether or not this judgment is itself true, and regardless also of the degree of confidence with which he makes it. Thus not merely those of our judgments that are uncertain or completely incorrect, but also those that we make with full confidence and that fully conform to the truth, are here called *opinions*.

here, always find themselves in an enviable state of good fortune, that punishment in the afterlife is dubious, and so on, must exercise a very damaging influence on our virtue. In the former case, conflict between the demands of our reason and the desires resulting from our drive for happiness will arise far less frequently, and even when they do arise the desires will not be so violent and unbridled as in the latter.

4. There are also concepts and beliefs that exercise a general influence *on our happiness*:

a) the concepts that we have *of the true nature of the happiness that is within our reach, of its conditions, and of the means for attaining it* have obviously the greatest influence on our happiness. It can only be most beneficial if these concepts are *correct* and *complete*. On the other hand, if we form false ideas of the true nature of happiness, if we know nothing of the various ways and means that lead to happiness, and hence look upon many things as means for attaining happiness that are in fact nothing of the kind, this can only cause the greatest harm. In this case it is to be feared that we will leave many things undone that would have increased our happiness and do many things that in the end only make us unhappy.

b) *certain pleasant or unpleasant concepts that we form of things completely beyond our control*, e.g. of death and its terrors, the afterlife, and so on, also have a great influence on our happiness. Whoever forms *pleasant conceptions* of such things gains in cheerfulness, while those who worry that these things, which they cannot possibly avoid, will be thoroughly bad, will be needlessly tormented by their own terrifying ideas.

c) Finally, *all beliefs that have an influence on our virtue* have, for that very reason, a *mediate influence* on our happiness. For because, as shall be shown more precisely in what follows, there is a God who rewards each good action and punishes each evil one, so that every rational being that is capable of being happy and virtuous will be happy over the course of its existence to the extent that it lives virtuously, and unhappy in the measure that it becomes vicious. Thus what virtue requires is also indirectly required for our happiness, and what takes away from our virtue also makes us less happy.

5. Incidentally, it requires no special proof to show that there are also concepts and beliefs to which no such general influence on our virtue and happiness may be attributed. Who would deny, for example, that for the purposes of the virtue and happiness of men, generally speaking, it is a matter of complete indifference whether they deem the dark patches on the moon to be valleys or mountains? etc.

6. Should it be necessary to adopt terms to mark the distinction we have just noted between human beliefs, perhaps the most reasonable thing would be to call the latter sort *indifferent* and the former *important* or *generally important.*

§. 17.

We sometimes wish that we had certain beliefs

From what I have just said about the ways our beliefs can have a lesser or greater influence on our virtue and happiness, it follows that we must often be in a position to notice this influence, and indeed to judge (i.e. more or less correctly to represent) what influence beliefs we do not hold would have were we to hold them. As a result, it can often happen that we wish in fact to hold certain beliefs. When in particular we foresee that a certain belief, e.g. in the immortality of our soul, would be very conducive to our virtue, then, if we sincerely will the good, we will at once feel the wish in fact to hold this belief. In this case it is our moral feelings that give rise to the wish that a certain belief was our own. Still more often it happens that we foresee, or at least imagine we foresee, that were we to adhere to a certain belief, this would free us from certain burdensome obligations, or would bring us other true or merely apparent advantages. One who is not very virtuous will have a hard time fending off the wish that he really believed it.

§. 18.

Our will has considerable influence on the formation of our beliefs

1. It is true, however, that the process of *judging*, and thus all our beliefs and opinions, are not *immediately* dependent on our will. We cannot directly bring ourselves to judge that things are thus and so just because we

will it. Rather, the fact that our faculty of judgment forms precisely this or that judgment depends on the constitution of the *ideas* then present in our mind. This occurs with a kind of necessity. Nonetheless it remains certain that our will has a significant *mediate* influence on the constitution of our judgments, and consequently on the formation of our beliefs. Our will, namely, has an undeniable influence on:

a) our *attention*. We can, when we so will (I will not here look into whether this occurs mediately or immediately) direct our mind's attention towards certain ideas, keep it focused on them, by so doing make them more vivid and strong, etc. On the other hand, we can move our attention away from them and thus make them gradually disappear from our consciousness.

b) Furthermore, our will has an undeniable influence on our *body*, and consequently on a number of *external objects*. If we want to we can bring about a variety of movements in our limbs, and thus bring about changes in the bodies and objects around us, bringing them closer, moving them away, and so on. It is clear from this how our will can exercise a considerable influence on our beliefs. According to whether we direct our mind's attention to this or that sensible object, these or other sensible ideas, experiences and cognitions will arise in us; according to whether we reflect longer on these or those ideas, or compare them, etc., these or other convictions arise in us; according to whether we stop at this or that place, associate with these or other people, read these or other books, and so on, we shall develop these or other concepts and beliefs.

2. I make yet a further claim: we are often in a position to foresee the influence that our freely chosen behaviour will have on the formation of our concepts and beliefs. Do we not in fact *foresee* that we will not succeed in attaining certain knowledge and insights if we do not apply the means that lead to it, or the attention and reflection required, or do not consult the appropriate books, etc.? So too many people can know in advance that they will adopt the beliefs of those they associate with, since they know from their previous experience that they usually accept the opinions of the company they keep.

3. Finally, I claim that the influence that people have on the beliefs they form extends so far that if we want to we can even *deceive ourselves* or, as it is said, *talk ourselves into something*. That is, we can intentionally

behave in such a way that we in the end come to believe something we originally held to be incorrect or at least unproven. In particular, people can:

a) (as we saw in the previous §) form the wish that they truly adhered to a certain belief; and because they can influence their beliefs, and know in advance that they can do so:

b) they can attempt to truly bring about this belief in themselves; they can intentionally direct their attention towards all the true or merely apparent grounds that support it; they can intentionally disregard everything that counts against it; they can frequent people who adhere to it, read books in which it is defended, and so on. Through all these means, finally,

c) bring it about that they in fact hold this belief with more or less confidence.

4. Several *objections* may nevertheless be raised against the claim that such intentional self-deception is possible, which I must briefly set out and reply to. In particular, one can say that:

a) it would go against the natural *drive towards truth* were anyone to form the intention to deceive himself. Admittedly, it occurs all too frequently that people, without knowing or willing it, deceive themselves; but they can never *wish* to be deceived. But even supposing that he really *wished* to deceive himself,

b) it would not be possible to carry it through. For it is a contradiction *knowingly to deceive oneself.* If someone knows that an opinion is false, it is precisely for that reason that it is not *his* opinion; at most he could *pretend* that he believed it, but could not really do so.

c) Finally, all judging or opining that takes place follows certain necessary laws. If we recognize the grounds of a truth, it is impossible for us to deny it; and on the contrary, if we have no grounds for it, we cannot possibly believe it.

5. To this I reply:

a) The natural drive towards truth is not so strong in men that we are incapable of wishing in certain cases that we *didn't know* something, or imagined the opposite of what really is. Thus for example, it is only all too well known that someone who has done wrong would happily convince himself that he did not do it, or that what he did was not really all that bad, etc.

b) It is admittedly impossible for someone to deceive himself at the same moment that he forms the intention to do so. But it can happen later on. As long as we are distinctly aware of our intention to deceive ourselves, we have of course not succeeded; but we subsequently forget this intention, and then the actual deception first appears.

c) Judgment of course follows necessary laws, but our attention can be freely directed, and according as we direct it here or there, we may believe to see grounds either *for* or *against* a certain opinion.

§. 19.
The concept of a moral proposition

As was shown in the previous §, there are beliefs that we wish we had, or, what amounts to the same thing, we sometimes feel in our hearts a wish (some also say an *interest*) for the adoption of a belief. But as for every belief there are others that contradict it, it is easy to see that there are also beliefs that we wish not to have, but rather find repulsive and that our heart resists. Because, for example, it is pleasant to think that one has rendered service to others, it is by contrast unpleasant to be shown that one has harmed rather than helped, and so on. Thus we can say in general that there are beliefs that are *not indifferent* to our faculty of desire, beliefs that it either speaks for or against. But as our will has a considerable influence on the constitution of our beliefs (as shown in the previous §), it stands to reason that in a great many, though indeed not all, cases there will arise in us a particular temptation to adopt or reject such beliefs without sufficient justification. Thus, for example, when we have done something bad we not only feel tempted to deceive ourselves into thinking that we were not as culpable as all that, but all too often actually succeed. Closer inspection reveals, however, that there is hardly any proposition so indifferent that various accidental circumstances could not at least sometimes produce a wish either for or against its adoption and consequently a longing either to claim it or to reject it without sufficient grounds. What, for example, could be more indifferent in itself to our faculty of desire than whether a particular truth of pure mathematics runs one way or another? Nevertheless if we ourselves have discovered it, and if we must fear to be mocked should it turn out to be false, we wish it were true, and are tempted wherever possible to convince others that it is correct. However, there are also propositions that lead our faculty of desire to push for or against them, thus engendering a temptation either to accept them or reject them without sufficient grounds, not on account of purely accidental circumstances but because of grounds that lie in our nature and are generally operative. Of this sort are, for example, the important propositions stating that no lie is permissible, or that our souls are immortal, that a single evil action undertaken by us with a distinct consciousness might well bring upon us eternal misfortune as a punishment, and the like. I find this kind of proposition so remarkable that I would like to have a special word to designate them, and since I know of no expression more suitable, I will allow myself to call them *moral* or *ethical propositions*. Thus I call a proposition moral if there is something grounded in human nature that gives rise to a temptation either to accept it as true or reject it as false without sufficient justification. I have chosen the term *moral* because the behaviour we observe in connection with such propositions (our acceptance or rejection of them) may, generally speaking, be called *moral* in the more general sense of the term, i.e. it consists of acts that may be called either morally good or morally bad. For should we withstand the temptation to either accept or reject such a proposition without sufficient grounds and examine it with all possible rigour, while yet wishing that we could find it true, then our conduct is certainly very praiseworthy. So too should we be censored if, in the opposite case, we give in to temptation and convince ourselves of the truth of the proposition because it pleases us, or else fight against establishing it, because we find it unpleasant.

§. 20.

Concept of the word religion

Only after all these preliminaries do I believe myself to be able to define the concept that in my opinion should be connected with the word "religion".

1. We have seen (§16) that there are many concepts and opinions that are not indifferent to men's virtue and happiness, which rather exercise a beneficial or a pernicious influence sometimes on a person's virtue, sometimes on his happiness.

2. It is easy to see that a large number of such opinions are of the kind that I dubbed *moral* in the previous section, that is, opinions for which there is a special cause grounded in our human nature which gives rise to the temptation either to accept them as true or reject them as false without sufficient justification.

3. This is not always the case, however, for there are propositions that have a considerable influence on our virtue and happiness but do not give rise to such temptation. This is the case, for example, where new knowledge does not impose any new onerous duties upon us, but rather simply indicates welcome new means for the satisfaction of our needs, as for instance medical discoveries. This is also the case where we do not yet have any idea at all of the new duties that accepting a proposition imposes, or of the unpleasant consequences these duties may have for our sensual nature, and also where it is immediately apparent that we cannot possibly refrain from acknowledging a proposition because its truth is too plainly visible.

4. But as there are propositions that have a considerable influence on our virtue and happiness and yet are not moral, so too are there some propositions that must be counted as moral, even though they do not considerably influence our virtue and happiness. This holds, for instance, when an illusion that comes naturally to us humans makes it appear that a certain proposition, if only it were true, would free us from burdensome duties, while closer consideration shows that nothing of the sort follows from it.

5. Thus a proposition can have either of these attributes, that is, being *important* or being a *moral* proposition, without having the other. Propositions that combine the two attributes, however, that is propositions whose earnest consideration engenders a specific temptation to declare for or against them, and the acceptance or rejection of which causes a change in the measure of our virtue and happiness, are especially worthy of notice. I allow myself to call such propositions *religious*, and

accordingly understand by the word *religion* in the *subjective* sense the collection of all of a person's religious beliefs. In other words, I call a person's religion the collection of all of his beliefs that have either a beneficial or detrimental influence on his virtue or his happiness and at the same time are so constituted that there is a particular temptation to opt for or against them without appropriate grounds.

6. The *subjective* sense of this word easily yields its *objective* sense. In particular, when we think of a collection of religious propositions with the determination that they *might* well comprise a person's religion, without however assuming that they are *really* believed and accepted by anyone, we think the concept of religion in the objective sense.

7. In both cases however, we take the word with a *wider* meaning than is customary. For on the common understanding, if I am not mistaken, religion is understood to be nothing other than the belief in God and the collection of all the moral beliefs of a man concerning his relations to and duties towards God.

§. 36.

Concept of the most perfect religion

1. Since we only reckon a doctrine to be religious if it is not indifferent to virtue and happiness, it is easy to see that different religions will have markedly different impacts on people's virtue and happiness. Among all conceivable religions, however, there must be one (or perhaps there may be several) which are so conducive to the virtue and happiness of a given individual (at least at a given period in his life) that no other religion exceeds them in this respect. Please allow me to call such a religion the *most perfect* for this person at this time in his life.

2. Similar considerations apply to entire collections of persons, for an entire people, or to any other society with several members. There must be in each case a set of religious teachings that have such beneficial effects upon the whole (if not upon each individual taken singly) that no other religion would produce more beneficial effects. I shall call this religion the *most perfect religion for the given society.*

3. Finally, I shall call a religion the *most inherently perfect*, or simply the most perfect, if it contains all the teachings and opinions that are so beneficial for people *in general* (that is, disregarding the imperfections that can only be found in individuals) that no other religion exceeds it in this respect.

4. In giving these three definitions I have intentionally refrained from saying that a religion that deserves the name of the most perfect (whether it be for a single individual, several people, or for mankind in general) is the *most beneficial*, that is, that every other religion must be *less* so, but rather only that there is no other that is *more* beneficial than it. In this way, no one will be able to deny that this concept has *objects* (is a real concept), that is, that there is something of the kind represented by the concept. For there is doubtless at least one among all conceivable religions that is so beneficial that no other is more so, because a human being's capacity to understand is finite, and consequently the set of religious beliefs that he can grasp is only finite. Were I to require of the most perfect religion that every other must be *less beneficial* than it, one could reasonably doubt whether there was such a thing. For in that case one could say that it is conceivable that two different religions might both be so highly beneficial that no third exceeded them in this respect, and in this case no religion would merit the name of the most perfect.

5. I have also intentionally refrained from saying in these three definitions whether all the individual doctrines which make up these religions must be *truths*. For one might certainly dispute whether this is so, especially when it is a question of the most perfect religion for a certain person, or a certain society. But a definition should always be framed in a way that someone who disagrees with us finds as little occasion as possible to begin his criticisms with the concept we have set out.

6. It is readily seen, moreover, that these three concepts differ not only in the components contained in their definitions, but also in their extensions, that is, they do not designate the same objects. A religion which is inherently the most perfect is not necessarily the most perfect religion for every individual. As everyone has his own particular circumstances and needs, it is possible that in addition to the doctrines contained in the most perfect religion a great many further details and explanations

must be added for his sake alone. It is also possible that certain truths that belong to the most perfect religion are not yet beneficial for him—should, for example, he still be a child and not yet be receptive to them, and so on. And just as with individuals, so too there may be entire societies or peoples that are not yet prepared to grasp with advantage all the teachings of the religion that is inherently the most perfect.

7. The last of the three concepts, namely, that of *the most inherently perfect religion*, is precisely the one intended in the concept of the *science of religion* set out above. For the most perfect religion that this science is supposed to acquaint us with is none other than the *inherently* most perfect religion. The science of religion should instruct us not on the religion that happens to be most perfect for this or that individual, but rather concerning the one that is most perfect for *mankind in general.*

§. 37.

A person's highest duty with respect to his religion

In §18, it was already shown that the human will has a considerable influence on the production of our beliefs and convictions. And it is clear from the way that the meaning of the word religion in the widest sense was set out that this influence is especially strong and important in the case of *religious* beliefs, since these are beliefs that are not indifferent to our happiness and virtue, and that give rise to a particular inclination either to accept or reject without sufficient reason. This leads us to the following question: *what use are we obligated to make of this influence of our will on our beliefs?* Or, in other words, what duties do we have with respect to our own religious beliefs and convictions? If I had to sum up *all the duties* we human beings have in this connection in a *single rule*, I should state it roughly as follows: *Everyone should strive to obtain knowledge of the religion most perfect for him*, that is, everyone, as far as lies in his power, should grasp only those concepts and opinions that are most conducive to his own virtue and happiness, or at least as conducive thereto as any others. Each of us should, namely, do everything possible to promote his virtue and happiness. Now as it is by no means a matter of indifference for our virtue and happiness whether we adhere to some religious beliefs rather than others, given that there are concepts and opinions that have a generally beneficial influence on our virtue or our happiness; and as it is frequently in our power to decide whether we acquire or fail to acquire these beliefs, there is no doubt that we should strive to acquire all the concepts and opinions that are maximally conducive to our virtue or happiness.

§. 38.
A more detailed exposition of the particular duties contained in this highest duty

The duty I have just indicated, which we might call the human *duty of belief*, contains so many important particular obligations in itself that it is necessary to present these in greater detail.

1. From the moment that we are have the full use of our reason, we are duty bound to be especially attentive to all the opinions that we suspect might have an influence on our virtue or happiness, particularly when they are also of the kind that gives rise to a temptation in our heart to accept them or reject them; to test the nature of their influence from time to time, and to separate ourselves as much as possible from beliefs that are detrimental to our virtue and happiness. It is obvious that this duty only begins once we have *the full use of our reason*, for before then we were not able to judge which opinions have an influence on our virtue or happiness, nor whether this influence was beneficial or detrimental. From the moment we can do so, however, we have the duty to be especially *attentive* to such beliefs, as they are the most *important* of all, indeed, in a certain sense the only important ones. We must investigate this influence *from time to time*, because:

a) this influence may *change* with time, and a belief that was once beneficial for us may later become harmful. This happens because

b) our knowledge *increases*, and in a later examination we may find something that earlier escaped our notice; and finally, because

c) we are continually adopting new concepts and beliefs, whose influence we could not previously *gauge* because we did not yet *have* them.

2. If it should happen that we are unable to find fully decisive grounds for the truth of a given view, but were nevertheless in a position to judge

that the adoption of this opinion, even should it prove to be incorrect, would only have a beneficial influence on our virtue and happiness, it would not only be permissible but indeed commendable if we were to use all means at our disposal to convince ourselves of its truth. We would do well, for example, frequently to call to mind all the genuine or even apparent reasons that speak in favour of this view, or to draw our attention away from the reasons that speak against it as much as we can; to frequent people who adhere to this view, to read works which defend it, and so on.

Through such behaviour, regardless of whether the belief is erroneous, we shall harm neither ourselves nor others, supposing that we in fact succeed in gradually coming to accept this opinion as truth. On the contrary, all will gain because our virtue and happiness will become more perfect thereby.

Objection: Error can never be beneficial, only *truth* can. But if error is the opposite of truth, how can it produce the same effects? Can *light* and *darkness* produce the same effects?

Reponse: 1. Opposite things can in fact bring about the same effects, under different or sometimes even under the same conditions. In the objection, light and darkness are mentioned as opposite things, yet both can produce the effect of hindering clear vision, for light that is too strong does this just as well as darkness. Thus it by no means follows from the fact that truth and error are opposites that they cannot produce the same effects under different, or indeed under the same conditions.

2. Furthermore, it is also certain that *not all* truths have beneficial effects on people. For even though new truths would only produce beneficial consequences in a being whose reason was completely unencumbered by error, and whose *faculties of sensation and desire* had no weaknesses, this is by no means the situation in which we *human beings* find ourselves. Even the *wisest* among us is saddled with so many errors, even the *best* among us has so many weaknesses in his faculties of sensation and desire! But where there is *error* and *weakness*, the addition of a new truth can undeniably produce such pernicious consequences that the condition of ignorance would have been more advantageous. If a *truth* is added to *errors* already present, it can easily lead to new and most pernicious errors. If for example, someone harbors the erroneous

view that the Bible could not be the work of God if even a single one of the dates it mentions or some other historical statements should prove incorrect, will he not fall into the far more damaging error of believing that the Bible is not God's work once someone points out to him that in fact certain historical statements in the Bible are unreliable? So too where weaknesses of our *faculties of sensation or desire* are present, the recognition of a new truth can cause damage rather than the hoped-for benefit, since it causes us sorrow we might have been spared, or inflames desires in us that should not be satisfied, or provides us with the ways and means to commit some offense or other. Thus for example it can be very detrimental when a man who is ill is told of the recent death of his friend; or to tell a man incurably blind from birth of the many advantages sight might bring; or to teach a scoundrel obsessed with thoughts of murder the secret method of preparation for *aqua toffana*.

3. But if *ignorance* is beneficial in many cases, why should not *error* be as well? Why should *errors* not sometimes be an excellent way to remove the bad effects of another, difficult to avoid error, or the evil consequences of some flaw in our faculties of sensation or desire? If someone is unable to overcome the revulsion he feels whenever he contemplates the ingredients from which a certain medicine is prepared, is it not the case that the pernicious consequences of this flaw in his faculty of sensation are most easily overcome through the erroneous belief that the medicine is in fact prepared from different ingredients? If someone is unable to suppress a forbidden desire so long as the means of satisfying it are before his eyes, are not the dangers of this flaw in his faculty of desire most securely removed when he imagines that there is in fact no possibility of satisfying this desire? In the same way, when a very uncultivated man can only with great difficulty be disabused of the error that physical pains are the greatest of all, will not the belief that the punishment in another life is physical, even should it be incorrect, be of great service to him, in that it prevents evil consequences that the first error can create? Will he not now be all the more careful to avoid all sin?

Objection: Even were one to concede that a certain error might be beneficial in a *single* case, its detrimental consequences would make themselves felt in a hundred others.

Response: But perhaps it is possible to conceive of errors from which no bad consequences follow, or at least for which the bad consequences do not outweigh the good. The last-mentioned example concerning physical punishment in the afterlife may well be of this sort, along with many others.

Natural Morality

§. 86.

Contents of this part

There is not enough time to sketch even the briefest outline of the *particular duties* of men that can be discovered simply by reasoning. I will accomplish only two things in this part: *first*, I shall set out the truth that is in my opinion the highest principle of moral theory, or the *highest moral law*; afterwards, I will derive several especially important consequences that follow from this truth for the theory that deals with the *cultivation of virtue.*

§. 87.

Concept and existence of a highest moral law

1. By the *highest moral law* I understand a practical truth from which every other practical truth (thus, every human duty) may be *objectively* derived, i.e. as a *consequence* from its *ground.*

2. I prove that there must be such a highest moral law as follows:

a) There are certainly some practical truths. Whoever denies this goes against the judgment of sound human understanding, which assumes with great confidence the world over that there are certain actions that one *should perform*, and others that one *should not*. This opinion can hardly be an empty prejudice, given that closer attention shows the concept of *obligation* to be not complex, but completely simple. Now only complex concepts can sometimes contain an inner contradiction, for which reason it is impossible to attribute them to any object as a predicate (though this contradiction may only come to light after long reflection). An example of such a concept is that of a triangle with two right angles, or the concept of a god who, although an unconditioned being, nevertheless has *passions*, etc. Simple concepts, however, can never contain an inner contradiction, precisely because they are simple. Consequently they are all real [*reell*] that is, can be applied as predicates to certain objects. Thus the concept of *obligation* must be applicable to certain objects, that is, there are actions of which it may truly be said that they *should*, and others that they *should not*, be performed.

b) All practical truths have the form "**A** should be willed." For it is not the actual *performance*, but rather merely the *will* that is the immediate object of every practical judgment (§ 15, Nr. 11).

c) When there are two truths, one practical, of the form "**A** should be willed", and one theoretical, of the form, "Whoever wills **A** must also will **B**" (namely, because **B** is a means for bringing about **A**, or at least is believed to be), the following new practical truth is a consequence of these two: "**B** should be willed." And this new truth is *objectively* grounded in the previous two; accordingly, it is a mere *derivative truth*.

d) If the truth "**S** should be willed" is objectively grounded in the truth "**R** should be willed", and this in turn in the truth "**P** should be willed", and so on, then there must be a truth in this series, say "**A** should be willed", that has no further condition. For it is certain that in the realm of truth there can be no series of consequences without a first ground. There are only conditioned truths because there are unconditioned truths. Now a truth such as "**A** should be willed", which cannot be derived from any other in the way described, I shall accordingly call an *original* or *unconditioned practical* truth.

e) Thus there exists at least one original practical truth. And should it turn out that there is *only* one, this must be the *highest moral law*, since all the others may be objectively derived from it.

f) Supposing that there are several such original practical truths, e.g. "**A** should be willed", "**A**′ should be willed", etc., one could combine all these into one: "**A** and **A**′ and . . . should be willed." Then from this truth all the remaining practical truths could be derived, and it would be the highest moral law. In either case, therefore, there is a highest moral law.

§. 88.

Derivation of this highest moral law

1. Whatever someone should *will* must be *possible* for him, or at least he must *believe* it to be possible. If now we run through all the varieties

of action that are *possible* not only for men but even for the most perfect being, we cannot fail to come across *one* or *more* that reason *unconditionally* commands. Once we have uncovered this, we will by the same token have found the highest moral law. Let us therefore consider each kind of action one after the other, and ask whether sound human reason commands it unconditionally.

2. From the discussion in § 75 one may gather that all actions that a rational being can undertake may be classed under the following headings:

a) *Creation*, through which a substance is brought into existence

b) *Influence on the condition of lifeless beings*

c) *Influence on the condition of a living being*; and this either

α) on its *faculty of sensation*, in that one gives rise to pleasant or unpleasant sensations in the being; or

β) on its *faculty of thought*, in that one causes it to have this or that idea, concept or cognition; or

γ) on its *faculty of will*, in that one causes it to form this or that resolution; or

δ) on its *faculty of desire*, in that one either helps or hinders the development of some desire.

Any form of activity not mentioned here may be traced back to one or several of the ones listed here. Thus, for example, the influence we have on the externally directed action of another may be brought under one of the previously named kinds of action, depending upon whether we induce him to bring about a change in a lifeless substance, or in the faculty of sensation, cognition, desire, or will in a living substance, etc.

3. In order to discover *one* or *several* of these kinds of action that are unconditionally commanded by reason, and in whose conjunction the highest moral law consists, I shall begin with the investigation of those that obviously do *not* belong in this class:

a) *Creation is never unconditionally commanded by reason.* The creation of *lifeless* things clearly can only be commanded by reason for the sake of living things; and the creation of *living* things that feel nothing but *pain*, and at the same time are not *beneficial* to anyone, is certainly forbidden by reason. From this it clearly follows that the command *to create* is a conditional one, that it depends on *other* commands, and that even in the cases where reason (namely, God's) demands it, it is commanded for *some other* reason. The command to create is thus neither the highest moral principle, nor any part of it.

b) *Neither does an original law command changes in the lifeless parts of the universe.* All the forms and structures one may give to lifeless matter are in and for themselves, i.e. apart from any influence they may have on living creatures, entirely indifferent to practical reason. When it demands of us to make such and such changes in the lifeless part of the world, it does so only because something else, a certain change in the condition of *living* things, may be accomplished by this means. Thus all such commands are merely *derivative*. If some commands of this kind should seem unconditional, it would be, perhaps, only the following ones: *prefer beautiful to ugly forms*, and *never destroy an organic body unnecessarily.* But even these commands have a ground. We should prefer beautiful forms to ugly ones because the contemplation of the beautiful affords us and our fellow men pleasure, and because the orderliness to which such things habituate us has a beneficial influence on our virtue. We should not destroy organic bodies unnecessarily either because they are living and capable of enjoying happiness, or else because they can be put to better use by the living part of the world than inorganic bodies; and also, in part, because they are more beautiful to contemplate than inorganic bodies. Whoever is unwilling to admit that the grounds I have cited are the genuine ones must at least recognise that these commands cannot be unconditional because they have *exceptions*, and must often be relaxed. For exceptions can only be governed by a rule when they follow from something higher, and thus do not follow from the original rule with complete strictness.

c) *Neither are actions on the cognitive faculty ever unconditionally commanded.* If any action on the cognitive faculty either of oneself or of others might seem to be unconditionally commanded, it would be this one: *promote the recognition of truth by yourself and others.* But it is clear that this prescription is not unconditional simply because reason demands that we distinguish truths that are more useful from those that are less useful, and that we show a preference for the former over the latter. Furthermore, there are truths that reason forbids us to seek and to spread, e.g. other people's secrets, when the exposure and spreading of these would be detrimental to their honour, or would only cause offence to ourselves and others, etc. It is sufficiently clear from this that the command to promote our knowledge of truth and that of others stands under some other, higher command, and thus is derivative.

d) *Neither are actions on the faculty of desire ever unconditionally commanded.* Sound human reason recognises with the greatest distinctness that while we are sometimes duty bound to engender certain desires or wishes in others, this duty always derives from some higher ground, e.g. in order to increase the pleasure that the attainment of some good would afford, if one had felt a desire for it; or in order to influence the will and behaviour of a person by acting on his faculty of desire.

e) *Neither do actions on the faculty of will belong in the content of the highest moral law.* Any action on the faculty of will of a being must consist in one of the following two things: either one attempts to bring it about that this being wills what he should will, or else one seeks to prevent this. The latter is without a doubt forbidden by reason. The former, however, is commanded by reason, which wants us *to bring it about, as much as this lies in our power, that every being will what should be willed* or, what amounts to the same thing, that it become virtuous. Only one should not believe that this command is an *essential component* of the content of the highest moral law. For the proposition: *one must endeavour to bring it about that others will what should be willed* is an *identical proposition*, i.e. a proposition whose predicate is the same as its subject. The expression "one should endeavour" just means " one should will" or " it should be willed". Thus the proposition "One should endeavour to bring it about that others will what should be willed" is at bottom no different from the proposition "It should be willed that what should be willed be willed." Who can fail to see that this proposition is *identical*? But from an identical proposition no truth can be objectively derived. Consequently, the highest moral law cannot be an identical proposition, nor can it contain any identical proposition as a part.

f) *The promotion of happiness is an original command of reason.* If reason does not unconditionally command any of the actions considered so far then nothing remains except that there is some unconditionally commanded action upon the faculty of sensation of beings. For if no such duty existed, there would be no unconditional, and hence no conditioned duties either. Now clearly there are only two states in which the faculty of sensation of a being can be put, one *pleasant* and the other *unpleasant*. To promote one or the other of these must therefore be an unconditional duty. No one will want to say that reason demands that we cause unpleasant feelings or promote pain. Rather, everyone is certain that it demands the production of pleasant sensations or happiness. Admittedly, the worry arises here that the rule telling us to promote pleasant sensations suffers at least from apparent exceptions. Thus for example, there is no doubt that when a free being has done something evil, we are permitted not merely to cause him to have pleasant sensations, but also to visit unpleasant sensations upon him as a punishment. But since there is only this one original duty, it follows that these exceptions must be only apparent. And we may assume that further reflection will show precisely how one must proceed in order to follow this rule. Thus it is clear in the example I adduced that one punishes evil only so that by reducing evil one may increase the happiness of the whole.

4. The promotion of happiness is thus the single genuine original command of reason, and consequently the sole content of the highest moral law. If now one asks *which beings' happiness should be promoted*, it is entirely clear to sound human reason that we certainly have a duty to promote the happiness of every sensate being *at least* when this can occur without doing the least harm to the happiness of *other* beings, including the one *performing* the action. If it should be asked, however, *to what degree we should promote the happiness of such a being*, the answer is obvious: *in the highest degree that is possible for us.* If, further, it is asked what is to happen when there is a choice between two or more actions, each of which renders some being happy, but in differing degrees, then everyone will reply (as long as it merely concerns animals that do not differ in respect of virtue) that one must choose the action that maximizes the sum of happiness produced, no matter in which individuals. If, finally, it is asked whether one should privilege the promotion of one's *own* happiness over that of *others*, when the gain in happiness is greater for others than for us, then perhaps *self-love* will want to answer *yes*, but *reason* will say no. For if we wished to grant ourselves the permission to favour our own advantage over the greater advantage of others, the new question would arise whether we are in all cases justified

in sacrificing the advantages of others for the sake of our own, no matter how much the former may surpass the latter, or (in case this should not generally occur), at what point our own should begin to prevail. The claim that our own advantage may prevail in all cases over that of others is one from which every good man shrinks in horror. Concerning the second, there is no known measure that would allow us to determine the degree of preponderance. Thus we cannot avoid demanding even of ourselves that we always sacrifice our own advantage to that of others whenever it is smaller. And so the highest moral law may be expressed roughly as follows: *Among all possible actions, always choose the one that, all things considered, most promotes the well-being of the whole, no matter in which of its parts.*

5. Without essentially increasing the content of this proposition, we can interpolate the concept of virtue, and say: *Among all possible actions, always choose the one that most promotes the virtue and happiness of the whole.* It is clear from what was said in (3e) that nothing essential is changed through this addition, for "promote virtue" is an identical proposition. But even though this addition does not improve scientific precision, it makes the statement more serviceable in the social context. For through the express reminder that one must always act so as to further not only happiness by also virtue, a dangerous misunderstanding is prevented, namely the thought that an action that does harm to human virtue could really promote genuine happiness, and thus be permissible. For this reason, I will henceforth always use the highest moral law with this addition.

Note. As obvious as the highest moral law set out here seems to me, I must nevertheless admit that so far only a small number of scholars have expressly accepted it, and indeed it has been contested by several. Accordingly, I may not present as a proven thesis of the natural religion of the human race the truth that the ultimate ground of all duties and obligations, not only of men but of all other beings as well, consists in nothing but the promotion of the virtue and happiness of the whole. Those who defend this principle have been called, not without pejorative overtones, *cosmopolitans*, or *citizens of the world*, while it would be more suitable to call this principle the *law of the general well-being*. One of its principal adherents was *Jean Jacques Rousseau*, who actually stated it as follows: *Promote your own well being with as little damage to that of your fellow men as is possible.*[2] Also: Struve, Bernhard Basedow (who went over it most rigorously in his *Practical Philosophy for all Estates.*), Leß, Meiners, Trapp, Herder, Wieland, E. Plattner (who deduced it in his *Philosophical Aphorisms* with the greatest acuity), and several others.

§. 89.

Objections against this highest moral law

I hold it to be my duty to indicate the weightiest *objections* that have been raised against this highest moral law, accompanied by some remarks in response.

1st Objection. There are several duties to whose genuineness both *sound human reason* and our *innermost feelings* attest, that nevertheless cannot be derived from the proposition: *promote the general well-being.* For example, when I can help only one of two people who ask me to do something for them that is of equal value, I have the duty to privilege the one who has previously done me a favour.

Response. Everything that sound human reason, and our innermost feelings (our conscience) declare to be our duty, I also believe to be our duty (§14.7). Nevertheless, I think that, more carefully considered, it can also be derived from our principle. Only one must pay attention not only to the immediate, but also to the more remote consequences of an action. The duty adduced in the objection is easily derived from our principle, for only the immediate consequences of the two actions are equal, and only on this basis would our principle fail to decide between them. But if we consider the more remote consequences, we soon see that the common weal gains far more when we reply in kind to a service we have received. For such behaviour promotes the virtue of charity, in that we show that whoever has done good for others shall be rewarded when the opportunity arises. Etc.

2nd Objection. According to this principle there can be no *general moral rules*, no duties that do not permit exceptions; or can anyone point to a type of action that *always*, without a single exception, promotes the

[2]*Sur l'origine et les fondements de l'inégalité parmi les hommes.*

common weal? Yet reason recognises a variety of moral laws that are valid without exception, e.g. the duty of veracity under oath, the rules of chastity, and the like.

Response. I counter that many of the rules that the teachers of morals set out as *universally valid* admit of reasonable exceptions in certain cases. Human reason in general agrees with me, and sees no obstacle in declaring such exceptions to be permissible when the well-being of the whole is thereby promoted. It is for precisely this reason that *every rule is said to have its exceptions*. Yet there are, I believe, *several moral rules that admit no exceptions whatsoever*, and the ones mentioned in the objection are of this sort. But this *freedom from exceptions* may itself be shown from our principle. In particular, if a rule is such that it must be followed in most cases in order to retain its force, where any exception granted inevitably leads to the granting of further exemptions, so that the rule becomes all but useless, then one must on this account consider and follow it as a rule *without exceptions*. The rule of veracity under oath is of this sort. This rule is entirely necessary if people are to be able to trust the statements of anyone who has been recognised as a *morally good* person. This usefulness of the rule would almost completely disappear as soon as one permitted exceptions in certain cases; for then no one would know whether someone who testifies to something was in one of the situations where lying was permissible, or at least believed himself to be in such a situation. And many would convince themselves that they were in such a situation without really being so. Thus it is necessary that humanity should possess a means that in the most important cases provides the highest conviction that a certain statement is the pure truth. This means is the *oath*—but only so long as the duty to be truthful under oath is regarded as a rule with absolutely no exceptions. Doubtless, then, that it must actually be considered to be thus! It is equally obvious that the *rule of chastity* applies without exception; for can the small advantage that the transgression of this rule might bring in individual cases, a fleeting moment of pleasure, ever outweigh, or even be measured against, the unspeakably great and diverse disadvantages that would flow from allowing exceptions in individual cases, which would naturally be extended to many others? Etc.

3rd Objection. When it is a question of *duty*, sound human reason does not ask: is it *useful*?, but strongly believes these two questions to be distinct. Already among the ancients the Stoics marked a distinction between the *honesto* and the *utili*. And the jurists say: *Fiat justitia, et pereat mundus!*

Response. There is indeed a difference between the *useful* and the *morally good*, when by the former one understands what is useful for the *agent* alone, or even useful for the whole of humanity, but only in its *immediate*, not in its *further consequences*. It is only this that common human understanding means by *useful*, when it opposes the useful to the *morally good*. This is also what the Stoics meant, if, indeed, they understood what they were saying. The jurists' proposition, however (*Fiat justitia, et pereat mundus!*) is a bit of an exaggeration, if by *mundus* one means the entire universe. *True* justice never demands, and *can never* demand, that the whole world be destroyed.

4th Objection. According to this principle the moral worth of our actions would depend on *mere chance*. If someone stabs his neighbour with a knife, intending to murder him, but by chance lances a boil and thus cures him, he will have done something good.

Response. By no means. For the *moral goodness* of an action (i.e. its claim to be worthy of praise) always depends only on whether the action was undertaken in the *belief* that it was in accord with this law, and was undertaken *for this reason alone*, as well as on the greater or smaller advantages that the agent sacrificed for the sake of his duty. Every right thinking human being recognises this, and it follows quite naturally from our principle. For precisely in order to promote the general well-being, one must promote *virtue*, i.e. the frame of mind that aims at doing what the general good requires, as much as possible. Thus every action that is undertaken with this intention deserves praise, since it promotes the common weal, and deserves more praise the more will power it requires, etc.

5th Objection. We humans are rarely if ever in a position to judge what is compatible with the well-being of the whole. We survey only the smallest part of the world, know only the immediate, and not the more remote, consequences of our actions. Thus the principle of promoting the general well-being is unworkable for us humans.

Response. It is admittedly true that we are unable to foresee all the remote consequences of any single action we perform. But this is not necessary in order to proceed according to the principle of promoting general well-being. This principle only demands of us that we always opt for the action that seems most conducive to the common weal, according to the consequences *we are able to foresee.* Incidentally, we have every reason to believe that the consequences of our actions we are able to predict with more or less probability are generally the most *important* ones, and those that we are in no way able to recognise are for the most part unimportant. If this is so, we can in any event claim with sufficient assurance that certain actions are compatible with the common weal, and others detrimental. Thus, for example, no reasonable person would dispute that lying, stealing, murder, and the like are forms of behaviour that harm the whole, and that the forms of behaviour opposed to these are conducive to the general best, etc.

6th Objection. Even if this principle is true, it is at least *dangerous*, for it can be abused to justify the most evil actions, provided only that their bad consequences are not obvious at first glance.

Response. I do not deny that the reckless dissemination of this principle could become dangerous. One must in particular take care to warn anyone to whom one communicates this principle that he should never reject a duty that his inner *feeling* (or, as one says, his conscience) announces to him just because he cannot see the underlying reason for this duty distinctly enough—i.e. how it is that following this feeling might promote the well-being of the whole. Let him think things over a little longer, and most of the time he will find the reason. But whether he finds it or not, never let him believe that this inner feeling is mistaken. For it is generally known that we recognise (sense) a good many truths with complete certainty without being in a position to be distinctly conscious of the reasons that support them.

§. 90.

Brief assessment of the most common differing opinions on the highest moral law

In order to become all the more convinced that the principle set out here is the true one, I will present the most common *differing* opinions on the highest moral law, adding a couple of words by way of assessment of these views.

1. First I must remind you that there are *philosophers* who declare all of our concepts of *good* and *evil* to be mere prejudices. Among them is, for example, *Michel de Montaigne*, when he claims that *education* is the only source of our concepts of good and bad.

Had he only said that education has a considerable influence on the specific ways and means people use to develop and form the concepts of good and evil, we could certainly agree. We must remember, however, that this influence of education has done less to change our *moral* concepts than any other kind, as becomes clear from the *uniformity* of these across the entire globe, despite all differences in education. If, however, one wants to claim not only that *many* of our concepts concerning what is good or evil in certain cases are *prejudices* planted in us through education, but indeed the *concepts* of good and evil themselves (i.e. the belief that there is such a thing as *obligation*) are such, then all of ethics would be overturned in one stroke. The error of this view has already been shown (§ 87, Nr. 2 a).

2. According to *Mandeville*, virtue is nothing other than the *effect of the desire for praise*. From desire for public admiration we strive to promote the general well-being.

Even if it were indeed true that people for the most part, or even always, perform good deeds from the desire for praise, it would not follow in the slightest that the concept of the good is identical with that of *praiseworthiness*. Consequently, it would by no means be proven that the highest moral law could not take approximately the form I have stated.

3. *Thomas Aquinas* believes that the totality of our duties can be summed up in the formula: *Do what is good.* A few years ago another scholar set out the same formula.

The proposition is quite true, but merely identical: for by good (only the morally good can be intended here) one understands nothing other than what should be willed. *Do what is good,* therefore, just says: *What should be willed should be willed.*

4. *Follow reason*, said *Richard Price*, always do what reason immediately recognises as right and true.

Also identical. By *reason* one clearly understands here nothing other than the ability to recognise truths, and by the reason that one should always *follow*, the ability to recognise *practical* truths. *Follow reason* therefore just says: Do what you should do. Incidentally, the principle has the dangerous feature that it can so easily be misinterpreted to mean that only the duties that (as one says) can be recognised through mere reason, i.e. without the intervention of external testimony, e.g. from God himself, are binding for humankind.

5. Several *English philosophers*, e.g. *David Hume, Jacob Oswald, Henry Home, Hutcheson*, and others claim that the duties of men cannot be derived from *concepts*, but that instead there is a special sense for them, called the *moral sense.* Accordingly, they present the highest principle of ethics as follows: *follow your moral sense.* Among us Germans it was especially *Friedrich Heinrich Jacobi* who sought to ground in feeling all our practical as well as theoretical knowledge of non-empirical things.

This proposition is, like the foregoing, *identical*. For by *moral sense* one understands here, just as *reason* was understood in the previous case, an ability to recognise practical truths, only with the difference (which does not matter here) that one imagines these truths to be *immediately* evident rather than being inferred from others. This last opinion is, in my opinion, incorrect. For I believe instead that only the highest moral law must, as a principle, be recognised immediately, and that it is not impossible, through extended reflection and with the help of purely theoretical minor premises, objectively to derive all other practical truths from it. I do not, however, deny the benefit of this principle's claim that we recognise every one of our duties immediately, since it protects us from that dangerous *moral scepticism* which rejects as prejudice every duty whose basis one cannot clearly set out.

6. Some say that the good is *what all men concur in declaring good.*

It is indeed true that actions declared good or evil by the common judgment of mankind must in fact be so. It is also true that noticing such a general agreement on a judgment lends uncommon confidence to our belief that it is correct, and that as a consequence it is advisable to think about this agreement whenever our passions bring us to doubt a universally acknowledged duty. Only this means cannot always be put to use, since there are also cases where the judgment of mankind is not so unanimous. But even were this not the case, one could never present the proposition "The good is what all men concur in declaring good" as the highest moral law, for not a single duty can be *objectively* derived from it, i.e. as a consequence from its ground. For certainly something is not good *because* all people *recognise* it to be good; rather the converse is true: all people *recognise* it as good because it *is good*.

7. Others say that something is *good if the laws of the country say it is.*

The objection raised against the last proposition may also be applied to this one, only one must add that it is by no means as certain that everything declared to be good or evil by the laws of a country really is so. Should, however, one wish to understand the expression "what the laws of a country declare to be good" as meaning "what they do not threaten with punishment", i.e. interpret it as meaning legal (in the juridical sense of the word), then the proposition would be utterly false, since there are innumerable *morally evil* acts that are *tolerated* even in the best states, i.e. are and must be declared legal.

8. *Act in accordance with your circumstances*, teaches Frint, among others.

It all comes down to the question of what one means by an act that *accords* with the totality of one's circumstances. If by this one means nothing other than an action that is good under prevailing circumstances, or, what amounts to the same, is approved by reason and declared to be one's duty, then the proposition: act in accordance with the totality of your circumstances is quite correct, but obviously *identical*, and thus cannot serve as the highest moral law in the sense I assumed. It is useful, indeed, in that it reminds us of the truth that we are not in a position to judge whether someone's action is good or evil when we do not know everything concerning the *circumstances* in which he finds himself. But it is equally true that this proposition can be easily misunderstood and shamefully abused, if it is interpreted to mean that anything is permissible that, as one says, circumstances *demand*, that is, whatever is difficult to avoid doing in these circumstances is permitted. What sins could thereby be excused! And how often one hears really evil men use such an excuse!

9. *Follow nature* was the principle of the Stoics.

This principle does not seem essentially different from the one we just considered, in that it may well mean nothing other than: one should do what appears to be best after considering all the arrangements of nature. Incidentally, this proposition has the merit of reminding us of the important truth that one must diligently observe the arrangements that nature has hit upon—a reminder that is all the more necessary the more often, alas!, we forget about nature and its inalterable laws.

10. *Aristotle* set out the following proposition as the highest moral law: *Always observe the mean.*

Here the question is: how is one supposed to understand this *mean*? If by this we understand the *correct* measure, i.e. what reason approves of in each case, then the proposition is identical. If one the other hand, one interprets it as the *mathematical average*, i.e. an action equally distant from two extremes, then it remains to be determined what these two *extremes* are. If in order to say something definite, one says that the *smallest* and *greatest* possible activities of every kind are to be called the extremes, then it is certainly quite false to say that man should always maintain the mean. Or should one even when one has a chance of *benefitting* someone choose the mean between the least and the most *beneficial thing* one can do? Incidentally this proposition is quite useful for reminding us that with almost all kinds of things it is not merely a matter of their constitution, or the end sought, etc., but also of how hard we strive, and that we can do too little as well as too much. We can, however, judge the *correct measure* only by considering the relation between our activity and the common weal.

11. Various theologians teach that *good is what God wills*, and the highest moral law is accordingly: *Follow God's will.* This is the view of *Melanchthon, Crusius*, and others.

If this is taken to mean that God's will is the *ultimate ground* of why something is good or evil, then I believe it to be mistaken. For although the *individual* duties of men, e.g. the duty that I should give this poor person alms, certainly rests on circumstances that the will of God has introduced into the world, yet there is at least one practical truth, namely, the highest moral law, that is not conditioned by God's will, but rather, like all purely *conceptual truths*, holds completely independently of this will. Otherwise, how could one say that God is holy, i.e. that his will always accords with what he recognises as good, if being good depended on his *will alone*? If, by contrast, one takes the proposition: "Good is what God wills" to mean that everything that God wills, i.e. *commands* (thus in a figurative sense of the word "will") *is morally good*, then the proposition is certainly true. It is also at bottom a practical proposition, in that it says as much as: *Do what you know to be God's will*, i.e. *God's command*. All the same, it is not the highest moral law, for not *all* practical truths can be derived from it, namely, not those that are determined by God's behaviour, and also because the practical truths that can be derived from it cannot be derived from it objectively, i.e. do not follow from it as consequences from their ground. For it is not because God wills, i.e. commands, something that we should will it, but rather conversely, God wills or commands it because we *should* will it. Incidentally, this proposition is very useful for us, as shall be shown in the proper place (in the section on Catholic morality).

12. Just as some theologians have raised God's *will* to the highest moral law, others have raised the *glory* of God to the highest moral law.

There is no doubt that we have a duty to promote God's glory. I also admit that many, indeed *all* human duties are partly grounded in the duty to promote God's glory, or at least can be derived from it, since every morally good action promotes God's glory. Yet one cannot consider this duty as the highest moral law, for it only *partially* and thus not *completely* grounds most human duties; also because this duty itself has a further *ground*, namely, the usefulness that the promotion of God's glory has for his creatures; moreover, because in most cases our actions are not duties because they promote God's glory, but rather promote God's glory because they accord with duty; and finally, because not all practical truths can be derived from this rule, namely, not those that determine God's own deeds.

13. Still other theologians set out the *imitation of God*, or the proposition: *strive to be like God,* as the highest moral law.

If one assumes that the similarity to God that people are supposed to strive to attain is holiness, divine activities that people can and should imitate, then the proposition is certainly true, but at the same time *identical*. For then it says nothing other than: *If reflection on divine perfection tells you that you should do something, then you should do it.*

14. *Plato, Wolff, Baumgarten, Daries, Eberhard, F. V. Reinhard* and many others introduced the *principle of perfection*, i.e. the proposition: *strive towards perfection.* Most of them understood by this only the perfection of the acting subject, so that the principle can equally well be stated thus: *perfect yourself* (*perfice te ipsum*, Wolff). Several, however, e.g. Daries, meant the *general perfection*, and thus demanded not only that *one's own* perfection, but also that of *others*, be promoted.

We must ask what was understood by *perfection.* Plato did not express himself very clearly on this, in that he appealed to a simile, and said that the perfection towards which men should strive is like that found in a well-constituted state. *Wolff* gave the more precise definition: perfection is the agreement between the constituents of a thing and a goal. Hence the formula "strive towards perfection" means: *All of your actions should be directed towards one and the same ultimate end.* Now this is certainly true. Because if the magnitude of the result whose production is commanded by the highest moral law knows no limits other than those imposed by possibility, i.e. if we should promote the happiness of the whole as much as possible, then in order to do justice to this proposition, all our energies, and all our actions must be referred (directly or indirectly) to this end—and the principle of perfection, thus interpreted, reminds us of this important truth. But however true this principle may be under such an interpretation, it cannot be regarded as the highest principle of the entirety of ethics, since in order to derive any duties from it, one must first have determined this *ultimate end* towards which all our striving must be directed. But the proposition that determines this end will also be a practical proposition, of the form: "The ultimate end of all striving should be this and that." Once one has found it (and I believe actually to have shown that this ultimate end of all our striving consists in the promotion of the common weal), it is obvious that all human duties may already be derived from it alone, and the proposition "all of your actions should be directed towards a single goal" is superfluous.

If one defines *perfection* more precisely by saying it is the agreement of all the attributes of an object with the end that it *should* have, then the proposition "strive towards perfection" would be *identical*. Several recent scholars appear to understand the concept of perfection roughly in the way I defined *absolute perfection* above with reference to *God* (§ 74), i.e. they appear to think of the perfection of a being as the greatest possible development and efficacy of all its powers. Then the principle "Strive towards perfection" would really mean "Everything that is possible (every possible being and every possible condition of these beings) should be made actual, or, better, should be willed. Against this many will raise the objection that what is morally *evil* is also possible. But this objection can be easily countered by pointing out that everything that is morally evil (e.g. causing someone unnecessary *pain*) is indeed something *actual*, yet an actuality that prevents many *other* actualities from coming to be. This response is quite plausible. And if we assume (as remarked already in § 77) that the awareness of every power affords us a pleasant sensation, then the principle "strive to make actual everything that is possible" is in essential agreement with the one set out here: "strive to bring about the greatest possible sum of happiness." The only point in dispute would be which principle of the two was the ground of the other, and thus more basic.

Several scholars—e.g. *Eberhard*—defined *perfection* as a being's ability to enjoy happiness. Now if they were to require that one should promote not only one's *own* happiness, but that of *others* as well, then their principle would not differ fundamentally from mine. If, by contrast, they believed that everyone should care only about his own perfection, their principle would be the same as the following.

15. *Prodicus, Aristippus, Epicurus and his followers, Lucretius, Gassendi, Buddeus, Helvetius*, the author of the *System of Nature*, d'Alembert, and many others besides claim that there is no other duty for man than to *make himself happy*. "Make yourself happy" is, in their view, the highest principle of all morality. Several of these scholars, who are tagged with the pejorative epithet "Epicureans" (although it is probable that Epicurus himself was not of this opinion), placed the happiness towards which one should strive in mere *sensual pleasure*. Others, by contrast (who were accordingly called "Eudemonists") understood by happiness not merely sensual but also mental pleasures, in brief, everything that makes people happy. Before the appearance of the critical philosophy, most philosophers in Germany, especially among the Protestants, ad-

hered to this Eudemonism.

For the following reasons, however, I believe I can show that this principle is false and deserves to be rejected on either interpretation of the word happiness:

a) If the goal of all our striving were solely our *own happiness*, then someone who found himself in a position to save millions of lives without the slightest personal sacrifice would have no duty whatsoever to save them, unless he could find some advantage *for himself* in this. Whose feelings do not rebel against this claim? But if the claim is outrageous, then the principle from which one seeks to derive it must be false.

b) This principle cannot be applied to God, for God cannot increase his own happiness through any of his actions. For what reason, then, would God have created the world, if no rational being *should* ever will anything, or even *can* will anything, that does not promote his own happiness? In what sense could one call Him *holy*?

c) If the *virtuous person* according to Eudemonism seeks nothing but his own happiness, then there is no difference between him and a *scoundrel* as regards ends, but only as regards the means they think will lead them to this goal—thus in their understanding. Virtue is then nothing but cleverness, vice just foolishness. Sound human understanding, however, locates this difference elsewhere.

d) According to the system of eudemonism, the three concepts: *wish*, *obligation*, and *will*, which sound human reason sharply distinguishes, have the same extension. For everything that reason deems conducive to our happiness, and thus declares to be our *duty*, we must also *wish* due to our drive towards happiness, and thus must doubtless also *will*.

e) For just this reason, the system of eudemonism allows for no freedom whatever, at least not in the sense of indeterminism. For such freedom can only obtain when we consider two actions to be possible, one of which we *should* do, and the other we *wish* to do, thus when there is a contradiction between *wish* and *will*.

f) Were there no freedom, however, then everything that is *actual* would also be *necessary*, and everything that is *not actual* would be *impossible*. The *possible*, the *actual*, and the *necessary* would therefore be three coextensive concepts—this sounds strange indeed.

g) Some eudemonists declared the approval of one's *conscience*, the *inner joy* one feels when performing a good deed, to be the *principal*, indeed the *only* element of that happiness towards which men should strive. However, in order to feel this joy we must first have seen that a certain act is good, i.e. accords with the highest moral law. But then the formula would be an identical proposition. Incidentally, it would remind us of the truth that the joyful state of mind that the performance of good deeds affords us is actually one of the most important elements of our happiness.

16. Immanuel Kant expressed the highest moral law as follows: *Act according to a maxim of your will that you can will to be a universal law (thus also a law of nature)*, or: always do what you can rationally will that everyone else would do if put in your place, indeed be compelled to do by a law of nature. In the second statement there is, however, an ambiguity in the words: *rationally to will something*. This can mean: a) to will something as reason bids us, or b) simply to will something that is possible, not self-contradictory. If one adopts the first meaning, the Kantian principle has the following sense: *In every situation do what you must admit everyone else should do in this situation.* This principle is certainly true, but does not constitute the highest moral law, but rather is a consequence of it. Indeed it is a consequence that follows from the highest moral law no matter what one may think that law is, so long as one assumes it to be an *a priori* judgment, a purely *conceptual truth*. For such a law, being composed solely of *concepts*, must be *universally valid*, i.e. must demand the same thing from all individuals that can be subsumed under the same concept, and thus demands the same thing from all acting beings that find themselves in the same circumstances. How little this proposition can serve as the highest moral law becomes clear from the fact that from it we cannot judge how someone should act without the help of *another* practical truth of the form: *In such and such a situation, such and such should happen.*

If, on the contrary, one takes the second meaning of the expression "rationally to will something", then the Kantian principle means: *In every situation you should do something that could be required of all beings in the same situation without giving rise to a contradiction.* Kant seems himself to have adopted this second meaning, as one can see from several of his examples. Thus he demonstrates the duty to return a borrowed good by remarking that the opposed maxim, were it made into a universal law, would negate itself, as there would be no more loans since no one would lend something to another were the latter not duty bound to return it. In my view, there is no doubt that a proposition that contradicts itself is false, and thus its contradictory opposite must be true. But I do not believe that any practical truth can be demonstrated in this way. For it seems to me that no practical truth is so constituted that its contradictory opposite is a self-contradictory proposition. The contradiction that Kant believed he observed in the example I mentioned as well as in several others, is only apparent. In order to show this first of all for the example Kant himself cited, I remark that it is not completely true to say that there would be no more loans if there were no duty to return the borrowed items. For as long as it was not a duty not to return them, many could still hope to have the goods they loaned to others returned. But even supposing there would be no more loans, the rule: "you may keep goods that were entrusted to you" does not yet contradict itself. For it only says that we may keep goods that *have been loaned to us*, not that we may keep goods that *have not been loaned to us.*

The Kantian principle also allows many completely false rules to be defended, e.g. the maxim: *Do whatever you can to make those around you unhappy.* For without contradicting myself I can prescribe this rule to all beings that find themselves in my situation. For if everyone applied all conceivable means to create unhappiness around them, the world would by no means perish, rather creatures that can be tormented and tortured would persist for a long time. And even supposing that there were not a single creature to whom this law could be applied, it would still not *contradict* itself, for it only says that one should torment others for as long as it is *possible*.

As unsuitable as the Kantian principle is in my opinion for the highest moral law, it cannot be denied that it reminds us of a very important truth, namely, that one can often plainly see the *damaging consequences* of an action, and why it is *forbidden*, by imagining it to be generally performed.

17. Kant also thought the highest moral law could be expressed as follows: *Never treat a rational being as a means, rather consider each one to be an end in itself.*

This formula seems to have the following meaning: For every action you undertake that will bring about a certain change in the condition of a rational being, you should consider the character of this change, and this must be one of the grounds determining whether you decide to perform the action or refrain from performing it. This is indeed very true, only it is certainly not the highest moral law. This is already apparent from the fact that not all human duties can be derived from it. For there are certain actions that have no observable influence on the condition of rational beings, even though they do influence the condition of other animals, and sound human understanding commands us to observe this influence, so that, for example, when confronted with a choice between two actions, which have an equally beneficial influence on rational beings, but one of which causes pain to an animal while the other does not, we should prefer the latter. Thus it is incorrect to claim that humans may use living but non-rational beings as mere means, and that these should not be recognised as ends in themselves.

18. Fichte teaches: "*The principle of morality is the necessary thought of Intelligence that it must determine its freedom only according to the concept of autonomy, without any exceptions.*" That is, every free being should bring its freedom under a *law* that is supposed to be nothing other than the concept of *absolute autonomy*, i.e. not determined by anything outside of itself. Or (as he says elsewhere): the ultimate end of all actions of a morally good man is that *reason and only reason rule in the world of the senses.* Thus, for example, he demonstrates the duty to maintain our own life and the lives of others by pointing out that we are instruments for the realization of the moral law in the world of sense, and the like.

If I understand this expression correctly, this principle is a purely identical proposition, something which was to be expected given the singular method Fichte uses to deduce it. Reason and reason alone shall rule in the world of sense, really says nothing other than: everything that depends upon the freedom of men should be directed according to the principles reason sets out concerning them, or, they should be directed as they should be directed!

Note. Anyone who hears enumerated, one after the other, the formulas set out here, and many others which were meant to express the highest moral law, will find it difficult to understand how people could have committed so many errors, and how they could have overlooked the *true* law, which is so near to hand and which presents itself so naturally. The causes of this phenomenon lie, as I believe:

a) principally in the circumstance that only a very few scholars were distinctly aware of *what* they should understand by the highest moral law. Most of them appear not to have correctly grasped that it must set out the ultimate *objective ground* of all obligations and duties, or, more generally, of all practical truths. They seem to have confused the highest moral law with a proposition that only sets out a *subjective ground of knowledge* for our duties, a means for recalling them. This is the only reason that helps us to understand how formulations such as "Do what is good", "Follow reason", "Act in accordance with your circumstances", "Imitate God" and the like could have been presented as the highest moral law.

b) That the *true* principle (that is, the principle that I hold to be true) was not more widely adopted stems from α) the notion that it is a dangerous idea, β) from the belief that not all duties can be derived from it, and γ) abhorrence of eudemonism, with which it is often confused.

c) From the errors into which contemporary scholars have fallen, among these the desire to distinguish themselves by setting out a hitherto unknown principle, but even more the logical prejudice that every correct, non-contradictory derivation of a truth must start from the principle of identity $A = A$.

d) That the highly pernicious principle of *eudemonism* has nevertheless attracted so many adherents can be explained as follows: α) Man's physical nature makes it very natural for him to wish that he had no other obligations than to make himself happy, and this wish gave rise to the conviction that it really was so. Especially since β) the difficulties involved in going against the drive for happiness often appeared to be wholly insurmountable—and admittedly, if it were impossible to resolve to do anything but what our drive for happiness demands, there could be no duties; or, if one still wanted to assume there were duties, their highest principle could not say anything other than "Do what you wish, or whatever makes you happy." For whatever reason presents to us as a duty must be possible, but on the above assumption it would not be possible to do anything other than follow our own wishes. γ) Others thought that the great vividness of the drive for happiness was a hint from God that we should follow it, even though it is itself no proof of the impossibility of resisting this drive. δ) Furthermore, some thought they had noticed (and it is indeed true) that most of the actions people perform spring from a more or less distinct consideration of their own advantage, and concluded that this was always the case, that is was indeed impossible for things to be otherwise, and that one's own happiness was the only conceivable motive for all actions—yet in fact, such selfish considerations are often only contributing factors, and sometimes play no role at all. ϵ) More than any of the preceding factors, what counted in favor of eudemonism was that most, indeed almost all human duties could be grounded (at least apparently) in the wish to make oneself happy.

§. 91.

Uncertainty of all human virtue

Now, as promised (§86), several of the most important propositions of the *natural theory of the cultivation of virtue* shall be derived.

1. First of all, I must demonstrate the truth that *human virtuousness is always unpredictable*, i.e. I must explain that and why no one can be completely certain in advance that his virtuousness shall persist, no matter how earnestly and vividly he now intends to remain true to all precepts of virtue. It is clear that here I

a) do not speak of offenses of some particular kind, but rather of violations of the moral law *in general*—for we can certainly say of some offenses—e.g. ones that we would never have an opportunity or the power to commit—that we shall never commit them. I also exclude

b) the case of someone who himself has learned through divine revelation that he shall remain virtuous throughout his life.

2. Having thus explained the *meaning* of my claim, I now proceed to its *proof*. It follows immediately from the experience we have all had *ourselves* (when we look back upon the bygone years of our life), and what we may observe in others, that it is by no means unusual for people to hold certain principles in the most earnest and vivid manner, and yet soon afterwards to act in a way directly contrary to these principles. Not only faults that have unfortunately become habits and so to speak second nature to us often (alas!) lead us to violate even the most firmly held principles: this also occurs with new faults we had never before felt

inclined to commit, but often are guilty of when an unexpected temptation comes along. Even people who have followed the path of virtue to an advanced age sometimes in their final days stray onto the path of vice. These all too sad experiences must make every rational person pay heed, and he must worry that what has happened to so many others might well happen to him, or that what he himself has already experienced may well come to pass again in the future. Thus no matter how firm his principles may be, he may never hold himself to be completely assured that he will never be in any way untrue to the precepts of virtue.

§. 92.

What leads us to be untrue to our virtuous principles?

1. According to an observation already made several times, we human beings consider ourselves free only when it is possible for us to violate the moral law, that is, when reason and the drive for happiness enter into conflict. Thus one can say that it is only the desires of our drive for happiness that lead us to be untrue to our good principles and make us depart from virtue. The more frequently this conflict between the wishes of our drive for happiness and the commands of our reason occurs, and the more vivid our wishes are, the greater is the danger that we shall follow them, even though we are in no way forced to do so.
2. But based on his drive for happiness man can only form desires for things that seem to him (at least at the moment) to be suitable means for promoting his own true happiness. If a man believes in the existence of God, or is convinced by some other means of the important truth that virtue alone is the most certain path to true happiness, and that every evil deed sooner or later inevitably makes one unhappy, then the question arises: how can such a man feel tempted in any way to depart form the moral law? To this I answer: only insofar as he does not remember this important truth at certain moments, or else recalls it, but does not find it compelling enough. This in turn is only possible because of the way our mind is constituted, namely, in such as way that it is only capable of being vividly conscious of a single idea, or a group of several related ideas, at a given moment. Should a man represent the pleasure of sin more vividly, the idea of God, and of punishment in another life, fades at the same moment; only in this way is it possible for us to look upon

the evil deed as advantageous to us and therefore *desirable*. According to this explanation, therefore, the freedom of men is grounded in the association of ideas and the limits of his consciousness. According to this claim, one can look upon every sin as a way of being *unmindful of God*, even when this does not go so far as to produce a doubt or indeed a denial of the existence of God.

§. 93.

There are means of promoting virtue.

Whatever can contribute something to the protection, facilitation or perfection of our virtue I shall call a *cultivator of virtue*.

It is easy to show that this concept is not without its objects, that is, that there really are means for promoting or protecting our virtue. In particular, everything that contributes to a more perfect and ready knowledge of our duties, as well as everything that causes the wishes of our drive for happiness to come less often into conflict with the commands of our reason, or that weakens or moderates these wishes when such conflicts do occur, all of these things contribute to the protection, facilitation and perfection of our virtue. But there are doubtless many means that can do the things I just mentioned. Thus, for example, frequent reflection on our duties must make our knowledge of them ever more complete and fluent; frequent reflection on the truth that only virtue can make one truly happy, associating a variety of pleasant ideas with our obligations, and the like, must surely reduce our reluctance to fulfill them. Hence, without doubt, cultivators of virtue do exist. Among others things, it is obvious that *calling to mind certain advantages* to fulfilling our duties will make it more certain that we observe them, and make their fulfillment easier for us. It is thus a *cultivator of virtue*. This particular kind of cultivator I shall call inducements to virtue, and indeed *inducements based on our drive for happiness*, or, briefly, *physical* [*sinnliche*] *inducements*.

§. 94.

It is not only permissible but also a duty to make use of all the means at one's disposal for the cultivation of virtue

1. No reasonable person will doubt that we should do everything we can to perfect our virtue, since this claim is at bottom an identical proposition (§88, No. 5).

2. But we should also make use of everything that serves to protect our virtue. For since we can *never* be *entirely* certain that we shall never be guilty of departing from our virtuous principles (§92), we should do whatever we can to *increase* their reliability.

3. Finally, it is obvious that we should do whatever we can to render the fulfillment of our duties *easier*, because:

a) When the fulfillment of our duties is made easier, it increases our *own* happiness without adversely affecting the happiness of others, so that the sum of well-being is thereby increased.

b) Whatever is *easier* for us is also more *certain* to be done; thus in order to secure our virtue, we have a duty to do whatever we can to make it easier to do so.

4. As obvious as all of this is to sound human understanding, *scholars* have nevertheless raised many strong objections to it. We must acquaint ourselves with the most important of these.

1. *Objection.* Through the use of such means for cultivating our virtue, our virtue is only made more secure because we find it easier to act virtuously. But the easier it is to exercise virtue, the less worth it has. For it is a generally recognized proposition that *the harder the struggle, the worthier the triumph.* The use of cultivators of virtue thus reduces the worth of our virtue.

Response. The proposition, the harder the struggle, the worthier the triumph, is only valid when the struggle was something we ourselves could do nothing to avoid. When, however, someone, neglecting the cultivators of virtue at his disposal, is himself the cause of the severity of the struggle he has to endure, then God will surely not reward him more for this reason, but will instead punish him for needlessly exposing himself to so great a danger. Conversely, one who through assiduous use of cultivators makes fulfilling all his duties ever more easy with the passage of time, and consequently sins less often, shall not be rewarded less by God. Rather, he shall receive a separate reward for having made his virtue as secure as possible.

And how self-contradictory this objection is! They fear that the worth of virtue shall be reduced when it is made easier by such cultivators—but at the same time, when for this reason (that is, by laying claim to a greater reward) they want to make virtue more difficult to attain, they base their act on an egotistical inducement.

2. *Objection.* When we are frequently exposed to the temptation to commit evil acts, our moral fortitude is exercised and strengthened, so that we become better able to defeat unavoidable temptations.

Response. Insofar as exposure to certain temptations (impulses) serves to exercise our moral fortitude it too deserves to be called a *cultivator of virtue.* In fact, however, this is only very rarely the case, and we shall do better to avoid all temptations to evil that are in themselves avoidable. In any case, the avoidance of situations where temptation is likely to be felt is not the only cultivator of virtue, as is assumed in this objection. Rather, there are many other ways of strengthening our virtue, e.g. by increasing our conviction that virtue alone can make us happy, etc.

3. *Objection.* If what you say is true, a virtuous person will never be clearly aware of the strength of his virtue.

Response. He can still be aware that he loves virtue for its own sake—but to demand that he know the exact *measure* of his virtue is in part impossible, in part unnecessary and indeed harmful, since this might well lead to pride and arrogance.

4. *Objection.* At least the use of those *inducements to virtue that are drawn from our desire for happiness* are not permissible, for by this very use our virtue is destroyed, as contemptible selfishness supplants it—the very least one can say is that the purity of the motives—which should be nothing other than pure respect for the law—is tainted with by the admixture of physical advantages.[3]

Response. I assume that those who make use of such inducements do not embrace the principles of virtue merely *for the sake of* these advantages, but rather have already resolved to follow the moral law because

---

3

> *Gerne dien' ich den Freunden, doch thu' ich es, leider! mit Neigung;*
> *Und so wurmt es mich oft, daß ich nicht tugendhaft bin.*
> *Da ist kein anderer Rath, mußt' suchen, sie erst zu verachten,*
> *Und mit Abscheu dann thun, wie es die Pflicht dir gebeut.*
> (Schiller)

(The verses are from the *Xenien* of Schiller and Goethe. Crudely rendered, they read: Readily serve I my friends—but alas! I enjoy it;/ This lack of virtue rankles constantly./ There is nothing for it, you must try to despise them,/ And act with disgust as duty bids.)

they have recognized that it is the *right* thing to do, and use these ideas merely as a means for better ensuring that they will actually follow these principles. If this is the case, then it cannot be said that their virtue is transformed into a *contemptible egoism* by the use of such inducements, nor even that the *purity of their motives* is thereby compromised. For even when someone makes use of all possible means for assuring his virtue, he can never bring it about that the continued exercise of virtue will cost him no effort, nor that his drive for happiness shall never again enter into conflict with his reason. There will always be cases where he acts freely, and intends to do what is good only because it is good. But even in those cases where his drive for happiness concurs with his reason, where he no longer acts freely, his actions still count as *meritorious*. For the action is one that is conducive to the well being of the whole, and it is indeed—if not immediately, at least mediately—a result of his free choice. At the time, namely, when he freely gave the direction to his drive for happiness, which resulted in its agreement with his reason, at that time he laid the ground for the action he now performs. And the reward that he merits for this shaping of his drive for happiness must be set higher than the sum of all the praise he would have deserved for performing the same action, but only after a struggle with his physical nature. For precisely because he has freed himself from this struggle, his performance of good actions is all the more assured, and the well being of the whole gains thereby; and the reward that God allocates to him must be correspondingly greater.

5. *Objection* Even though the use of inducements to virtue drawn from the drive for happiness may bring forth actions that accord with the moral law, this increases the mastery of the drive for happiness over the will, which from then on will result in more actions running contrary to the law.

Response. I do not deny that there can be inducements to virtue to which this objection applies. But for this very reason they should not be numbered among the *cultivators of virtue*, nor should they be applied as such. At the same time there are other inducements to virtue drawn from the drive for happiness to which this objection does not apply, of which one cannot say that they will lead us in the future to ever more violations of the moral law. Among these belongs the thought, for example, that only virtue makes one truly happy.

§. 95.

Several rules that may be applied in determining the relative worth of various cultivators of virtue.

From what has been said it is clear that the worth of different cultivators of virtue varies. Now I say that a cultivator of virtue is more beneficial, all other things being equal:

1. *the more certainly it attains the sought goal.* The more certain the efficacy of a given means, the more our virtue is promoted though its use, for departures from it are correspondingly fewer. Thus, for example, the precept of completely avoiding situations that give rise to temptation (whenever this is possible) is to be preferred to any precept concerning how we should behave when tempted, no matter how solid and definite, since such intentions have a tendency to remain unfulfilled.

2. *the more generally applicable it is.* The more often a cultivator of virtue is applicable, the more benefit its use will create when we make it a habit. Thus for example, the use of various *proverbs* is a better cultivator of virtue than the use of posted reminders confined to *one place*, which can only be used when one is there.

3. *the less prone they are to be abused.* With certain cultivators of virtue, especially with *inducements* it happens that they can occasionally be abused, and instead of urging us towards the good can lead us to commit evil acts. Now if the danger of harm is greater than the expectation of usefulness, such means should be completely rejected. But among cultivators of virtue, one that is less prone to abuse is always to be preferred. Thus for example, the inducement of approval from the wise is a better cultivator of virtue than the inducement of the approval of the crowd, etc.

4. *the more its use is pleasant rather than painful*—for it thereby contributes all the more to the promotion of our happiness. Thus for example, hope is a more valuable cultivator of virtue than fear, when both would be equally efficacious.

5. *the more closely related it is to another, more noble one*, that is, the easier it is to shift from the one to the other. Thus for example the fear of a harm that is remote, perhaps only to be encountered in old age, is a nobler cultivator of virtue than the fear of an imminent punishment, for

the former makes us more receptive to the very efficacious cultivator of virtue that consists in the fear of punishment in another life.

6. *the more it promotes the cultivation of the mind.* For the reasons just enumerated, since it makes us all the better able to make use of the *most excellent cultivators of virtue*, which require a highly cultivated mind.

Note. From the above it follows that the most excellent of all inducements to virtue is that which follows the contemplation of God's will.

Part IV

Political Philosophy

On the Best State

The little book on the best state

or

Thoughts of a friend of mankind

on

the most suitable institutions

for

civil society

Foreword

The author of this essay can in all truth declare that he has always loved his fellow men as brothers, and from his youth has occupied himself with no other question as much as this one: "In what way can the many ills and the suffering that weigh upon our kind here on earth be most effectively remedied?" Whenever some misfortune befell him, or he heard of one that plagued someone else, it was always his habit either to consider quietly by himself, or to discuss with other people who seemed qualified, whether and how people might be either completely spared ills of this sort, or at least be troubled by them less often than at present. As he grew older, it became increasingly clear to him that the perverse arrangements we still find more or less in all civic constitutions are, if not the only, certainly the most powerful obstacle to the improvement of things on earth. From this time on, he dedicated many of the hours he devotes to solitary reflection to the investigation of *how a state must be organized in order to accord with the most perfect advancement of the general well being.* Although he is under no illusion that he possesses a complete solution to this extremely difficult problem, he decided, already somewhat advanced in age, to write down as briefly as possible what presented itself as correct after a thorough examination and unbiased comparison with everything others have so far said on this question.

He decided this not in the expectation, and not even with the wish, that in a country where his thought became known people would immediately tear down its existing constitution and erect a new structure according to his plan. Such an undertaking he must rather declare in advance to be rash, and because of the disastrous consequences which it might entail, indeed criminal. No, he entrusts his thoughts only to his pen, with the sole intention that knowledgeable and unprejudiced men may examine what is new, keep what is true, correct what is in error, and fill in what is missing (assuming that in some state or other it is declared permissible to distribute this work either in print or even only in manuscript). Before one is allowed in a civil society to venture changes as far reaching as most of those proposed here, one must first have considered them from all sides, and all wise and good people of the country must have declared themselves unanimously in favor of them. Nay, even this is not enough; even if the wisest among a people are agreed that a certain institution should not be absent from the most perfect state, even then one can raise a reasonable doubt about whether it should be introduced in a certain country right on the spot—and this either because not all the other institutions that must be introduced simultaneously with it have been thought through; or because at present too strong an opposition is to be feared from those who—rightly or wrongly—think that they personally will lose by it; or, finally, because the gap between what has been in place and what will follow from the new institution is too great for it to be fair and advisable to jump abruptly from one to the other. Before one is allowed to introduce the institutions which belong in the best state into any presently existing state, one must have launched a complete sequence of *intermediate changes*; one must have, I say, devised measures that will only last a short time, and have the purpose of preparing people for what is to come. The transition must be so gradual that not only will no one's rights be violated, but also none will have grounds for complaint that he had to undergo a hardship that he would have been spared in a longer process. But it is only possible to implement these measures if people are in complete agreement concerning which institutions must be present in the most perfect state. In addition, it is easy to see that *different* intermediate institutions will be required for different states, for the character of these institutions depends not only on the common goal, but also on the various situations in which the peoples of the earth currently find themselves. For this reason the author has merely concerned himself with the first problem, that is, with the question of which institutions are appropriate for a state that deserves to be called the most perfect. He has not concerned himself at all with the second question, namely, how such a state might be brought about. It will be sufficient for him if it is admitted at some future time that he has produced a response to the first question, a contribution not to be discarded. This, however, he believes to be in fact the case; and although the number of these pages is small, he nevertheless sets a certain value on them—indeed, it seems to him that this little book is the best, most important legacy he is capable of leaving to mankind, if they will accept it.

For this reason, whoever you may be who sometime lays eyes on these papers, know that their author wishes to demand an account of the use you make of them, before you and he stand before God's seat of judgment. As little as he wants you to agree with his views without examining them, or rashly to attempt putting his recommendations in place using unjustified means, just as strongly does he demand that you impartially examine, and not contest merely out of passion, what perhaps will appear to your innermost self as truth. Even more strongly does he warn you against the offense of suppressing such truths. It is certainly an easy thing to throw these few pages into the flames (especially as long as they remain only in manuscript), and thus to nip in the bud all the good they might have brought about. But consider whether you could so easily answer for it if in doing so you were to blame for people recognising even a single beneficial truth later than they had to.

Introduction

To investigate which institutions would be the most appropriate for a civil society, one must be motivated by the belief that it is not a matter of indifference whether a civil community is organized in this way or that. Now there really are people who not only claim to believe the contrary (for we need not worry any further about such people here), but earnestly believe it, if not always, at least at certain times when they fix their eye on events that seem to confirm it. For in fact, when observation teaches us that so far roughly the same number of unhappy people live in almost all states, however their institutions are constituted (whether the will of only a single person, or the will of all, is law); when history teaches us that the most reasonable peoples have changed their institutions so often, never finding the well-being hoped for, so that after many unsuccessful attempts they not seldom considered it best to revert to one of the previously abandoned measures; when on top of this we consider that everything has a good as well as a bad side, and that to a certain degree it lies within human nature that people, finding themselves oppressed by no one, become their own tormenters; then perhaps all of us feel a bit tempted to believe that in the end it makes no great difference whether we give the state one set of institutions or some other.

Nevertheless, I claim that nothing is more incorrect than this idea. For however true it may be that there are people in every state who are dissatisfied with their lot, and that even in the very best state that might be designed, there will be no lack of such people, it can by no means be demonstrated nor even shown to be probable, that the *number* of these people will be everywhere approximately equal. In Europe, for example, there are incontestably more unhappy people than in the United States of America. But even if this were not so: what would it show except that all constitutions up to now have been defective in roughly equal degrees? It in no way follows that a significantly better constitution than all prevailing ones is impossible, and that the same result would also occur with a wiser organization of civil society, with an organization as has nowhere been found up to now. Nor is it even true, as has been said, that under the present constitutions one finds roughly the same number of unhappy people everywhere. Where a gentle prince shows the love of a father towards his subjects, there will perhaps be some one or other who grumbles because he was dealt with justly; but a hundred thousand consider themselves happy. On the contrary, in a country ruled by a despot one reads the expression of misfortune on every brow, and while the smoldering fire of rebellion may barely be put out in one place, it flares up again in another. Nor should it be forgotten that a person's complaints are *no exact measure* of the degree of his suffering and unhappiness. People can be very unhappy and yet—whether from a sort of lethargy or from fear—bear their suffering with silent pain. On the other hand there are people who, because they are more alert, because they fear nothing, but instead expect that complaining will better their lot, gripe about this or that without even feeling themselves especially unhappy. How rash it would be, therefore, for someone to want to infer immediately from the circumstance that more complaints may happen to be heard in one country than another that there are more or even roughly the same number of unhappy people in the former as in the latter. No complaints ring out from the grave, but are corpses happy?

To be sure, history teaches us that reasonable peoples have often changed their laws and after many attempts have sometimes reverted to an ancient original. But does it really follow from this that the different measures that were tried out—and not only these, but also all the other possible ones that haven't yet been tried—had an equal influence on the general well-being? First, the many attempts that have been made are just so many proofs that the common understanding of mankind has at all times recognized the truth that it must be possible to attain a higher degree of general well-being through an appropriate change in prevailing constitutions. When, however, one has scarcely introduced an institution before moving on to another, this teaches us at most that people haven't yet happened upon the right thing—and should this surprise us, when it is so difficult to think up what is right, and having thought of it, so difficult to introduce it? When, finally, we see that after many changes a people returns to an old institution, this may well show that they were wrong to depart from it, but by no means that all institutions are equal. Anyway, strictly speaking, we never see the old accepted again in unaltered form; rather, it is only *similar*, and occurs not in the same but in changed circumstances. And so we may not claim that it must have been a mistake either to abolish or to reinstate it, for both decisions may have been right when they were made.

Moreover, it cannot be denied that every institution has its good as well as its bad side; only one may not imagine that the good and the bad always balance each other. Rather, in some cases the one outweighs the other. Thus for example, there is much good and some bad when no one is compelled by force to acknowledge a certain faith; but here the *good* decidedly outweighs the bad. So too there is some good along with much bad when offices and titles are hereditary in a state—but how strongly the *bad* outweighs the good in this case!

Finally it is not to be denied, alas, that we humans are foolish enough to become our own tormenters; and since not even the best constitution can make everyone wise and good, and since on top of this so many inevitable ills are grounded in our finite nature, it follows that even in the best constituted state we will still experience plenty of suffering. But it does not follow that the number and magnitude of these sufferings will always remain the same. On the contrary, the longer we reflect on this matter, the more clear it will become to us how many of our sufferings and especially their causes could and should be removed or at least reduced by appropriate institutions. How weak is our body, and to how many diseases is it subject, not because some inalterable law of nature demands it, but rather because we are born to weak parents, are poorly treated in our childhood, sometimes spoiled, then again completely neglected, because neither the food that we eat, nor the activities we pursue, nor our clothing and housing is in accordance with the rules of health. Can it really be doubted that a rational improvement of all these conditions of our health and strength can have beneficial effects? How many thousands of our brothers—O! even at the very moment I write this—go without the means for satisfying their most basic human needs, perish in their need, not because the great earth isn't rich enough in goods to supply all her children with abundance, but only because counterproductive institutions in the state allow these goods to be divided among us in such an unequal way, and because most of the earth's surface remains virtually uncultivated. How many other kinds of suffering, attacks on honour, insults, abuse, we inflict upon each other, and the state lets this happen, or at least doesn't apply all the measures at its disposal to fight these disorders.

Considering all this, can one really still hold the opinion that no conceivable changes to the constitution of civil society could improve the happiness of our race? Even to find this probable, one would really have to assume that some kind of higher being through its invisible activity prevented things from becoming better here on earth; a being which would always take away exactly as much happiness from us as the improvements to our civil institutions might have brought about. As certainly as it is foolish, even blasphemous, to believe in the existence of such a being, just as confidently may we expect to become happier as soon as we have given our civil community a more rational direction. But here perhaps someone will say: if things are really this way, if our race could be fundamentally helped by the introduction of a more appropriate constitution, why is it that God hasn't long since led us to a knowledge of this constitution? How is it that He, who does not deny himself extraordinary means in order to instruct us in the truths that are necessary for our well-being, never called forth a man who would make known to us the most appropriate institutions for civil society? Should we not conclude from the fact that God has never let us know what these institutions are that this knowledge would be of no use to us?

I think it necessary to attempt to put *this* doubt to rest as well. And for this end scarcely more is needed than to recall what everyone at bottom knows, namely, that it will never do to reason that because God has not yet allowed a certain piece of knowledge to appear, that it would also not be useful for us. The most absurd consequences would follow were this inference valid and permissible. Or do we not find even in these days entire peoples in a condition of such raw savagery that we gather more from their similar human form than from their behaviour that they belong to our species? And because these people up to now have had almost no inkling of their moral worth, of the true essence of virtue, of the existence of God, of the immortality of their souls, and of thousands of other highly important truths; because up to now they have remained ignorant of even the most common means for bettering their earthly condition, even perhaps the uses of fire and metal; should anyone on that account earnestly believe that learning about these things would be of no use to them? If things were thus, all reflection and all use of reason would be pointless and futile. But it is not like this; rather the good and wise creator gave us the glorious gift of reason so that we, his servants, could progress more and more in the improvement of our condition on earth by using it. As certainly as he has given us eyes in order that we might see, so too has he given us reason to be used for everything to which its nature suits it, including among other things, to devise the most appropriate institutions for our civil communities. But why has he let it happen that we learn of one truth sooner than another; why has God arranged things, for example, so that we have known the healing powers of one herb for centuries and only now become aware of the beneficial effects of another? We must not demand to understand this, since it depends upon reasons that lie in the context of the whole; only He who surveys the infinite universe knows this. If we have used our reason appropriately, if we have spared no efforts of reflection, and still have not succeeded in learning the truth, then it must be that the knowledge of this truth, as useful as it might appear, is not yet beneficial for us. It is certainly unjustified to claim that the fact that up to the present moment we have not succeeded in finding a truth implies that we will never be able to discover it in the future, and that accordingly it would be more reasonable to give up the search for it—especially when we cannot avow that we have sought the truth, and sought it with all possible diligence. To say that the fact that this truth has remained hidden up to now is proof that God himself wills that we do not recognize it; this is just trying to put the blame for our own laziness on God's decrees—and this is to misuse the belief in God in the most shameful way. If up to the present day we are still not agreed on which institutions would be the most appropriate for a civil constitution, this is only because we haven't yet done everything we could and should have done long ago in order to bring us closer to an answer to such an important question. Or can we really boast that even one of us has occupied himself with this question as often as it deserves? That we have engaged in these investigations with the necessary impartiality? That we have never rejected a plainly appropriate institution because it offended our self-love, pride, or some other passion?

And what should I say about general discussions of this subject? In most countries it is not even permitted to raise the question of the best state as a matter of public investigation, or else one is only permitted to affirm that the constitution that exists there and then is to be praised as the most appropriate. And in such circumstances is it any wonder that we haven't yet found the truth? Should we desire that God make known to us through revelation institutions that we could devise through our own reflection? Or should we, in case he hasn't done this, be permitted to infer that their discovery would be of no use for us? No, none of you will permit yourself to make such an inference.

Dear people who read these papers! If it pains you (and you have a *right* to be pained) that our race is already six thousand years old, and still has not reached any substantial agreement on which institutions they should give to their civil societies, then go forth and correct the errors as best you can, so that at least you will have considered with all possible diligence and without prejudice or passion a subject that merits our consideration more than a thousand others. If your judgment in this matter has not already been led astray by wrong-headed schooling, if you consider the matter with your own sound human reason, then I am certain that at least you will not long remain indecisive concerning the first point that must be addressed here, namely, the *goal* towards which all institutions of a civil constitution must aim if it is to earn the name of the most perfect. I believe, in particular, that you will all agree with me when I claim that such a society must have as its goal the greatest possible promotion of the virtue and happiness of the whole; each law, each decree and institution must only be constituted in the way demanded by the promotion of virtue and happiness. In fact this is such an obvious truth that one could scarcely find it comprehensible how there could be learned people who have not admitted it, if one were not aware that there is nothing so absurd that it has not been claimed by some philosopher or other. If, however, it is certain that the only state that merits the name of the best and most perfect is one whose institutions are so conducive to virtue and happiness that no other arrangement would be better in this respect; then so too is it certainly not the case that exactly the same institutions belong to the concept of the best state in all places and times. For according to the differences in the conditions, one and the same institution can be sometimes more sometimes less conducive, or even completely detrimental to the general well-being. What is very easy to bring about in one place is attended by heavy difficulties in another, indeed, may even be impossible to bring about. As, however, despite all these differences in the circumstances of time and place, there is much in common to all these circumstances, and since human nature is essentially the same everywhere, it follows that alongside these variable institutions there must also be others that are invariable, and must have a place in every single state that makes a claim to perfection, no matter in what part of the world it may be found. Only the latter sort of institutions will be discussed here; I will only attempt to furnish a concept of those laws and arrangements that must be found in any genuinely well constituted community. And even here I do not promise any exhaustive completeness, but rather furnish only fragments which, if they are usable, may be supplemented by others to make up a whole. It should scarcely be necessary to recall that in deciding the question whether or not a certain arrangement belongs to this most appropriate constitution, we must by no means suppose people to be as they *should*, or as the teachers of morals would like them to be, but rather must only take them to be as they really are. For if we were already perfect, then admittedly even the most defective constitution would still be tolerable. But precisely because we are imperfect it is necessary to maintain constitutions in which these imperfections are taken into account and all is arranged so that despite these faults we feel inclined to do precisely what the good of the whole requires. From this it already follows what one should think of the famous saying that the best constitution is the one which is best administered. Whether a constitution is *administered* well or poorly, i.e. whether that which the constitution leaves to the discretion of its citizens, is carried out well or not, does not belong to the essence of the constitution, precisely because it is determined not by the constitution itself but rather by other circumstances, and thus cannot either raise or lower its worth. However, a constitution may certainly be said to be faulty if it depends only upon its *administration*, and thus on chance, whether or not its citizens are happy. A good constitution should not surrender the well-being of its citizens to such a chance, but rather must be so arranged that even when the people who are entrusted with a certain power do not always do what is best but rather pursue only their own interests, their actions are still not harmful to the whole.

CHAPTER 1

On the citizens, the extent and the divisions of the state

I think that the first thing one may ask of me is whom I would like to be recognized as a member of the state. To this I first reply in general that in a well-constituted state one must regard everyone as a member of this state if his membership and its consequences (namely, that one extends to him all the advantages but also holds him to all the duties of a citizen, by the application of force if necessary) produces more good than harm. From this principle it follows that one considers as

1. genuine citizens:

   (a) all who themselves ask to be regarded as citizens, and not only promise to obey the laws of the state, but also give reason to hope that they will keep this promise; likewise

   (b) all their children up to a certain age of majority, at which point they will publicly declare whether or not they wish to remain in the state, in roughly the way prescribed by certain religions; in which case they must solemnly swear to obey its laws.

   In addition to these genuine citizens, one can also allow in a well constituted state

2. many other people as aliens, as long as they:

   (a) Can cite a valid reason why they cannot formally join the state, e.g. because they do not yet have a complete knowledge of its laws, or are only thinking of traveling through its territories, and the like; and as long as

   (b) it does not appear that they will be harmful to the state, e.g. by causing harm to others through their way of life, or attempting to make them disobey the laws, and the like. Should they do any of these things, one is allowed to punish such foreigners for their offenses, and in any case to deport them.

A foreigner must also follow the laws of the state for which no exceptions can be made without causing harm. He will not, however, be bound by the others; but by the same token he will not enjoy the benefits which flow as a reward from these very obligations.

Whoever has once declared that he wishes to be regarded as a citizen of the state, and who as a result of this declaration is accepted as such, cannot withdraw from the state as he sees fit, and by withdrawing evade punishments his offenses have earned him. Once he has served his sentence, however, he can indeed leave the territory of the state, i.e. *emigrate*; and so too can any other citizen under certain conditions, namely, where no danger thus arises for the remaining citizens.

What has just been said assumes that there will still be places and perhaps whole societies which the best state does not include. I hope, however, that there will come a time when the entire human race considers itself only as a single whole, in that every single person will be committed in certain matters to conform to what is known as the will of all the others, and that one will have means (including, if necessary, force) to hold them to this commitment. I would say at that point that the entire human race constituted only *one single state*. It may be thought that an appropriate organization of so large a whole would not establish close enough connections between the parts to justify calling this collection a single state. I will not dispute this, as it seems to be a merely verbal matter. Rather I will be satisfied if one concedes that a certain unification of all the people living on earth, a sort of general alliance between all states, is a goal towards which we must strive.

But whatever one's opinion may be on that matter, it is beyond dispute that in every well-constituted state, however small its extent, a number of other smaller societies and communities will be not only tolerated in its midst, but their formation must be encouraged, and care exercised to maintain them. Thus, surely, in every state there must be very many *families*, i.e. societies in which husband and wife, or parents and children, or siblings, live together. There must also be a number of societies that have been formed in order to carry out some activity better and more easily—e.g. the cultivation of the earth, a voyage, or a scientific investigation. In every good state one will also tolerate *religious* societies, i.e. societies which people feel it their duty to join for no other reason than that they are convinced of the truth of a certain religious doctrine, etc.

It will also doubtless occur in the best state, just as it occurs in current states, that families that live near each other either by choice or by chance, for precisely that reason enter into closer relations with one another and form their own *munici-palities*. If these municipalities are not too small—if, e.g., they consist of approximately one hundred families—many phenomena which occur in single families more or less at random will occur within the municipality according to an almost constant law. Thus for example, provided there is no inequality in their circumstances that might produce a difference, any group of hundred families will have a nearly equal number of children, etc. If the municipality is not too spread out, it will not be too difficult to survey, and everyone will be able without too much trouble to become acquainted with the peculiarities, circumstances, and needs of the other members. From this it follows that they will be able to be helpful to one another in many ways, and that a great many of advantages may be had if certain numbers of families living in close proximity entered into an association. It is no less evident, further, that between several such municipalities a somewhat looser association would be of great use, since there are a great many needs that a municipality could not meet by itself, but could meet in cooperation with others. In an association of approximately one hundred municipalities, phenomena that still occur randomly in individual municipalities will be observed quite regularly, e.g. the number of children whose outstanding talent makes them suitable for advanced study, and the like. Still other phenomena that occur with no regularity in such associations, will in groups of a hundred of them once again display regularity–e.g. damage due to fire or flood. It therefore is expedient to form associations consisting of approximately one hundred neighboring municipalities (let us call these *counties*), and again other associations consisting of approximately one hundred counties (I will call these *provinces*), and so on.

CHAPTER 2

On legislation

The next question that presents itself is:

Who must be granted the power of *legislation* in a well-constituted state?

Here it is my opinion that no adult member of the state should be wholly excluded from participation in legislation. By the same token, not everyone should have a say concerning every piece of legislation. Rather, it is my wish that for any given decree that is to be introduced the right to have a say should be extended to all and only those people whose character, opinions and morals, as well as external circumstances, promise that giving them a vote in the case would be of benefit. Thus some decrees will be justified through the will of merely a few; then there will be decrees that will be legally valid only when approved by many hundreds, and finally there will be decrees for which each member of the state, provided he has reached maturity and is not a criminal, must be consulted. Which of these cases applies in a given instance will sometimes be decided in advance by general regulations, at others by taking into account the nature of the case at hand.

The following people will be denied the right to vote:

a) anyone who clearly knows nothing about the matter under consideration; as well as

b) all upon whom it would have no humanly detectable consequences, either positive or negative, were the matter to be decided one way or another; unless, that is, the parties who have an interest in the matter cannot reach an agreement, in which case the disinterested parties could be consulted as arbitrators;

c) all who because of offenses of various sorts are suspected of lacking the necessary good will for judging the question at hand.

In order that those who have sufficient insight to propose an appropriate measure or law shall be encouraged as much as possible, the right to make proposals will be freely extended to everyone. Not only that, the service rendered by disinterestedly proposing measures that have turned out to be good and generally beneficial will be gratefully acknowledged in the annals of the community, or if appropriate those of the entire province, etc. In order that no one will have cause to fear that he will gain enemies through his proposals, people will be able to submit them under seal (with code number) to the community, provincial, etc. authorities, as is already done in various states. Whoever breaks open or suppresses such a proposal without authorization will be harshly punished.

In order, however, that the nation not be bothered by the examination of proposals that do not merit it, the submissions will receive a preliminary examination by several (e.g. six) completely independent persons. If they are unanimous in declaring that the proposal is not worth consideration, it will be rejected. Should, however, the originator of the proposal believe that he has not been treated fairly, that his proposal has been rejected only through malice or misunderstanding, he shall be permitted to demand that a document containing the proposal be kept in the library of the municipality or province. In order to further minimize the concern that the group of people responsible for the preliminary examination might abuse their authority, those who have rejected such a proposal will be required to record their names. On the other hand, those who have recommended a proposal, perhaps even suggested a few improvements, etc., will share the honour of introducing it.

If persons responsible for examining a proposal judge it to be good enough to merit further consideration, then everyone eligible to vote on it according to the above will be notified, by printing the measure if necessary (in urgent cases, the telegraph can be used).

Then in every municipality, at appointed times, all who find it worthwhile to vote on the issue will gather. If opinions differ, and some think that the proposed measure would have an adverse effect on them, than they will have to say what harm would be done. And if it is not clear enough to the other party what damage will be done, then an impartial group of specialists will be called upon to give an estimate. The party in favour of the measure will now consider whether the benefit they hope for will be great enough to compensate for that loss. Should they undertake to pay the compensation, its distribution among the affected individuals will be determined in the same way that the damages were estimated, namely, everyone provides his own estimate of the size of the benefit due him, which is then assessed by others.

Should someone remark that the proposed measure might have an adverse effect on people who are unable to vote on it, perhaps because they are not present, or even because they have not yet been born, then some people must be chosen to represent their point of view, and their reasons for and against made more or less widely known depending on the importance of the case, in order that the judgment of the public and even of posterity may provide a further motivation for proceeding conscientiously.

The most plausible objection that might be raised against this distribution of the legislative power among so many, indeed all, citizens is that such an arrangement assumes a much higher degree of intellectual and moral culture than is now met with in any state, or indeed ever will be attained. However, as I have expressly stated that one may only extend the right to vote to those who through their insight and moral character give reason to hope that it will be beneficial to heed their voice, this objection cannot really be made against me, since I deny the right to vote to those who do not have sufficient insight or honesty. At most, one could say with some plausibility that determining who would be accorded the right to vote would be extremely contentious. Only it should not be forgotten that I have expressly remarked that there must be various regulations determining the matter more precisely, regulations that decide in cases that can often be contentious in a way that most often is the most appropriate. It is good to consider, too, that a certain intellectual culture could be far more common than is the case in any state that has hitherto existed, as I plan to make clearer in the sequel. As far as morality is concerned, one should by no means believe that only those will have the right to vote who are supposed to possess such a high degree of morality that they will completely disregard their own interest and only propose what the general best commands. No, they should by all means allow themselves to vote according to their own interests; for it is precisely through such votes that one will learn which measures are advantageous to the majority. One would only deem unfit for voting on account of their bad moral character, therefore, those who out of sheer malice would thwart something that held no disadvantages for them simply because others would benefit, or who were so dishonest as to exaggerate the harm that would come to them because of some measure.

With all this in mind I claim that in a state where any law might be introduced or repealed as soon as a majority of citizens had united for or against it, no matter how appropriate all the other measures were, one would have to be concerned that sooner or later many beneficial measures would be repealed and many pernicious customs might be sanctified by the mere appearance of lawfulness—merely because human sensuousness would be gratified by such a change. For even if men are brought up in the most appropriate way possible, it is to be feared that the greater part of mankind, when faced with a struggle between sensuality and reason, will follow the former rather than the latter—and this is especially the case with young people, who always form the majority within a state. In order, therefore, to prevent any such abuse, which is to be feared with an unlimited legislative power placed in the hands of the majority of the entire people, the following measure is, in my opinion, necessary. *No decision of the majority attains the status of law if it is rejected by a part of society I shall call the* Council of Elders, *and not simply by a mere majority of votes, but nearly unanimously, i.e. with about 9 to 1 against.* Now I understand by the Council of Elders a number of people of both sexes who are elected to this honour by majority vote every three years in the municipalities in which they live. After three years, they can either be reappointed, or else removed from office—if, for example, they have been guilty of some offense or have become less capable through age. The members themselves shall also be free to request that they be relieved of their duties because of increasing infirmity of age. Only persons who are more than, roughly, sixty years old should be chosen for this office, and among them only those who have through repeated tests given evidence of their uprightness as well as their insight, and who have shown themselves resistant to strong temptations. As one can be both good and wise without having been tested in ways which bear witness to the qualities required for admission to the Council, no one is disgraced by not being chosen to serve, even though he may have reached the appropriate age. For precisely this reason too, no one shall belong to the Council of Elders solely on account of his profession, not even a pastor or a preacher. People under sixty years of age who have given extraordinary proof of their uprightness and extensive knowledge can be chosen for this office, but in no case should anyone under forty be chosen. On the other hand, people who have been guilty of some offense, or even suspected of an offense, are irrevocably barred from the office.

Finally, every municipality has the right to elect at least one, at most five people to this Council. The right to demand a certain resolution passed by a municipality or a larger part of the society to be put before the Council of Elders for that part of society shall be granted to council members themselves. It is to be stipulated, however, that a Council of Elders must have at least ten members. In any case, it is clear that the Council of Elders should not only be able to *prevent* the repeal of already existing measures or decrees but should also have the power to *introduce* necessary new measures that are still lacking. For, like all citizens, the members of the Council of Elders have the right to propose new measures and laws. Should such a measure be rejected by a majority of the citizens to whom it must be submitted, this would not prevent its introduction, which could still proceed even though it does not enjoy majority support, provided that the Council of Elders agrees to consider the measure again, and gives it not merely a majority, but near-unanimous approval.

After some reflection, the advisability of a Council of Elders furnished with such rights and duties will, I hope, be evident. Should it not be obvious at first glance, however, why such decisive power as is here granted to the Council of Elders is necessary or even useful, in order to examine the votes of the remainder of the society, I remind you that from what has been said about the Council of Elders it does not follow that this power exists in all cases; rather, the Council shall have decisive power over the voice of the majority only when there is no division of opinion among the members, but unanimity prevails. Should someone wish to conclude from this that it would be more efficacious always to consult the Council of Elders first and separately, and only to consult the rest of the population where the Council is not unanimous, I counter that it must always be more gratifying for a people when they have chosen a certain measure for themselves, and that they will be more inclined to obey a law that exists because of their own choice. One must not rob a people of the credit of giving themselves a wise law, but rather give them every opportunity to do so. To this end, then, in every case where the Council of Elders has decided in favour of a law, even if by a heavy majority, one should attempt to convince the preponderance of the remaining citizens through all means of instruction at one's disposal to vote for it of their own free will. One might, for instance, distribute essays among the people that set out the advantages or the necessity of the measure, ask those citizens whose subjective conviction is already in favour of the measure to use every opportunity when they meet with others to refute the prejudices against it, etc.

One might ask, however, why I wish to grant the Council of Elders the power to overturn a majority vote of the people only in those cases where the Council has not just a simple majority, but when universal agreement can be obtained, since the entire people by a simple majority of votes can introduce a law (at least in certain cases, viz., when the Council of Elders is not opposed as a body to it). I have already said that even with the best educational institutions and laws of all kinds it could not be avoided that among the totality of people entitled to vote on public matters, there would be a considerable number weak enough to allow their better judgment in certain cases to be blinded by their passions. We can, therefore, not expect that, whenever a truly good thing comes along, we can convince *everyone* of its goodness, and persuade them to vote for it. On the other hand, one can confidently expect that when a truly good measure is under consideration, then not just a majority, but all, or nearly all or that part of society from which the Council of Elders is drawn may be won over to it. We have therefore no reason to fear that a truly beneficial measure might never be introduced in the best state only because it is not possible to bring the members of the Council of Elders to vote for it. Also, it would seem very oppressive to the part of the people who are not in favour of such a measure, if any slight preponderance in the Council of Elders were to have the power to compel them to obey, especially in the case when their number is so much greater, and when they can see that even those who are accounted the best and the wisest in the country are not unanimous in their opinion. When, on the contrary, it is said that a minority can only overturn the vote of the majority of the people when the Council of Elders speaks with one voice for the minority position, then the majority could not in truth find it unfair. Rather they must themselves feel that they must have made a mistake in making a judgment that, as now appears, the best and wisest are unanimous in contradicting.

Chapter 3

On government

It is obviously difficult to decide, for individual men as well as for states, what would be the best and most reasonable thing to do under certain prevailing circumstances. The most diverse kinds of knowledge are often required in order to answer this important question even somewhat correctly; and sometimes nothing at all can be said on the subject without first obtaining an overview of the conditions in the state, without, that is, knowing all of its needs and the totality of resources available for satisfying them. One might wonder, for example, whether an expensive project that the society's men of learning wish to undertake should or should not be permitted, e.g. the recent circumnavigation of the north pole. It might well happen that not all scholars are capable of assessing the usefulness of such undertakings, but rather only those who are specialists in the field. But it is not only a matter of this usefulness, but rather also of the state's assets, what other expenses need to be covered, whether there might not be other, much more necessary or at least more useful projects, and so on.

From this it will be gathered that a state requires people who are expressly put in a position to acquire as much knowledge concerning such matters as is possible for a single person—thus people who are not only schooled from their youth in the general principles of judging such matters, but as well are made familiar with all the detailed circumstances of the state. The more people in a state who can be trusted to possess the appropriate knowledge without neglecting their other activities, the better. It is obvious, however, that not everyone is able to spend the time required to acquire such exhaustive knowledge, especially a comprehensive overview of all the needs and resources of the state. In order, therefore, that there never be a lack of people who have an intimate knowledge of the affairs of the state, and in order that such people will always be available, it is necessary that there be in every state a special society composed of citizens, who in part already possess such knowledge, in part are required by their office to acquire it on the job, and who are appointed to make their views known whenever a resolution is at issue that can be rationally drafted only on the basis of such knowledge.

And just as there are cases where the other citizens will not be able say what is to be done, because they lack sufficient knowledge of the true state of things, so too there are other cases where even those who actually possess enough knowledge cannot be consulted, because there is not enough time, or because the matter, on account of its minor importance, does not merit the expense of time and energy of such an extensive consultation. Here too, then, there must be certain people with the right and the duty to decide in the name of the remaining citizens. I call the collection of these people, in brief, the *government* or the *directorate* of the country, or the *state officials*, and an individual official a *director*. In every municipality there will be many advantages to having one or several officials to look after the affairs of the municipality. Still more will have to be appointed for each county, in order to make decisions that can only be made with an overview of the entire county. The same holds for entire states, and insofar as several states enter into general alliances, so too there must be *officials for the entire alliance of states*.

It is obvious that the knowledge and qualities these officials must have in order to fill their positions properly are extremely diverse. It also goes almost without saying that these officials, should their duties occupy all their time, must be supported by the general population, and most appropriately by the part of the population with whose well-being they are most directly concerned–i.e. the officials of a municipality should be supported by that municipality, those of a county by the county, of a province by the province, of the entire state by the entire state. Should some officials only devote part of their time to public service, it will be sufficient that they receive support for that portion of their time from those whose well-being is their concern. It will, moreover, be expedient if the duration of the appointments of officials is not uniformly determined for all. For since they learn their business gradually and only become better at it with time, as they acquire more skill through practice, we should not wish to replace them unless it is necessary. On the other hand, it is not good to appoint them with the prospect of lifelong tenure, partly because their character may change, or because through changed circumstances or age they might lose their ability to do the job; finally, because other people might come along who—no matter how competent the incumbents were—justify still greater hopes. It therefore seems most expedient that the people be given the right to choose their officials either annually, or at least every two or three years; and that they be given the opportunity to retain the old officials or else to try their luck with new individuals, in which case it must be expressly stated that no dishonor should attach to a civil servant who is not retained, unless someone has been removed from his post on account of actually proven dereliction of duty.

These paid officials or civil servants will have the right and the duty to find all the arrangements that further the best interests of the state. They will be guided in this by certain regulations. Among other things, these regulations will indicate how far their power to make laws extends, and in which cases, by contrast, it will be necessary to submit a contentious matter to the decision of the whole, be it the municipality, the province, or the entire country; and, finally, in which cases they will indeed have the power to decide, but not before having heard the opinions and advice of certain other people, or even entire groups, e.g. of scholars. Among the things that no civil servant, not even those concerned with the entire state, shall have the authority to decide, but rather can only be decided by the entire mass of the people in the way already discussed above, belongs each and every law that is to be *valid in perpetuity*, and that is to be adopted as *an element of the constitutional charter of the state*.

In every department containing *several* civil servants one shall be the *head*, and direct the business of the department. Apart from this role, he is to have no other special rights or duties than those concerned with maintaining the orderly progress of department business. The civil servants will make their decisions by majority vote; should there be a tie, the opinion of one party shall prevail over that of the other according to certain rules—e.g. because the most *experienced* are to be found on one side, etc. Only in cases of urgency should decisions be taken on matters during the first meeting in which they are brought up. Otherwise, they may and should take an appropriate time to consider and discuss the matter. Should the importance of the matter require it, and should it be possible—i.e. if the nature of the matter does not require secrecy—the matter should be made known to the entire public, and the public encouraged to express their opinions either individually or as entire communities. But however the voice of the people may speak, if it is a matter that by its nature cannot be decided by the great mass of the people, the department is not required to obey it. Yet even when one is not compelled to heed an opinion, it can nevertheless be a good thing to hear it. Also, people will be far more ready to accept a law when they are shown that their opinions have been taken into consideration, even if they were not the only guiding principle. And if many of the opinions that are voiced on such an occasion are incorrect, then a good deal of truly useful advice may be given. Accordingly, the government must be required to make generally known the matters that are up for decision, and to hear the opinions of the people, whenever this is possible—which is not to say that they should be formally accorded a vote on every such case. In any case, the government must at least publish an annual record of their decisions and negotiations *afterwards*, and its members are, obviously, to be held responsible for their contributions to the government. In this way, the people will receive a report on all the activities of their government and will at the same time receive an account of government revenues and expenditures.

With these institutions, in association with others to be mentioned later, we should not worry that civil servants will even feel tempted to embezzle large sums of money or to enact measures harmful to the whole from mere self-interest. Should it be suspected, however, that one or another official is not dealing honestly, or lacks sufficient insight, then either he won't be chosen the next time, or he may indeed be investigated and prosecuted in court.

The number of civil servants is to be determined by two considerations. First, there must be at least as many as are required properly to discuss the decisions they must take, and so that they will not feel forced to rush their decisions due to the lack of time. On the other hand, there must be as many as are necessary to allow us to expect that all matters may be considered from all the appropriate perspectives, and decided honestly and conscientiously—for if some were to decide in a partisan and impassioned manner, others will be present to counter them. A larger number than is required for this double goal would be too burdensome, and would only hinder the government's business and create unnecessary expenses for the state.

Doubtless, the most expedient thing is to have the people themselves choose their civil servants, each municipality, each province choosing one or several depending on its numbers. It may indeed not be necessary that each *profession* and each *trade* have their own *representative*. Nevertheless this may be a good thing, something that will promote people's willingness to obey the laws. In a well-constituted state it will certainly also be easier to find individuals in every trade and profession who have the ability to serve as officials, since the entire mass of the people will receive a much more uniform education, and especially because the knowledge required for the administration of a state will be far more widely distributed than is now the case in most developed states. From this circumstance it follows that each and every municipality will have in its midst enough people to form their administration (i.e. that of their municipality). It follows, further, that it will be best to leave to each municipality the choice of their own officials. Naturally, if allowed to do this, they will almost always choose someone who lives among them. But they will not make poor choices, for precisely because these people live among them they will all be well enough known, and one need not fear that a completely incompetent individual will be chosen, for there will be no lack of competent ones.

It is more difficult to decide how the officials who are to be concerned not just with a municipality, but with an entire county or province, or even the entire state should be chosen. On the one hand, it seems very fair that each individual municipality should have a vote here, since the choice will have an influence on their weal and woe. On the other hand one may not suppose that one and the same person, no matter how suitable for such a post, could be well enough known to every individual citizen in a county, still less in an entire province or state, to possess their trust, and thus have a solidly grounded claim to their vote. Only men who have already served for a long time in a post, in which their behaviour could be observed by many thousands, and in which their influence extended over many thousands of people, could be known by reputation in the entire country. But this reputation does not always conform to the truth, and accordingly cannot be a secure way of determining such a choice. And how are those who have not yet occupied a post to acquire a reputation, no matter how great their aptitude? Further, it must be admitted in the end that the great mass of people, even in the best-constituted state, will hardly be in a position to judge whether even people they think they know well enough have the qualities required of a competent civil servant in the higher levels of administration. From all this, I draw the conclusion that it would be most rational if it were not left to the entire mass of the people, but rather to the officials [of the next lowest level of government] to choose, or, rather, to nominate people for these posts, and this so that always more, roughly twice as many, people are nominated as are required—at which point it will be left to the nominees themselves to decide who shall occupy the various posts. It is indeed to be expected that those who are themselves officials will know how to assess the qualities required of a future official, even one who is to serve at a higher level of government. They will also have far more opportunity to get to know the people who may possess these qualities. It is therefore to be hoped that the people whom they nominate will for the most part be worthy. Finding the most worthy among these worthy nominees is something one can safely leave to the nominees themselves, provided that one extends to them the right to institute the examinations and tests that they consider necessary to decide who should be appointed, and in addition that the annals of the state contain, next to a record of the achievements of officials, the names of those who, though elected, ceded their places to them. As for elections, whether of officials or any other sorts of people, if it consists of a simple vote, the most natural procedure would be to have the group of electors meet the first time only to allow each member to make known to the others those people who seem to him especially suitable, bearing witness to their qualities, talents, principles, previous performance, etc., precisely so that anyone who finds these recommendations incorrect or one-sided, or who thinks he knows of an even more worthy candidate, may speak against him. After these preliminary discussions, a vote may be taken during the next meeting. It would be an easy matter here to devise a procedure that would eliminate any suspicion of fraud in the collection and counting of votes, and also, if one wishes, prevent it from becoming known who has voted for whom. It would only be necessary, for example, for each elector to write the name of the person he is voting for on a folded piece of paper and to bring it to the meeting; children could be chosen to collect these pieces of paper in an urn, and afterwards to pull all of them out, read them, sort and count them, and so on. This could all take place in a large room in which the little ones carrying out the business would be separated from the spectators by a grid, and on an elevated platform so that they could be observed by everyone, etc. But as no one should be compelled to accept an official position, especially at the higher levels, i.e. one that requires a great deal of good will to be appropriately filled, it is obvious that people (officials), however they may have been chosen, must in every case remain free either to accept or to decline the post they have been offered—indeed anyone who merely thinks that the electors might consider him must be allowed to request in advance that others be considered, since he does not feel himself to be suited for this post.

CHAPTER 4

On means of coercion

It would not be much use for a state to pass the best laws without at the same time taking care to ensure that they must be followed. It is to be expected in advance, however, that not all citizens will be willing to follow the laws of the state, even when they clearly see their benefit, and indeed have themselves voted for them.

In every state, then, there must be a power that threatens those who do not wish to obey with an appropriate punishment, and compels them to do as the law commands when they do not follow it willingly. Were there a society completely lacking such a power, one that utterly lacked all means of implementing the general will, if necessary by force, we would say precisely on that account that it did not merit the name of a state, or that the state had been dissolved. Therefore, means of coercion must not be lacking even in the best state. First of all, there must be certain people (*judges*) in every individual community to whom some of these means are entrusted. Even when these people do not themselves carry out the business of enforcement (corporal punishment and the like), they will have some others with them (*bailiffs, police, guards*) who do so at their behest, and for this purpose are issued weapons and tools of punishment. The expediency of such a division, whereby one person merely determines what sort of force is to be applied, and another only applies the force as instructed, is obvious. So too it is clear that only men who combine a good deal of knowledge with an irreproachable character should be chosen as judges. As for their assistants, one should be more concerned with their physical strength, but should also take care that their way of life is not repugnant, and also that they are not given to violent bursts of temper, which might lead to a misuse of their weapons and tools of punishment. Any use of these weapons that does not conform to official instructions shall be considered such a misuse, which must be punished with the utmost severity from the very first, and which must entail the loss of permission to carry weapons ever again. Incidentally, it scarcely needs to be said that neither the judge nor his assistant will have this work as their only occupation, and the latter will by no means be required to have his weapons with him at all times. This being said, only certain less severe coercive measures shall be at the disposal of the judges of individual municipalities; more severe punishments may only be imposed after legal proceedings before a higher official (county judge)—and always according to regulations governing such cases, which should be few enough in number so that their main points can be made known to everyone through public instruction.

However, such means only suffice if there are only one or a few people who refuse to obey the state and must be compelled to do so by force. Should the idea of overturning what the state demands occur to many people at the same time, a different, far greater power will be necessary in order to instill fear into them and overpower them. Such an eventuality does not seem impossible, for even in the best state there are measures that are not pleasant for everyone, measures that have been introduced or maintained with the support of only part of the population, perhaps even only by the Council of Elders. Is it not possible, then, that at some time many, even the majority of citizens, might rise up to declare that they no longer intend to obey such a law? And just as the best state is not secure against the possibility of the fire of rebellion flaring up *within*, it is even less safe from an attack mounted by an *external* power attempting to destroy it. As long as there exist alongside the better-run states others not so well-run, it may be really or at least apparently advantageous for the latter to bring down the former where possible. What can be done when entire armies advance on all sides in order to force the peaceful citizens of the best state to submit to a foreign power, and to live not under their own laws but rather under those of another state? I admit freely that I know of no means by which the citizens of the best states could fend off this danger always and everywhere, and this is one of the principal reasons why it would be by no means prudent for every society of people, no matter how small and in whatever environs, to seek to form a state according to principles that seemed best to them. Where it cannot be hoped that a better order can be preserved, it is better not to begin something that can only end with the spilling of human blood. On the other hand, in order that we will not have to wait longer than is necessary for the introduction of an appropriate constitution, and that we will be able to protect such a constitution, once introduced, from both internal and external threats of subversion as well as is humanly possible: all citizens, provided that they are not physically incapable, shall be trained and drilled in the use of weapons and techniques of defense. Further, there must be sufficient stocks of weapons and military equipment—not, to be sure, to be left in the hands of the individual citizens, but rather stored in secure places, where they can be immediately put to use if needed. By means of such precautions we will be able to put the entire nation under arms, and should a foreign state have the courage to launch an attack on us, they will have to raise an army as numerous as our entire people, and then will have to expect that their mercenaries will not fight as courageously as those who are fighting for their own hearth, for their freedom, for their wives and children, even for their own lives! They will have to be satisfied with conquering corpses instead of men, and a smouldering ruin instead of a flourishing land. Should we be able to bring it about through such measures that foreign powers will not think lightly of trying to impose another constitution on the citizens of the state than the one they have given themselves, we will by precisely the same token have provided the surest means of protection against the disturbance or even the complete overthrow of the state by dissatisfied people within its *own midst.*

All too often, unfortunately, it has occurred that even better states that have withstood external powers for many centuries, have finally succumbed to the rebellion of their own citizens—or, even if the rebellion did not result in the complete overthrow of the state, at least could not be stopped until the blood of many thousands had been spilled. Let us inquire into what brought about such sad events, events whose memory always brings tears to the eyes of friends of mankind. We find that every rebellion comes from one of the following two causes, or from their combination: either the rebels were men who had been reduced to the most extreme poverty by the bad constitution of the country, or in part by their own dissipation, and did what they were doing out of desperation, from the conviction that they had nothing to lose but their own lives. Or they were followers of a powerful man, won over by money and promises, who hoped either that a radical change in the existing constitution would afford them great personal advantages, or else had convinced themselves that rebellion would be the quickest path to a better state of things. It will be granted that a rebellion due to the first of these causes is not to be feared in a state that is even moderately well-run. Citizens who through no fault of their own lack the most basic necessities of life and only feel tempted to shake up the state in order to obtain something for themselves, will certainly not be found in a well-constituted state, for there everyone will be given the opportunity to earn the necessities of life honestly. By contrast, even in a well-run state people who are starving by their own fault, through their own laziness and dissipation, will not be wholly absent. But such people will be quite rare, and their malevolence, no matter how great, can never become dangerous for the whole, provided only that one pays as much attention to such people as is customary in all the better-run states today. But the other usual cause of rebellion will not come into play in a well-constituted state either, since it presupposes that there are citizens who possess such an outrageous amount of wealth and influence that thousands live from their munificence and can hope to win advantages for themselves from their patronage. Something of this sort can never occur in the best state, as shall be shown in the sequel. Thus we can already see that the kind of rebellion that one might fear here would have to be of a completely different nature than all that have so far been experienced.

What can happen even here, though, is that a considerable, or even, if you will, the greater portion of the citizens is dissatisfied, not with the entire constitution, but rather with an *individual* measure or decree (whether it be a new or an old one), and insists that it be repealed. At the wish of these citizens, the matter will be taken into consideration once again (provided that this has not already happened recently or several times), and another vote taken. Let us now suppose that, despite all representations made to the public, the majority is still in favour of rescinding the measure—so that, indeed, the only reason that the contentious measure is still considered legally binding is (in conformity with the constitution of the state) because the Council of Elders has declared unanimously in favour of it.

Let us suppose, further, that the dissatisfied citizens are aware of the strength of their numbers, and that it is merely the Council of Elders that stands in the way of their getting what they want: should it then be feared that they will rise up *en masse* and employ violence in order to have their way? O! Even in our very imperfect states it happens only all too often that the larger part of the polity is dissatisfied with certain measures—measures which in addition obviously do not have the general good in view, but rather the interests of a single individual—and nevertheless they bear the yoke from one year to the next. Normally a rebellion does not arise unless offensive arrogance and scorn are heaped on top of the oppression. Nevertheless, let us suppose that the dissatisfied citizens immediately attempt to accomplish with violence what they could not through legal means. What will they accomplish, if in every community there are even a few better-disposed people, who will immediately make known to a higher official the plans of the others, plans that are as foolish as they are worthy of punishment; and indeed, in the meantime, will do whatever they can to impede the progress of this disorder? When, further, as we already know, only certain authorized people, but not individual citizens, will be permitted to carry weapons, all the rest of the stocks being stored by the government in special places? When, finally, the government issues a general call to all well-intentioned citizens to take up arms in defence of their country, in order to rout the rebels? Would not a power quickly appear in this way whose superiority would lead the unruly elements to surrender without great loss of blood, especially when they hope afterwards to be deemed merely mistaken, and judged with all possible leniency and consideration?

Let us also suppose that in the best state people will hear from their childhood on that anyone who opposes the arms of the government is contemptible; let us consider, further, that armed citizens shall be instructed to use them more as signs of their power than as actual tools for causing harm, and to use them to cause harm only when they themselves are in danger of being harmed; let us consider that during a rebellion, should one take place in the best state, it would not be a matter of bitterly opposed men fighting one another, but rather a company of soldiers meeting a company of citizens, in whose midst will be found all of those who enjoy the respect and love of all the people. If we take all of this to heart, we will all come to the reassuring conclusion that in the best state there will certainly be no need to worry about the occurrence of bloody scenes like those played out in states up to the present.

Chapter 5

On freedom

It is already included in the concept of any society, and all the more in that of a civil society, that by entering into it we restrict our *freedom of action* in certain respects. For above all else we pledge that in certain things we will behave not as our own will demands, but rather as the will of the whole demands. This restriction of his freedom, however unpleasant fools and scoundrels may find it, the reasonable person never sees as an evil, provided only that that which he is compelled to do by the will of the society is not evil in itself, and the happiness of the whole as well as his own is furthered more than it is harmed by it.

If, in particular, what society prevents him from doing, or even makes slightly more difficult, is something that is evil and unjust, but which he might nevertheless feel tempted to do, then he will consider this measure as a truly good thing not only for others, but also for himself.

Now in a well constituted state one must strive to restrict the freedom of the citizens in no other way than that which has just been described; thus insofar as it is possible, one must arrange everything so that no one might be led to do something that is evil in itself (indeed even if this is only according to his own opinion), either by the prospect of something to be gained, or by means of threats of hardships to be endured or some other bad consequence, and least of all by means of actual punishment.

If this condition is met, then one can boast that true freedom prevails in the country.

CHAPTER 6

On equality

Nothing is more often and more forcefully criticised by those dissatisfied with current constitutions than the great *inequality* of rights and duties of citizens that is to be met with almost everywhere.

"*Freedom and equality*" is, accordingly, the battle cry that can be heard ringing out from all sides, whenever an enraged mob rises up in some unfortunate country in order violently to overturn the existing order on account of its faults, in the belief that this would be the fastest way to bring about improvements. Let us see how much reason there is in this demand.

No reasonable person will demand a *perfect equality* in all rights and duties, if that is supposed to mean that all citizens shall be granted the same rights and also the same duties without distinction of persons. The rights and duties of people must indisputably be determined by their needs and abilities. If, now, the individual citizens who have united to form a civil society are not completely equal to one another, either in their needs or in their abilities, it would be foolish for them to demand exactly equal rights and to assume exactly equal responsibilities. Among us humans, there are a great many differences in the needs we feel as well as in the abilities we possess. Many come from inalterable laws of nature, so we can do virtually nothing to prevent them. There may well be other differences that can in some measure be *reduced*—yet even there one may wonder whether we are well advised to do so, whether this would do more harm than good. How many differences in needs and abilities are brought about by sex, age, or temperament! Should we ignore these, and impose the same duties on women and men, or give the same rights to children and adults? This has never occurred to anyone. From this it is clear that the *equality* on which we could reasonably insist must be understood in a completely different way than what the literal meaning suggests, i.e. to extend the same rights and duties to everyone.

No, if we are reasonable, we shall not wish that the state extend the same rights to all its citizens, nor that it make the same demands of all, but rather that no difference in what is demanded of or granted to citizens should be made that is not *justified* on the basis of differences in their needs and abilities; no inequality between citizens should be either introduced or tolerated that is not necessary for the best of the whole, or which rests on the merely arbitrary and baseless preference shown to some at the expense of others.

It is only all too true that such harmful differences between citizens and preferential treatment of some at the expense of others is to be met with in all constitutions that have existed until now.

Two especially pernicious inequalities are:

The inequality in wealth and in certain rights that are extended to certain people based merely on their parentage. I need to say a little about each of these here:

I admit in advance that a complete equality in the *wealth* of citizens would be neither possible nor desirable. No harm is done, rather there are many advantages, when a state is so ordered that it is possible for individuals, through diligence and thrift, especially when this is favoured with good fortune, to amass wealth somewhat greater than the amount that an equal partition of all goods would result in. Pernicious and not to be tolerated, in my view, are only such arrangements as allow for the possessions of a single individual to exceed a much greater level, e.g. greater than a hundred times the abovementioned average. It is certainly a good thing that someone who is more thrifty and diligent has the opportunity to acquire more property than others, to become richer than they, as this is one more incentive for people to acquire these virtues. And when the wealth that an individual amasses with the help of these virtues (indeed even if this wealth is merely the gift of fortune), does not exceed a certain limit, we will have no cause to complain that the wealth of one person impoverishes the rest. Nor need we worry that he will use this wealth as a means of bribing others to do as he wishes, and thus of exerting a corrupting power. Yet both of these will be the case if the inequality in the property of the citizens is so disproportionately large, as it is in almost all states past and present, where there are individuals who consider as their legitimately acquired and state-protected wealth a sum of goods that, with an equal division, would suffice for many thousands. Such wealth in the hands of individuals cannot possibly come about without impoverishing many others; neither can it endure without its possessors gaining a dangerous influence over their fellow citizens. And the longer this continues, the wider they will learn to extend this power. Whoever has the power to give to thousands, and can help them satisfy their wants, is he not for that reason alone, if he is not of the most sterling character, a very dangerous man? Can he not move thousands this way or that as he wishes, simply because he allows them some of his surplus, and promises more in the future? Something so obvious as this does not require many words to prove. But while speaking of this I by no means intend to deny that the inequality in wealth has had, in its time, many good effects, and indeed was necessary in order to raise mankind to the level of culture we find at present. In a time when the great mass of people still had no sense for anything higher than the satisfaction of their bodily desires and needs, it was indeed fortunate that several of those few who had by some chance succeeded in sensing that there was something still more noble found themselves in a position (thanks to the inequality in the distribution of goods) to finance things to which the great mass would never have contributed had it been up to them, since they never would have understood the benefit of such undertakings. How many of the most beneficial expansions of our knowledge in all branches of learning do we not owe to the propertied and the wealthy, who, be it from a pure zeal to do good or merely from a desire for higher pleasures, dared to undertake costly ventures whose goals the great mass could not even begin to fathom, and did so without any assurance of success, ventures which nevertheless in the end brought humanity blessings no one had dreamed of!

But should we draw the conclusion from this that an inequality that has proven so beneficial in the past promises similar advantages for the future, or that in any case the duty of gratitude bids us to leave undisturbed the wealthy who have helped us attain this blessing? Inferences from the past to the future are not, as everyone knows, always correct, for the circumstances may have changed mightily in the interim. An inequality in the wealth of the citizens as great as what I oppose for the best state is, given the level of general culture that we presently enjoy, e.g. in most European states, even now completely unnecessary in order to attain the good that could, I admit, in earlier centuries only be had through the wealth of individuals. Today we need not await the favour of wealthy individuals, to find out whether they are prepared to contribute the necessary sums to some generally beneficial undertaking; rather, we can raise these monies through taxation. And it should also be noted that given the way of imposing a tax or drafting a resolution regarding something generally beneficial that I propose in this book, it would not at all be necessary to make obvious to everyone the usefulness of the undertaking brought about through such expenditures. If we may assume that wealthy individuals are not necessary in order to bring to fruition certain costly projects for which the great mass of people have no sense, then in all other respects their existence has only damaging consequences.

That the overwhelming wealth of one individual must impoverish the others has already been pointed out several times. If we add to this that the presence of such a wealthy man is for the others, especially those who hold him responsible for their poverty, a constant temptation to envy, to resentment and to undertakings aimed either at becoming wealthy in a similar way or, if this is not possible, at avenging themselves by inflicting as much damage as they can upon him. And is it really possible that those who know how much their wealth is vexatious to others will themselves enjoy their riches, however these may have been acquired? What pleasure can the possession of a good give us, when everyone begrudges it? Yet you say: wealth is precious, since it provides us with the opportunity to do good. I believe you, and admit that this is the only reason why a rational and well-intentioned citizen under the present regime can feel pleasure when unexpected riches come his way. But you should know that it is already a bad thing, already something that can not possibly be tolerated in a well-constituted state, that it should depend merely on your *good pleasure* whether your wealth is to be used for good or for ill. Know, too, that those who live thanks to your benevolence will feel much more joy when under a wise organization they do not depend upon your mercy for what they will with full right demand, and may expect with certainty. Know, finally, that even if you are perhaps completely certain that your wealth would never lead you to do something evil, no one can ensure that this would also be the case with your heirs and descendants; that it is rather far more likely that, sooner or later, wealth will ruin them. But if this is the nature of wealth, there is no more cause for concern that we show ourselves *ungrateful* towards the rich when we introduce measures that lead to the gradual loss of their wealth. For it is in fact no good fortune that we take away from them; on the contrary we free them from a danger that would sooner or later lead to their downfall. Nor will anyone be able to object that we do the rich wrong by forcing them all at once to abandon a way of life to which they have grown accustomed—for we will not seek suddenly to redress the present inequality of wealth, but rather by a series of many steps that will take one or indeed even several lifetimes to reach the sort of equality required by the best state.

But a reasonable state not only demands a certain equality in the *property* of its citizens, but also, and still more strictly, the removal of all *hereditary privileges and responsibilities.* No citizen shall be accorded a privilege or expected to take on some responsibility simply on account of his stemming from such and such parents. It is by no means to be denied that the predisposition towards certain virtues and vices occasionally is passed on from parents to their children; for this reason some attention must be paid to one's heritage in the education of children in the best state. For example, in the education of a child whose parents were given to a certain vice, one would be especially observant to determine whether any inclination towards a similar vice could be detected in the child, and if so one would take care to nip this damaging inclination in the bud. It is equally appropriate to remind the descendants of people who have distinguished themselves through uncommon virtues of the example of their forebears, and to give them to understand that the same is expected of them. If it seems that this sort of procedure amounts to a tolerance of *hereditary nobility*, then I will allow that there is a sort of hereditary nobility even in the best state. For what I have just called for is something so natural, so salutary and so free from danger that it would be absurd to forbid people to do it. But one should not go any farther, and protect the bad use along with the good. You may remind the son of a great man of his ancestry as often as you wish; as often as you wish you may give him to understand that he shows promise of taking after his father; but you should never assume that it will be so, you should never accord him any of the rights that can only belong to those who have already clearly proven their outstanding virtue; you should not accord him greater wealth than anyone else merely on account of his parentage; you should not give any more weight to his voice than you would to someone of completely common birth when he finds himself in the same circumstances; you should not allow him to occupy a position when this would entail the removal of another who is there not on account of his birth but rather because his conduct has given far greater hope that he will fill it worthily; you should not cut off anyone, no matter how common his birth, from the means and ways of education nor from the most important posts and honours in the state, especially when an inner force pushes him to seek such an education and his teachers bear witness that he has the necessary aptitudes. It is only the abuses mentioned here, of which so many states have been guilty, indeed which are still to be met with in so many states today, it is only these that have made the institution of nobility so detested in the eyes of the true friends of humanity, and made them want to see all recognition of hereditary differences between people, even the most insignificant, banned from the best state. For it was feared that one would never stop at recognizing only these differences. In a state where all the other institutions are appropriate, however, there is no sufficient reason for such a worry. Thus I believe I may repeat here that the good customs should be retained, and only their abuses prevented.

CHAPTER 7

On freedom of thought and religion

The principle of freedom mentioned in the fifth chapter demands among other things that as far as possible no measure be tolerated that could tempt any citizen to convince himself of the truth of an opinion he had previously considered incorrect, merely out of self-interest or from fear of the consequences of believing the contrary, or even to profess a belief while in his heart he believes something completely different. If this holds for *all* opinions, then so much more for opinions that are considered *religious*. For the moral corruption is all the greater, one's condition all the more unfortunate, when one wrongly talks oneself into adopting or merely mouthing a certain religious opinion. It is therefore counterproductive for the state to favour, e.g., by granting privileges or preferment, or to disfavour people merely for professing a religion, that is, without regard to their *behaviour*. Still more wrong than trying to induce men to accept an opinion through *rewards* are attempts to bring this about through punishments or compulsion. Such means are not only futile, but counterproductive, and make men even more resistant to the opinions forced upon them. Even the heathen conversions carried out by Charlemagne *et al.* do not disprove what has been said. For in fact it was not the force exercised on the heathens, but rather the instruction their children received, that in time turned them into Christians. If a number of citizens believe it to be their duty to do certain things out of respect for God, the state shall allow it, even when this does not promote the general good (e.g. animal sacrifice, living in celibacy, and the like), unless the harm these citizens will suffer from a ban is greatly outweighed by the deleterious effects of their actions—should they wish, for example, to perform human sacrifice.

If a number of citizens wish to have their own *ministers* to lead them in worship, to instruct them more fully in their religion, and so on, this too will be permitted so long as they see fit of their own free will to live according to the laws of the state. It is thus not the state that appoints such ministers. Rather those who confess a certain faith must themselves choose their ministers, and look after their living expenses.

No one shall be allowed, however, to force his religious opinions on others, i.e. to preach to them against their will. Thus if a preacher changes his religious convictions, and preaches what his community does not wish to hear, they shall have the right to remove him from his post; so too, if they find his moral comportment unsuitable.

Nor will anyone be allowed to disseminate new opinions deviating from the current ones by *first of all* and *immediately* addressing them to the young through oral instruction. Rather, new opinions are to be introduced only in written works, under limitations to be discussed later.

Everyone shall be permitted to convert from one faith to another. He shall be required for his own good, however, to demonstrate his knowledge of the first faith as well as the one he plans to convert to. If, for example, he is not a specialist in theology, one will require that he undergo certain tests, or allow himself to be instructed for several weeks, and so on.

If someone should cause something generally harmful through his religious opinions, something that is moreover expressly forbidden by the laws of the state, he shall on account of this be punished, but more mildly if one is convinced that he acted in good faith. In addition, should it prove to be the case that many citizens share the religious belief that motivated his action, the scholars of the state shall be asked to consider how this opinion might best be refuted and cast out, and to write appropriate works on the subject.

Whoever finds the above not incorrect (and I hope that it is obvious if his judgment has not been clouded by the schools) will be able without much trouble to separate the true from the false in the following claims, still heard here and there even today. The state, some say, shall have no religion. Others, on the contrary, will have it that the state should adhere only to the most rational religion, which should be raised to a dominant status. Others should merely be tolerated, and religions containing obvious absurdities should be banned outright—e.g. no one should be permitted to deny the immortality of the soul or the existence of God, all superstition should be forbidden, etc.

Saying that the state should have no religion at all is certainly not to be understood as meaning that none of the citizens of the state should have a religion, not even that none of the members of the administration should have a religion. Nor can it be interpreted as meaning that the officials should completely set aside their religious convictions when attending to their business, i.e. in making decisions. Indeed, they must do exactly the opposite, for if it is the duty of all people to proceed according to their best insight and conviction in important matters, then so too it must be the duty of all officials to be conscientiously guided only by what seems true and good to them in those important decisions upon which the weal or woe of thousands depends—and this is what the religion they confess demands of them. Thus if the saying contains some truth, it must be interpreted roughly as follows: when drafting decrees that have to do with people who confess a different faith, officials should never fail to put themselves in their place, in order to understand the effect these decrees will have on them.

That the state should only adhere to a rational religion is certainly a very true rule, but not much is gained by stating it, since it is a very contentious matter to decide which religions deserve to be called rational, and which the most rational of all. However, it would be definitely wrong to claim that the state or (what here amounts to the same thing) the government is justified in raising the religion they think the most rational to a *ruling position*, if this means that those who hold this faith will, for that reason alone, be accorded certain privileges that other citizens do not enjoy. For, as has been said, this would lead those who think otherwise to hypocrisy or to talking themselves into something against their conscience. It is only true if it is understood as saying that the members of the government should apply all allowable means, especially instruction, in order to spread ever wider the religious opinions that they believe to be the most rational and beneficial. On the other hand, it is also true that they may and indeed should strive to banish through enlightenment all religious opinions that seem incorrect and harmful. It by no means follows from this that they should persecute people who are unfortunate enough to have such mistaken ideas or expel them from the state. If their behaviour is in accordance with the laws of the state, then they may be tolerated, until one succeeds in gradually teaching them something better. Should, however, they wish to do things contrary to the laws of the state, one will certainly be justified in punishing them. It is another question if and under which circumstances the government could justifiably count among forbidden actions the communication of religious opinions that seem mistaken to them. Here one must consider just how dangerous a teaching is, as well as the way one seeks to spread it and the people one addresses. Here the government should do less rather than more. How unfair it would be, for instance, to forbid the expression of an opinion that, although it seems incorrect to the government officials, nevertheless brings comfort and consolation to those who think it correct! How unjust to interfere with someone who seeks to spread his views not through tricks of persuasion but rather by peaceful explanation, regardless of whether or not his reasons are correct. How cruel to prevent parents from raising their children in what they think the only saving faith if it is in fact not entirely irrational. Thus one can claim in general neither that the government is justified in working in any way they please against everything that seems to them to be scepticism or superstition, nor that they have a duty to tolerate everything of this kind. Rather, it all comes down to a question of degree here, and only by considering all the circumstances and weighing as precisely as one can the good and bad consequences will one be able to decide what is to be done in a given case.

CHAPTER 8

On education and instruction

It naturally falls to parents to care for and raise their children, and what they can and almost always do accomplish in this respect, provided that they themselves have been properly brought up, cannot possibly be accomplished in any other way, in particular not in a boarding school. Thus in the best state, too, the care and rearing of children will be entrusted to their parents. Only when one or both parents show themselves unfit for childrearing (e.g. are given to depraved conduct or violent bursts of temper) may the children be taken from them and entrusted to different parents in another town—this so that the growing children do not learn too early and to their shame the true reason why they were taken from their parents. So too it is obvious that children who have lost their parents while young shall be handed over to other parents for the completion of their upbringing, people who perhaps have no children, or who wish to raise more.

All children who are mentally and physically capable shall be sent to schools that will see to their further education. There will be at least one such *elementary school* in every municipality of one hundred families or so, employing two or three teachers. The children shall attend these schools until they are fourteen or fifteen years old.

In my opinion, the instruction of every citizen, male or female, should cover the following subjects:

a) Instruction in the use of the senses, sensory discrimination, reflection, exercises in the use of the senses of touch, smell, sight, hearing, and taste.

b) Physical exercise, e.g. running, walking on a balance beam, swimming, climbing, sliding on ice, climbing up and down ladders, lowering oneself on a rope, jumping over ditches, etc. These exercises are for both sexes, but they will do them separately. They will be organized to promote health and skill in helping others in danger.[1]

c) Religion, namely the religion that the officials believe to be the most rational, provided that the parents give their permission.

[1] Although these exercises are done principally in childhood, they should be continued in later years as much as the promotion of health and the maintenance of the acquired skills requires.

d) Natural history: not the infinitely many genera and species, but rather the most noteworthy animals, plants, and minerals; especially as much knowledge of the human body as is necessary for

e) learning everything about hygiene and medicine that is useful for a person to know.

f) Arithmetic, geometry, mechanics, and natural science—as much of these sciences as can be usefully applied by everyone; also astronomy, principally the parts that serve to make the amazing size of the universe and God's wisdom in ordering it more obvious.

g) Reading and writing.

h) Singing, when interest and talent are present; so too instrumental music of various kinds.

i) Correct expression in one's mother tongue, and along with this instruction in another language, namely, the language that the nations may have agreed to use in their mutual communication,[2] as some once wished to promote Latin for this purpose.

k) From history only a few fragments, namely only the most instructive events, e.g. events in the lives of great men, in short only what truly instructs, encourages, warns and promotes contentment with the current state.

l) Some geography

m) The laws of the state, as far as they may be understood at this age.

n) Finally, every young person shall learn, if not in the school then from someone in the community, some handcraft or other that he can use to earn all or part of his living, or at least can put to good use in his free time.

Some will perhaps doubt that as many subjects as I have enumerated here can be taught in so few years. I will be so bold as to claim that with an appropriate method of instruction and the necessary aids it would be an easy matter to teach all of these subjects in a period of five to six years even to students of merely average ability, and this even with a teacher whose aptitude for his job is in no way extraordinary. Provided he has good morals, common sense, a cheerful disposition, a love of his profession, and is appropriately instructed in how his teach-

[2]Everything that should be read by educated people across the entire globe shall be written in this language.

ing should proceed, he will accomplish even more than I have promised. As I cannot possibly give an exhaustive proof of this claim here, I will only remind you of the following points. One of the most important conditions of the success I promised is that one must introduce the items to be learned in the appropriate order. This order is, however, by no means the one by which we classify knowledge as belonging to the different sciences, and present them in treatises. Rather, in educating children, at first we may and indeed should unite truths from the most diverse fields and present them together so that their variety will delight the child's mind and employ all its powers. In this way, each new truth is made more understandable and attractive by the ones that have preceded it, so that not merely dead learning, but rather a living and fruitful conviction, is achieved. Things would be made much easier were textbooks and readers available in which these truths are presented in the order that the children are supposed to learn them, and to this end are clothed in the form of stories or dialogues. This last feature is imperative especially for moral and religious truths, which can only be made vivid and thus usefully learned by leading the child through certain experiences, or by portraying them to his imagination in a lively story. Finally, it goes almost without saying that besides books there must also be many other aids to learning, pictures, models and the like, and that the children must be taught how to find out about all the things that they cannot find in their own surroundings.

Yet another worry arises here. For supposing that it is possible to absorb all the enumerated subjects through the instruction that every citizen receives from his earliest youth, one might still wonder whether it is *advisable* to do so. Could not much of this knowledge, if so widely known, cause more harm than good? This seems to be the case especially with respect to medicine. The little that one could teach here, it will be said, can only produce dabblers who, in the proud delusion that they can do without proper medical advice, will sooner of later attempt to treat themselves or others, only making worse an illness that has broken out. And isn't it a bad thing when people who are suffering from incurable diseases are themselves able to recognize the symptoms? How many people, finally, are struck with fear whenever they notice something in themselves that bears even the slightest resemblance to the symptoms of some disease, and indeed make themselves ill through their imaginings and their anxiety?

I too have no desire to produce people who have only smatterings of knowledge. But this does not always result when one knows only half of the propositions of a science. Rather, when we wish to reproach someone for being a dabbler, we should do so only when he has learned a few truths torn from the body of some science in such a way that he doesn't properly understand them and is incapable of applying them properly (or rather, that he draws false conclusions from them). But this can and should be avoided in any instruction, no matter how fragmentary. Above all, we must see to it that the students gain a proper understanding of what they learn, and warn them in advance against false conclusions they might draw therefrom by showing them that these by no means follow from those propositions. If one also proceeds cautiously with the few things that are to be taught concerning medicine, there will be no need to fear that anyone thus instructed will think the advice of a doctor dispensable when it is in fact necessary. Rather, they will set a higher value on their health than most people today, even the educated; they will be able to describe their condition to a doctor more precisely, to follow his instructions more conscientiously, and take more appropriate steps when things occur in his absence. Moreover, when knowledge of the symptoms of an incurable disease is of no use to a non-physician, e.g. if it can not help him to protect himself against the disease, then for precisely this reason the facts concerning these symptoms should not be selected from medicine to be generally taught. But we must never forget how many other truths there are in this science whose knowledge could have helped many thousands to preserve their lives and their health, had they only been conveyed to them. If, finally, we encounter people who are so fearful that any medical knowledge imparted to them will only upset them, we remark that such people are rare, and are in fact ill, which they most likely would not be if from childhood on they had better knowledge of the principles underlying the maintenance of good health. In any case, let us therefore include part of medical science among the subjects to be generally taught in the schools of the best state.

Children who show exceptional ability and desire for further education shall be sent to *higher schools*, but only with the permission of the county or provincial officials, for only they will be in a position to know whether there are already too many students. As it is impossible to learn everything that is useful for life at the young age for which the general schools are intended, it is necessary to make provision for further instruction after leaving these schools. For those who do not enter the higher schools, instruction shall be available in *holiday schools*. I will give this name to institutions where young men and women who have finished elementary schools receive instruction on the days set aside for rest from physical labour (for there must be such days in the best state, just as we have our Sundays). Here they shall learn about all the things they could not grasp as children. At certain times, the young women will be separated from the men, and taught by women. As this instruction is only to take place on holidays, it will be an easy matter to find a number of people in the community to help out here.

Now people should continue to develop their minds as long as they live. As the greater part of what is generally useful can be learned quite well from books, provided the ground has been well prepared by oral instruction in the elementary and holiday schools, every citizen shall be given the opportunity to read useful books. To this end, there shall be a library in every municipality containing all the books that may be of some use to this community, and several copies of the most useful books. In such a collection shall be found first of all works that are suitable for developing, completing and strengthening ideas of true wisdom, truths concerning the calling of mankind, our duties and obligations, the true essence of human happiness, and the different values of earthly goods. There will also be books that serve to fortify our belief in God, the immortality of the soul, and revelation. There will be books to teach parents and teachers the art of education and instruction, books that inform citizens on the institutions and laws of the state, the reasons why these have been introduced, and on the principles according to which they themselves should use the influence on government that is granted them, etc. In municipalities whose members are occupied with farming or other industries, there shall be no lack of books from which advice concerning these matters may be gleaned. Finally, there shall also be no lack of books whose principal purpose is simply to entertain, provided that they are not damaging to morals, and do not promote depraved ways of thought.

Now a word on the *higher schools*. I use this name for all the institutions in which something more is taught than in the elementary and holiday schools. It will be seen that there must be many such schools, and that they must be of various kinds. For however true it may be that much of what is read to students from the lectern at our current universities could be just as easily read by the students themselves, there are other subjects that are much more easily learned through oral instruction, and which accordingly merit the establishment of professorships. A few examples are: logic, metaphysics and other philosophical disciplines, mathematics, physics, and medicine. As the students enter these higher schools at an age that is still quite young (namely, 15 to 16 years old), it is necessary to supervise them carefully; this will be best entrusted to the teachers themselves, or in any case to certain assistants of theirs. Given the awakening of the sex drive at this age, and the fact that the young people will no longer be able to live in their parental home (that is, if the location of the institutions does not happen to be where their parents live), it will be most advisable to isolate them somewhat from the rest of the citizens of the town, especially from those of the female sex, and to restrict them to the company of other students, the teachers, and their assistants. On the one hand one must see to it that the young people make use of all the characteristic advantages that the *great number* of students coming from all parts of the country brings—namely, that they will make the acquaintance of all the others. Since this acquaintance continues in later years, it will put them in a position to nominate appropriate individuals for posts that require higher studies. Furthermore, the students will be able to emulate the good qualities they notice in others, and use their faults as a warning. Finally, those who are truly outstanding (and when there are so many students, there are always bound to be a few) will be able to set an inspiring example, and thus to exercise a truly beneficial influence on the rest. On the other hand, one must prevent a few bad people from taking advantage of the students living so close together to gain power to disrupt and torment the others; one must also make sure the students do not believe they are too closely observed or that their freedom is overly restricted—although in fact they must be observed and their freedom limited. All of this might best be achieved if the students were to be allowed to find lodgings in the city, living, say, three to a room, and allowed to choose their own roommates as long as no complaints are raised against them for abusing this freedom. Furthermore, the students should be required to have their midday meal together, at common tables, with their teachers and their assistants at the head. On days and hours set aside for relaxation, the students should amuse themselves together. Finally, the most reliable students shall be permitted from time to time to point out the misbehaviour that may have crept in here and there. It shall be the duty of the teachers and their assistants to visit students (either their own or the students of other teachers) in their lodgings, in order to see how they are living. They shall also have the right and the obligation to examine the students at least once every half year, and if they become convinced, from these examinations or otherwise, that a student is not applying himself appropriately, or is going astray, or lacks the talent required for study, then they shall be entitled to expel him, the sooner the better. If the young man believes that he has been wrongly accused of not having sufficient knowledge in his field, then several (perhaps two more) teachers will be asked to examine him together, since such examinations are always best conducted in the presence of several persons. It is stipulated, however, that in such examinations the student is not to be questioned on the system of this or that individual scholar (say, the teacher's), but rather on the branch of learning itself, and especially those of its doctrines that are demonstrably applicable. Incidentally, no grade for his knowledge of this or that field that a young man received in his early years of study is to be cited as conclusive proof that he still possesses this knowledge. Rather, if he is seeking a position for which this knowledge is an indispensable requirement, he must submit to a new examination.

Chapter 9

On caring for health and life

Life and health are goods of the greatest importance, since they are conditions upon which the enjoyment of almost all the others depends. For this reason, a well-constituted state will devote everything it can to ensure that its citizens enjoy these goods as long as they can. Concerning the sacrifices that the state is prepared to make in order to save a man's life, the following principle shall be observed: no sacrifice made in order to save a man's life is too great, unless it were to result in the loss of another *equally important* human life. I call two lives equally important when the sum of happiness that their possessors show promise of either themselves enjoying on earth or spreading among others is equal. Thus for example, I call the life of a mother more important than that of her unborn child, because the latter would have little hope of surviving and living to a mature age, even if it were to be saved through the death of its mother. According to this principle no objection would be made in the best state when an enormous amount of food stuffs were used up in order to save the life of one man—unless, that is, no other means were known of taking care of the needs of the people who could have been nourished by this food.

The most common causes of the illness and premature death of so many lie in the circumstance that not many people come to know the conditions for maintaining health and certain other generally useful medical truths early enough in life. Hence, as I already said, children shall be taught the portion of these truths that can be learned in childhood at the elementary schools of the best state. More shall be taught to adolescents in the holiday schools. And in the legally ordained libraries of each municipality books shall be available, from which adults may obtain further instruction and also advice for cases that arise. Besides these books, there will be at least one doctor for every municipality who shall be obliged to live in the community, to be on the lookout for anything that might be dangerous either to the life or to the health of the citizens, and to take care of people who have fallen ill. When contagious diseases break out, or in other cases where it can be useful to collect information, the doctor shall be required to make a report to the College of Physicians for the entire province, and so on. Whether there is something in the activities of citizens, in their nutrition, their amusements, briefly, in their way of life that is harmful to life and health shall be considered a perpetual problem for all doctors and also for anyone else who is able, perhaps by chance, to answer such a question.

A sick person may, if he prefers, be cared for at home, provided that this can be done adequately and he is not threatened with a contagious disease. Others shall be brought to the hospital, one of which shall be found in each municipality, where people shall look after them who, on account of their advanced age, have less to fear from infection. Every doctor has the right and the obligation to call in several other doctors from the surrounding area in difficult or particularly instructive cases. The most useful drugs and medical instruments, devices for reviving apparently dead people, suitable morgues, etc., will be found in every municipality.

No one who needs medical attention shall be required to pay anything either for the doctor or for medicines or the care he receives. These costs are borne instead by the municipality, which in case of need shall be further supported by the county or the province according to principles of which more shall be said shortly.

The more a doctor distinguishes himself through his diligence in the care for the sick, the acuity with which he removes causes that lead to illness, the successful outcomes of his cures, and through the decreased mortality in the municipality, the more he shall be praised by the community as well as the officials of the whole country.

CHAPTER 10

On citizens' property

I come now to the development of the principles according to which, as I see things, the *property* of citizens should be determined in a well-constituted state. I concede in advance that on this point my ideas diverge furthest from received views, but I may add that I have again and again examined in a variety of ways my claims that differ from the opinions of others. I thus have some right to demand that my readers not immediately reject what on account of its unfamiliarity will not at first glance seem reasonable.

It is quite obvious, and acknowledged even under the worst constitutions, that above all the state has the authority to determine the circumstances under which a thing may become and remain our property, or under which we may at least enjoy a right to its *use* for a certain time. It is well known that there have even been civil communities that did not wish to allow their citizens to own even the least amount of property. They certainly went too far, for much good derives from granting genuine property rights to certain things at least to those who are of age. If, however, one wishes to know what *highest principle* the state should follow in the business of granting property rights, it is easy for me to furnish one to which no one will have much to object. It runs as follows: a given object may only be declared to be the property of a certain person when it is more conducive to the good of the whole to grant rather than deny him this property right.

In my view a good many consequences flow from this principle. Until now these have only rarely been recognised, but I nevertheless believe that they should be regarded as just so many laws according to which property is allocated in a well-constituted state. Only the most general of these shall be set out here, each accompanied by a brief justification.

1. A thing that can be usefully employed only by a certain individual, and is of no use to anyone else, should for that very reason be recognised as the property of the first alone. There will be no great objection to the correctness of this first law. Indeed, people have followed this law in innumerable cases, whether or not they were clearly aware of it. Why else, for instance, do we declare the limbs of our body, indeed the body itself that our soul inhabits, our property, but for the reason that we can use our own body in a way that no one else can?

2. On the other hand, a thing that is either of no use at all or can provide only some insignificant service to a certain person, while it can be of great importance to another, may never be permitted to become or remain the property of the former in a well-constituted state. Thus for example, no one would allow a blind person who has no hope of regaining his sight to buy the most magnificent paintings, and thus to deprive others of their use. That one already proceeds according to this rule in today's states, albeit only in the most flagrant cases, can be shown from a variety of cases. Suppose, for example, that someone had bought up all the quinine in the world and out of sheer cruelty wished to dump it all in the ocean so that sick people could no longer make use of its curative powers. He would certainly be prevented from doing this in every state, by force if necessary. What else does this mean but that one does not consider this quinine to be truly his property? It is indeed true that I cannot do everything I like with my property, e.g. I am not permitted to do things with it that will interfere with others' use of their property. Nonetheless, if something is completely my property, then no one has the right to object to any changes I make to it merely on the grounds that these changes will reduce or destroy the capacity of this thing to be useful to others. But this is precisely what the state believes to be justified in the case of the alleged owner of the quinine, namely, to forbid him from making any changes to this product which would destroy its usefulness for mankind. It is, admittedly, true that in today's states such a buyer is allowed to make a great many changes to the goods he has purchased. Thus he is free to name the price at which he is willing to let go of them—unless, that is, he sets this price disproportionately high. For precisely this reason it may be said that in today's states this merchant is granted a certain property right (although not a complete one) over his wares. This merely indicates that the principle I have set out is not now followed in its complete scope. For the present it suffices to note that we follow it approximately, and without stating it. Indeed, perhaps without being clearly aware of it, we have introduced measures that can really only be justified by appealing to it. In the best state, it will be fitting to go somewhat further. Here this principle must not only be expressly stated, but all measures and laws dealing with the property of citizens must be directed by it.

3. It follows from this, moreover, that in the best state one will by no means consider the fact that *someone is the first to find something that had no owner until then* as a sufficient basis to give him the right to own it. For does it really follow that the person who has found something is also the one who will make the best use of it? As laughable as this is, it is equally foolish everywhere and always to make the discoverer of something its owner. In today's states people have actually recognised the unsuitability of this rule, and for this reason have not accepted it without a variety of restrictions. Thus, for example, someone who discovers a buried treasure is awarded at most a third of it as his property. But who can fail to see that this one third share is determined completely arbitrarily, and moreover, is often either too great or too little for the only goal one might reasonably have had in mind here, namely, to encourage people to seek such things and to report their finds. Thus, for example, one third would be far too much recompense for the pains of a farmer who happened to find a large nugget of gold while digging a well, yet still an insufficient incentive to cause him to report his discovery, as he may hope to keep the entire thing for himself undetected. And if, on the contrary (as would be the case under the arrangements of the best state) this hope were to fall by the wayside, then it would once again be excessive to give a third in order to encourage people to report their finds. A finder's right is therefore something that is entirely unknown in the best state. But the merit of *searching*, if it is intentional and based on unselfish motives, as well as of honest *reporting* of what has been found shall be recognised. If these activities are not their own reward, they shall both be appropriately honoured and compensated—the former even if it is not crowned with success. And do we really need yet another lengthy examination of the pernicious influence this prejudice of a finder's right has on people's frame of mind? For even if the state places numerous restrictions on this right, these are seen only as unwarranted intrusions, and people are not inclined to be subjected to them. Also, nothing is more natural for one who believes that his finding of something that had previously had *no owner* gives him a right of ownership than to convince himself that finding something that did have an owner but was *lost* entitles him to at least a very considerable *share* of this property right. And how strongly must he feel tempted to withhold what he has found, either in whole or in part, from its rightful owner.

4. In addition, the *labour* applied to an object, through which something is transformed from a useless into a useful item, may not be seen in the best state as a sufficient basis for the creation of a property right. It is certainly true that someone who has transformed an object into something useful through his labour deserves to be rewarded for this work. But it by no means follows that this compensation must take precisely the form of a right of ownership of the thing, for it is in no way obvious that this thing is most useful precisely for him, or even whether it has any value at all for him. Nor should one say that someone who manufactures a good must at least be recognised to have a property right in it when he made it precisely with the intention of enjoying it himself. Neither should one fear that were this not the case all incentive for work and for manufacturing useful goods from natural raw materials would fade away. No, in order to make people inclined to work, it suffices to give them the security of knowing that they shall not remain uncompensated for their labour, that they shall be able to enjoy, if not the good they have themselves produced with their labour, at least some other good of equal or higher value. For this goal it is neither necessary nor sufficient to make the object their property. Not necessary, because in most cases when a man makes something for his own use through work on raw materials, it does not matter to him whether in the end he receives precisely this thing or some other that serves equally well. Not sufficient, because in certain cases, even if we were to grant the person who had manufactured it from raw materials a complete right of ownership to the produced good, the enjoyment to be expected might be far too uncertain to motivate him to undertake this labour. Thus it little serves a poor farmer who is supposed to cultivate the earth to promise him the right of ownership of the fruits of his labour, when the probability that his work will result in something is not better than chance. The state, on the other hand, could promise the farmer full compensation for his labours in any case of failed harvest and still be certain of winning rather than losing on the whole, provided that such undertakings are successful more often than not. In fact, despite the wrongheaded ideas legal theorists have about this subject, in all states customs have been introduced that are more or less in line with what I have said. Only very rarely is the person whose labour transforms raw materials into something useful regarded as its owner; in most cases, he is simply compensated for his effort. And

even the scholars cannot downplay the appropriateness of this practice, but want to bring it into harmony with their systems. The state, they explain, only denies the producer of a certain good a property right over it when in producing his wares he uses something else (be it as a material, or a tool, or something of another sort), which, though useless in itself, is yet not his property, but someone else's. Thus for example, it was believed that the question of why the metal that a miner extracts from the bowels of the earth does not belong to him was answered by pointing out that the earth in which the metal was found did not belong to him, and so on. A little further reflection shows the insufficiency of such explanations. For if it is on this basis that the ore extracted by the miner is supposed not to belong to him, then with what right do we appropriate the fowl and the fish we catch, no matter where they may have come from? Quite generally, some consideration of the way in which we have divided the goods of the earth among ourselves will make it obvious to anyone who hasn't made up his mind in advance that we have in fact followed far different rules than those cited by legal theorists, that we have attempted to grant to each person as his property the things he can best make use of, and that we have only departed from this rule where the satisfaction of the greed of certain individuals demanded more. That the demands of greed will carry no weight in a well-constituted state goes without saying.

5. The principles I have spoken of in the preceding have not remained entirely unknown in today's states, and indeed have already been followed to a certain extent. Not even this much can be said for the further rules I have to add here. Indisputably there are a great many objects whose possession people value above all else, where yet the most painstaking research discloses no other reason for this evaluation than the *extreme rarity* of such things. This is so true, that we occasionally use the words *rare*, *valued*, *costly*, *dear* as synonyms. There is no need to inquire here into the reason for this. We must, however, ask whether the citizens of a well-constituted state may be allowed to abandon themselves to this human predilection for everything rare. Should a single individual, either by chance or for some other reason, e.g. by bidding the largest sum of money, be able to acquire a right of ownership over something that can have value for no other reason than scarcity? I believe I must answer no to this question. Anything that has a value for certain people merely on account of its rarity is for that very reason not

suited to be the possession of a single individual, but is rather to be considered the property of the entire community, and is to be used, depending on what sort of thing it is, either for public celebrations, or for decorating public buildings, etc. I believe I can offer the following reasons in justification of this rule: an object that we are moved to possess only on account of its rarity would by its very nature afford no real advantage to an individual who was allowed to own it, but might well lead him into vanity, boasting, foolish expenditures and many other faults. Other citizens, by contrast, would find themselves dissatisfied with their lot, which had denied them the possession of this object, and would feel envy and resentment against whomever happened to be its owner. Examples that prove this are daily before our very eyes. A diamond is, as everyone knows, of no more use than a piece of glass for the purpose we have in mind when we set so high a value on it; it is valued so highly only on account of its rarity. And what idiocies, what crimes many thousands have been drawn into because of the high value placed on them, and the permission granted citizens in all present states to acquire such jewels as their property! How much damage has been wrought by this single perverse arrangement even in the most developed states! All of this will be prevented once and for all as soon as the state declares that no object that is desired by people simply on account of its rarity may be the property of an individual, but must rather be turned over to the municipality by its discoverer, maker or present owner as a piece of property that only it is entitled to own. It will readily be seen that, with a few changes, this law can and must be extended to objects that besides being rare possess a certain usefulness, but which are valued and desired principally on account of the former. These too shall not be allowed to be the property of individuals, but rather shall be appropriated from their former owners for a reasonable price. These rules by no means cover things that are especially valued by an individual for reasons other than their rarity (no matter how rare they may be), e.g. a pocket watch of singular appearance that a son wishes to possess in memory of his father, who used to carry it, etc.

6. A still more important consequence that flows from the highest principle stated at the beginning is that everyone shall be free to renounce a personal legal property right to a certain thing, but not to transfer it to someone else simply because the latter is willing to accept

it. If this were allowed, i.e. if all citizens were permitted to exchange all the property allotted to them in any way whatsoever, then even if the state had originally distributed property in the best possible way, someone might soon come to own things he knows how to use only poorly or indeed not at all to further his own or the general good—in clear violation of the general principle and its consequences. Thus if property rights are to be bound to rational rules, the right to sell as well as the right to give away property must also be limited by certain reasonable rules, as the former are partly dependent on the latter. A certain dim perception of these rules may already be found in our states, since there are in fact several regulations that limit the right of giving or selling in certain cases (although these resulted from an entirely different intention).

7. And just as the possessor shall not be accorded the right to transfer his property to others as he sees fit, so too shall he not be allowed to *lend* it, i.e. to give it to another for a certain purpose or for a certain time, with or without payment. For such acts of lending already confer a certain kind of property right, namely the right to use the borrowed article for the specified time. An unlimited freedom of lending, misused by the citizens of a state, could cause many problems. Think, for instance, of the mischief that can result from an ill-considered loan of a book to someone for whom it is not written!

8. Thus in a well-constituted state it shall also not be permitted that someone advance *money* to others as he sees fit. For how harmful are the things that many could do with the *money* they borrowed from their fellow citizens without the knowledge of society! The state shall ban this in general, and mete out appropriate punishment to both lender and borrower when the law is broken. On the other hand, there must be an arrangement whereby anyone who has a surplus of money can invest it in the state (namely, in the municipality), and anyone who wants to have money can borrow it from the state, provided that he has adequate collateral, and there is reason to believe he will put the money to good use. Whoever invests money must receive a certain, quite moderate, amount of interest, (e.g. approximately 1/2 percent), and when he invests more, shall be paid a little less interest. The borrower, for his part, will have to pay a similar rate of interest.

9. Our principle has another consequence of considerable importance, namely, that in a well-constituted state children should by no means be seen as the rightful heirs of the property their parents owned. Rather, the state shall consider itself to be the sole heir and behave accordingly (first of all the municipality; but for items of more general usefulness, the county or even the entire province, etc.). This measure too is already to be found in the principle that only someone who shows promise of making the best use of a thing for himself and others should be allowed to acquire a property right over it. For it is as plain as day that it will not always be the children who show the most promise of making the best use of what their parents once possessed. Haven't we all seen enough examples of exactly the opposite? Granting children the right to inherit from their parents, which we unfortunately see in all present states, inevitably brings with it the most harmful consequences. When one allows children to inherit from their parents, is it any wonder that we find thousands of children who are depraved enough—I would not claim to promote, but at least to long for, their parents' death? When children know that they will inherit from their parents, then all children whose parents' wealth is impressive find themselves in constant temptation, wasting their precious youth, which should have been devoted to the acquisition of useful knowledge, in idleness and dissipation. And however one may encourage them to be diligent, they still lack the most powerful inner motivation, that of need. As a consequence, they with few exceptions show no real enthusiasm, and for the most part, despite the best external circumstances, learn very little. If children are allowed to inherit from their parents, then single families can through mere chance become enormously wealthy, while many others become poor; and we have already spoken about how harmful such great inequalities in the distribution of wealth can be. But if the wealth of parents is not to flow directly to their children upon their death, then it is obvious that it must come to the state (first of all, the municipality). It is quite understandable that no one has so far ventured to introduce such a measure in our present states, even though it must have presented itself to certain officials as a welcome opportunity for personal enrichment, and that on the contrary even very reasonable people, when they hear of this proposal, cannot at first glance come to accept it at all. There are two natural reasons that have given rise in all states to the children's right to their

parents' estate. First, the children are usually closest to the parents, and thus best able to take possession of what they leave behind. Second, it is generally the case that parents most prefer that their property not be left to strangers, but rather to their own children, and that this provides a strong incentive diligently to earn and save, for they believe themselves able in this way to look after their children after their own death. This certainly makes sense when the appropriate precautions are not taken, namely, when steps have not been taken to prevent the absurdity of having the inheritance that is taken away from these children misused to fill the coffers of people who need and deserve it far less than they; when the state does not find new parents for children who still require care and supervision because their parents died early, parents who will look after them as if they were their own; when there is not an inviolable law stating that the money the state receives from such inheritances shall not be applied to any other end until all children have been looked after. For woe to him who strikes down an existing institution without putting something better in its place! Only from the praiseworthy fear of making an existing evil still worse could so many reasonable people who did not completely overlook the imperfections of the customary right of inheritance still fail to recommend any changes to it. Others are perhaps moved by other reasons to leave everything as it stands. They saw that only in this way could their hope of holding on to inherited wealth through many generations come to fruition. But it is obvious that such self-interested reasons should not stop us from introducing a better arrangement once mankind is ready for it. Once this moment of readiness has arrived, when the measure that I here propose can be introduced, not by itself, but in conjunction with all the others that belong in the best state, will the worry no longer arise that one would be removing one evil only to replace it with a greater one. By the way, it scarcely needs mentioning that when I do not even extend to children the right to inherit from their parents, I deny this right all the more to people in other situations. Just as no living person is authorized to transfer ownership of his property as he will, so too he is denied this right in *death*, i.e. no one may take the liberty of stipulating who shall have one or another of the things he possessed while alive. The state alone has this right. To it flow the goods of those who have died so that they may be put to more general use. One may only *inherit* items that are solely of subjective value, objects that serve as mementos of their former owner in the eyes of his friends and admirers. Mementos that have in addition some external value can only be inherited conditionally, i.e. if the state approves, and is compensated.

10. Everyone knows that there are also objects that are not *destroyed* when they are used, i.e. do not become unusable for others, but rather can be used by many people, either simultaneously or at different times. Objects of this sort are: a painting, which can very well be contemplated by many people, either together or one after another; a book, which hundreds can still read after one person has read it; a house, which after one person has lived in it, can still provide lodging for another; a musical instrument, which only gets better through long use; and many others. I say of objects of this sort that in a well-constituted state they may never be considered the property of a single individual. Rather, only a right of use shall be granted, and this sometimes only for a certain period of time. When, as in present states, one does more than this, and grants individuals a true property right to such objects, this inevitably confuses people's ideas, and introduces a number of most harmful abuses. The owner now believes that he has the right to destroy the object that is called his property if he sees fit, to allow others to use only it under the strictest conditions, or indeed not at all. As a consequence, innumerably many objects that, if used by many people as their nature allows, would have been incomparably more useful to mankind, either lie about unused, or else produce less than a thousandth part of the benefit they might have. What is more, we are compelled at the very least to acquire a property right over (i.e. have to purchase) such an object in order to use it, which understandably gives rise to a great many difficulties. Such things are moreover bought up by the wealthiest citizens in order to flaunt rather than to use them. Finally, the people who could make the most important and generally beneficial use of them are precisely those who have to do without them. Who is not spontaneously reminded here of libraries, natural history collections, artworks, and other such costly things that, were they not the property of single individuals, could be used by all who have a sense for them? Under the arrangements that now exist, we should indeed be very happy and grateful for the magnanimity of our rich fellow citizens, who do not begrudge us at least a partial use of such things under certain circumstances. But we must

be horrified when we consider what the rich might do (and according to the current ideas of legal theorists are permitted to do), should they be malevolent enough to wish it. Could they not, if they wanted, commit the most excellent libraries to the flames after buying them, just like the famous Omar? Could they not buy up and suppress all copies of a highly important book just because they felt like it? Can not the same be said of paintings, artworks, and hundreds of other things, through whose suppression humanity would suffer an irreparable loss? Is it not terrible that we entrust the keeping and maintenance of such treasure to the discretion of a few, indeed to mere chance?

11. It is clear from the foregoing that a well-deserved property right to a given thing may *expire* in the course of time and as circumstances change. For certainly someone who up to now has been best able to make use of a given thing may later lose this ability, while someone else may show up for whom the possession of this thing is far more important. It might also be the case, finally, that it is entirely obvious that more benefit would be produced were the property right to be transferred from the former to the latter than would be the case were it left to the discretion of the former to give his right of enjoyment to someone else. It will depend upon the nature of these circumstances whether the state shall simply transfer the property right without any compensation, or whether the previous owner must be compensated for the loss he now suffers. If, for example, someone cultivates various trees in his garden in order to enjoy their fruits, but his sick neighbour requires such fruit for refreshment, indeed for medicine, and if it is not easily obtainable elsewhere, there can be no doubt that it would be right to require the owner to give the fruit to his neighbour, and that it would at most be necessary somehow to compensate him. If, on the other hand, someone had a monocle that he could no longer use, either because he had grown blind or for some other reason, it would be fair to maintain that he should hand it over to someone else without any compensation—for at bottom he loses nothing in giving away something he cannot use.

12. Finally, the *price* of every good that someone wishes to make his property must be set according to our highest principle, and so too the wages that are to be paid for any service rendered either to the state or to individuals. The most general rules that must be observed in this respect are roughly the following:

a) If someone is entitled to acquire a property right over something and wishes to do so, then the price at which this article can be had depends on two factors: first, whether the article is the property of the entire state (or of an entire municipality), rather than of a single individual; and second, whether the person who desires to own it has another dispensable item, or at least is capable of rendering a service to others through work.

α) If the article that someone wishes to own is not the property of an individual but rather of the entire municipality or the state, and the person who wishes to own it possesses no dispensable articles to exchange for it, then he shall simply be given the article without being required to pay for it, provided that no one else needs it more. If there are several people who are equally needy but the article cannot be given to all of them, then preference shall be given to the one who has thus far rendered the greatest service to the state. Should, however, the person desirous of owning the article possess other, dispensable ones, or should he at least be capable of doing some useful work for the state, then the state shall certainly be justified in requiring either that he exchange some of his dispensable goods for the one he wants to own, or that he incur an obligation to provide some service in the future. Now the question arises: "how much?" The answer to this is the universally valid and obvious: "one is justified in demanding as much as is required by the furtherance of the well-being of everyone." From this it follows that:

i) The demand must not be so great that the one who wishes to own something would rather abandon this wish than pay the price; for in such cases, clearly, no one comes out ahead.

ii) Nor should the demand be so great as to give rise to worry that the buyer will regret his decision, when he realises that he has sacrificed more than he has gained; for no one should be able to complain that the state has duped him, has taken advantage of his passions to get him to make a sacrifice he would never have made had he been thinking clearly.

iii) The more indispensable the desired article is, the more the wish to own it is based on moral reasons. Accordingly the state must do all the more in such cases to make it easier to acquire it. On the other hand, the more dispensable an item is, the more it serves simply to improve the enjoyment of life, or has a value merely on account of people's whims, the more the state can demand, provided that it does not fail to make the person seeking the article aware of this.

β) If the item that someone wishes to own is already the property of another individual, then the state leaves it up to these two to come to terms in the way they think best, provided that no law is broken. They shall be encouraged to make their transaction is a way that is most advantageous for the good of all. The current owner of the object shall, however, be asked to be prepared to give it away without compensation if he himself has no use for it, while the other, who has nothing to exchange for it, truly needs it. Furthermore, it shall not be tolerated that someone take advantage of another's current situation in order to extract something from him that he will later regret having given away. The state's authorized intervention in determining the citizens' property and its exchange is limited only by the concern that it should not go so far as to aggravate the citizens who find the attainment of their self-interested goals hampered by this intervention to a point where the peace and order of the whole is endangered. We should not forget that the citizens of a well constituted state will be all the more inclined to tolerate government intervention the more obviously the aims and results of its activity are good, and the greater their moral improvement through education. In today's states people already put up with a great deal of interference with the property of individuals, even though it is all too obvious that these interventions are made not for the common good, but for the selfish interests of a few.

b) If someone spends his time working on something that is not so much of use simply to himself but rather serves

α) the state or at least to an entire municipality (e.g. acquiring knowledge that will make him useful to hundreds of others), then it behooves the state or the municipality to look after his living expenses during that time at a rate equal to what he could have made had he worked simply for himself at the same level of exertion. We need not spend many words demonstrating the fairness of this rule, but it shows how wrong many other rules are that have either been expressly endorsed or at least tacitly observed. Consider, for example the rule that a service done for humanity deserves a reward directly proportional to its importance, to the scarcity of individuals capable of providing it, to the level of previous knowledge and preparation it requires, to the amount of strength and exertion it demands, etc. It is certainly both fair and intelligent for us to increase the reward we accord to the provision of some service according to these factors, *to a certain degree*. But that the reward should be *directly proportional* to them, that for instance we allocate one hundred times the reward to someone who does something a hundred times more important, is neither fair nor intelligent. For what purpose can such a lavish compensation serve? To encourage a competent person to render an important service to humanity, it suffices to ensure him that he will receive a somewhat exceptional reward, especially since the joy of knowing one has done such an important thing is a far greater reward. When worldly goods increase in direct proportion to the importance of the service rendered to mankind, this only destroys the equality of property that is so necessary in the state. It leads others to envy, casts a shadow over our altruistic impulses, lays snares for our virtue, and leads if not ourselves, then at least others into all sorts of foolishness and vice. It is even more pointless to use scarcity as a measure of the reward due for a service rendered. It is certainly true, on the other hand, that the previous knowledge and preparation required for a given task should not remain without compensation. But it should not be forgotten that in a well-constituted state, if someone devotes a stretch of time to prepare himself for generally beneficial undertakings or to the acquisition of the necessary knowledge, he will already have received encouragement and support during that time. He will not be rewarded for this preparation only when it bears fruit, but rather will already have been partially compensated for it. It is quite right, incidentally, that this compensation was only partial, for that he would be successful in the undertaking he was preparing himself for was by no means assured. But he should rest assured that he is properly rewarded, for he already received some support earlier, when he needed a contribution to his living expenses. But if he was already looked after while he prepared himself, why pay him for this again?

β) Some services that are provided for individuals, e.g. medical care, are often to be paid for by the state (the municipality or the county, etc.). This will be the case when:

i) people would not willingly bring upon themselves the conditions under which such a service is to be provided as soon as they knew that they would receive help free of charge, or at least

ii) it is clearly the case that a greater evil would arise were people compelled to pay for such a service out of their own pockets; and further

iii) only under such an arrangement can those who perform such services for people not depend on mere chance for their support, but rather enjoy comfortable security; and that moreover

iv) those who provide the service can be prevented from becoming lazy and slapdash in their work.

Where these conditions are not met, it shall be left to the individuals concerned to come to terms on the matter of compensation, provided that they break none of the laws of the state. They shall be encouraged to go about this in a way that is not only to their mutual advantage, but also to the greatest benefit of all. What was said above in sections α and β applies here as well.

c) It remains to be said by what means the state is to ensure that the rules enumerated here shall not remain simple pious wishes, but rather be followed by its citizens. Among these, first of all, shall be a small number of *decrees* that clearly set out what may or may not happen in certain cases, e.g. to set out the price of a certain good or the compensation for a certain kind of work at a given time and place. We should also mention here the *openness* that the state strives to ensure in all transactions and contracts between citizens. In particular, it shall be decreed that such dealings must always take place in public (in a marketplace or a bank) and in the presence of several witnesses who are capable of judging whether or not the transaction is fair. If it can be demonstrated that someone intended to make a deal of this sort in secret, e.g. if he had colluded with the other party in order to keep a certain condition secret, then the transaction shall not only be declared null and void, but the guilty party or parties shall also be severely punished and marked with shame.

CHAPTER 11

On money

The advantages afforded by the introduction of a general medium of exchange, or *money*, are far too great to renounce its use in a well-constituted state, since we know a great many more means of controlling its abuse than are currently employed. A *metallic currency* will be used for the most part only in trade with other states, that is, in so far as these states do not accept other forms of money. For internal transactions a simple paper currency or else some other worthless symbol of money will be used almost exclusively. Counterfeiting or imitation will be not be a great concern, as this almost always requires the collusion of several people, and could never happen on a large scale here.

Even in a well-constituted state circumstances could arise that result in significant changes in the *value* of money, i.e. the sum of goods that may be had for a given price. Therefore a law shall be established for individuals as well as for associations of several people stipulating that if they have committed themselves to pay a certain amount of money at a fixed time, they shall be obligated to pay not the nominal value of the debt, but rather a sum equal in value to the amount promised at the time the debt was incurred. But as some wares increase in price at the same time that others fall or rise less sharply, it may often be a contentious matter to determine what value the currency actually has. This decision shall therefore be left to the discretion of the state. It shall draw up a list of the most common necessities for every region of the country, and determine the value of the currency for that region at that time according to the totality of the prices at which these necessaries are to be had.

CHAPTER 12

On citizens' activities and ways of life

No matter how strong the conviction, even in a well-constituted state, that work is necessary and idleness harmful for mankind, still every discovery that makes it possible for some job that formerly required manual labour to be done as well without it and without additional expense of useful materials, shall be regarded as a truly good thing. This judgment will be based on the twofold assumption that (1) under rational arrangements it will always be possible to find enough useful occupation for everyone, and so (2) it will be easy to avoid the evil so often observed in present states, that the introduction of machinery deprives a part of the population of their income. With these assumptions, one of which is valid at least for an indefinite period of time and the other unconditionally, every discovery of the kind described must appear as a gain for mankind, since it puts us in a position to apply our strength to new production that formerly we didn't even have time to think about. Is it not proof how unwise our current arrangements are if on the one hand we must admit that many useful tasks remain largely undone because they require too much labour, while on the other hand we have cause to complain that introducing labour-saving machines leaves people unemployed? We cannot deny that an incomparably greater amount of foodstuffs could be raised on exactly the same soil, if only there were enough hands to plant the seeds one at a time,[3] to hoe the earth as in a garden, to weed at the right time, to clean, to water, etc., and yet we are horrified when someone wants to tell us how a job that presently requires hundreds of labourers could be done by a machine. No, in a rationally constituted state discoveries of this kind could never lead to unemployment; nor would there be any problem assigning to other useful tasks the hands formerly occupied with work that is no longer required.

For this reason it shall never be tolerated in such a state that someone who is demonstrably capable of accomplishing something useful either remain completely idle or else waste his time on useless tasks. Whether someone is working or not, whether he is working on something useful, and whether he could do more, in most cases all this is best judged

[3]How long will the European states allow themselves to be put to shame by the Chinese in this respect?

by those who are closest to him, i.e. the citizens of his municipality. Thus in all but a very few cases the right to judge such matters must be recognised as belonging to these people.

But in order for there to be a strong enough incentive for people not to tolerate laziness, idleness, or completely useless occupations, there shall be a measure according to which each municipality shall be entitled to distribute foodstuffs and other goods, or the general medium of exchange, money, among its members according to their contributions. Members who, on account of illness or weakness are unable to work, e.g. children or old people, shall live at the expense of the entire municipality. Only in cases where the municipality can show that it has a disproportionately large number of such people and is incapable of feeding them all shall it receive help from the county; and similarly the county shall in such cases be helped by the province, etc.

We can usually tell whether someone is healthy and capable of physical labour just by looking at him; in doubtful cases, the opinion of a doctor may be sought.

As for the requirement that an occupation be useful, there are certainly some for which this is difficult to decide. If the work is not physical, even people who are knowledgeable in the field are frequently unable to judge correctly whether or not someone is doing all he can. In such cases, the judgment of experts shall be requested, but also, those whose zeal for the common good and love of work has already been confirmed shall simply be trusted. People who are occupied with work of a kind not already known to be useful, work that is undertaken solely on account of the hope that something useful may come of it, are not always to be maintained only by the municipality, but rather by the county or the entire province, etc. It is obvious that this holds only for certain times, namely, when they are occupied with work that requires the consent of the county or the province. Since good health and a number of other factors require that no one remain continually in the same kind of job (mental work, especially, should not be done constantly, but rather interspersed with physical exercise), everyone in the best state shall learn several kinds of work in his youth, some of them manual, that can be interspersed with his primary work. A scholar, for example, shall not spend all his time at the lectern, but instead shall devote several hours of the day to suitable physical labour. Even today we find that scholars find it necessary to take a number of breaks from their work for the sake of their health and for diversion. But for the most part they waste these hours, e.g. in taking walks, playing chess, chatting over a glass of wine, smoking a pipe, etc. Activities that are demonstrably useless or at least activities that deserve to be supplanted by other, more useful activities, shall be banned by the state, e.g. threshing with flails after machines have been devised for this, the construction of toilsome implements, and the like. People who had hitherto made their living from an occupation that has now become redundant shall be referred to another. If they prove incapable of performing another job, however, or if what they can do does not bring in enough to cover their expenses, then the remainder shall be made up by those who have gained through the new invention. If the profit is not large enough, or if it is not a single individual, but rather the entire state that profits, then the state shall provide this compensation.

From what has been said it follows that many trades, arts, and ways of life that are tolerated in present states without hesitation, shall in a well-constituted state either be completely forbidden or at least so restricted that no one shall be permitted to make them his *sole* activity, i.e. to pursue them as the sole occupation of his entire life. First of all, I say that some occupations will be strictly prohibited in the best state. This includes all those that encourage vanity, lust, and other corrupting passions. Thus, for example, one may not and should not tolerate the production of food and drink that stimulate lust and destroy health and offer them to anyone who is willing to pay. Nor shall it be tolerated that innumerable hands be occupied to produce articles of the most foolish jewellery, such as rings, earrings, and the like, which often involves the destruction of valuable materials, and always involves an unspeakable expense of time and effort, etc. Other occupations are very much worthy of respect, but are of such a nature that they should not be anyone's exclusive occupation, either because this would be unhealthy, or would hinder the all around development of their powers and the progress necessary for one's improvement, or would diminish the enjoyment of life, or finally because it would interfere with the perfection of work that needs to be done. One or more of these cases inevitably arises in the ways of life followed by most of our peasants, labourers, craftsmen, artists and so-called professional scholars. Or perhaps you would care to explain how it is possible, for example, for a man condemned by society to perform physical labour from early morning to late evening throughout the whole year to develop and exercise his mind? How are miners, who spend the greatest part of their time underground, supposed to remain in good health? And what about the many craftsmen in their gloomy rooms, breathing the most toxic fumes, or whose work forces them to hold their bodies in positions that impede the circulation of the blood? An appropriate mixture of occupations would help all of these people immediately. And certainly most of them would opt for such a mixture of their own free will as soon as the wise provision of the state gave them the *opportunity*. The few who, out of ignorance, inertia, or self-interest, are not willing to change their occupations shall have no grounds for complaint if the state compels them to do so—for is this not in their own best interest?

Here the question arises whether poets should be tolerated, that is, people who wish to be nothing other than poets? I will in fact say no, because I believe that no one can successfully occupy himself with poetry exclusively for his entire life. I do not mean to say that the state would not be justified in granting someone who shows outstanding talent as a poet and requires several years to perfect a work an exemption from other obligations, since the same must be granted for other kinds of intellectual work as well. I would, however, claim with great confidence that in a well-constituted state no citizen should be allowed to look upon music, dance, acting, mime, conjuring, and other similar activities as a trade that he can earn a living from—this because, it seems to me, one can become adept enough at all these arts, insofar as they are useful to mankind, without devoting oneself exclusively to them.

In order that a spirit of laziness not insinuate itself into an entire community, in which case one person might find justification for his own inertia in that of others, the following measures shall be in effect: a) the young people shall be sent on trips where they can observe the activities of other communities; b) the judge of public morals and the provincial inspector (of whom more shall be said shortly) shall be charged with determining how diligent people are in every municipality; c) the total amount of work done annually in each municipality shall be published in its annals; d) members of one municipality shall be married to those of another, so that the new members will introduce a better spirit into the stagnant communities, etc.

There is understandably a limit to the number of individuals who can practice a given occupation for the true benefit of society, no matter how useful or indeed necessary it may be. Should too many take up such an occupation, some of them will find themselves forced into idleness by the lack of demand for their labour, or to take up other kinds of work for which they are not suited, or else they will make goods they cannot sell, destroying in the process materials that might have been put to good use. If this evil is to be prevented as much as possible, the state must make sure through surveys which and how many of its citizens intend to devote themselves to this or that occupation. It must from time to time announce which professions and occupations are looking for workers, and which on the contrary are overburdened with them. When more people apply for a given occupation or profession than there is room for, the state must try to make a good selection. Often nothing is more difficult than this choice, for it is not only a matter of which of the applicants is the most suitable for the post, but also of how capable the losing candidates are of doing some other job. It seems to me, therefore, that in the best states this will be done in different ways in different cases. Occasionally, e.g. when the individuals who have applied are well enough known in their municipality, and when there is a sufficiently strong reason to choose one over the others, the municipality itself shall decide. Occasionally, especially in the case of higher professions (i.e. those in which a person, guided only by his conscience, has a wide-ranging influence), when several of the applicants seem equally worthy, or when their aptitude cannot be accurately judged by the great mass of the people, they themselves shall be instructed to decide who shall fill the post. The names of those who voted for the one chosen shall be recorded in the annals of his community, provided that he has discharged this duty honorably. Sometimes one even conducts experiments, and allows one applicant after another to occupy the position for a certain time as a test of his suitability. Sometimes this is done not only as a test, but with the hope that each of the applicants will have his own merits, and so it would be a good thing to keep each of them in the job for a certain time, in order that each could create benefits according to his characteristic abilities. For professions of a certain kind, especially those that are bound up with many hardships, dangers, or sacrifices, as well as those that require qualities difficult to assess by outsiders, a general invitation shall be issued, stating that anyone who feels capable of filling these posts may apply for them. Of this kind are, e.g. the jobs of military leaders in war and the like. Occasionally, when no humanly detectable difference is to be found, the matter can be decided by lot.

If we want to recognise how much better things would be if professions and occupations were filled in this way rather than in the way they are in present states, we will have to remind ourselves of just how perverse present arrangements are. So very little is done to find out what people would be good at, and so little to help them find the path nature has marked out for them. The enormous inequality in the privileges that different professions enjoy, the innumerable distinctions of rank that have been introduced between them, could not have been better designed had one set out in the first place to mislead people in the choice of profession. Is it any wonder that people throng to become members of privileged professions, not wondering what they are good at, but where they are better off, when it is precisely the most arduous work that fetches the worst pay? When there are transactions that bring in a thousand times more than what is earned by honorable people working just as long and often harder? When one citizen enjoys so many privileges and distinctions that others are denied, not because the occupation he chose was more useful, but because it is seen as more noble and exclusive? When someone thinks that his occupation gives him the right to raise himself above another, and this one above a third, etc.?

Finally, it would be a very good arrangement if there were one or several houses in every municipality where there are opportunities to do various kinds of useful work, so that anyone with a spare hour, or someone who wanted a change of work, need only go into such a house in order to find useful work, and also to be rewarded for it. Such houses will be visited with as much pleasure as pubs are today, since there people will be able to look forward not only to activity, but also agreeable company.

CHAPTER 13

On the productive trades

The more certainly it is to be expected that the population of a civil society will increase when it has appropriate institutions, when no unnecessary wars are undertaken, when all due care is taken to ensure the fitness and health of every citizen, and marriages are supported and encouraged, etc., the more seriously one will have to think about how to produce what is required to feed, clothe, and otherwise provide sufficiently for all these people. For this reason, agriculture, the rearing of livestock, and all trades devoted to the production or preparation of such necessaries (I shall call them the *productive* trades) shall be regarded with special attention by the government as well as each individual citizen. And every discovery that increases the amount of goods available for meeting people's needs, or at least for making their lives more pleasant, shall be considered a benefit to the whole society. The same also holds for discoveries that make the production of such goods easier, i.e. make it possible to produce them using smaller amounts of materials, or less labour. In general, in the best state people are both accustomed to and practised in inquiring into the *value* any given thing has for mankind, and also into the *costs* involved in its production. In other words, one is both accustomed to and practised in asking: what can mankind gain in true perfection (in wisdom, virtue and happiness, no matter of which of its members), and what other goods must be given up in order to produce this one? Trades occupied with the production or preparation of objects that turn out on closer examination to cost mankind more than they are worth—e.g. if they serve merely to make life more pleasant (luxury), but involve the destruction of things that are necessary for life— shall be forbidden.

As almost all undertakings on a larger scale cannot be properly done by individuals, but only through the cooperation of many, so too is this the case with most trades, in particular, farming and livestock rearing. Already in today's states such work is rarely done by individuals, but almost always by several people in association. A farmer, for example, does his business in this way when his wife, his children, and several boys and girls help him out. This must also occur in the best state, or rather even more people will work together. But I don't think they will find themselves in such unequal relations to one another as are found these days, between the one or more people called the owners of an estate and their servants, as also between these servants and their subordinates, the so-called peasants and cottagers, and finally the labourers. Rather, everyone who is a member of such an enterprise and works full time on its business, shall also draw an approximately equal share of its proceeds (or if unequal, the inequality shall be in proportion to need); those on the other hand who only devote part of their time to the business will have to be satisfied with a proportionally smaller share. A piece of land small enough so that the work done on it can be easily supervised by one person (I will call it an estate) shall be provided with an appropriate number of workers under the direction of a manager. Again, several such managers shall work together if this is advantageous, etc. Who is supposed to direct, and who is to carry out a certain job, shall be determined in part on the basis of people's abilities, in part on the basis of their wishes. But no one shall be entrusted with the business of management who has not given satisfactory proof of possessing the necessary knowledge and other characteristics during a stay at one of the *model enterprises*, which are operated under the close supervision of the state. As, further, agricultural work has the peculiarity that at various times it requires dramatically different numbers of workers, e.g. at the time of planting and harvest far more are required than at any other time, other people who do not usually work on farms, e.g. craftsmen, artists, and the like, shall be asked to work there during these times, and indeed compelled to do so if they refuse. But they will be compensated for their labour, either by the farmers they helped out, or by the state. But since draft animals as well as people are required in larger numbers during these times, the farmers shall also be helped out in this respect, and it is decreed that in certain months all available horses and teams in the county shall be put at the farmers' disposition.

When damage occurs on an estate due to no fault of the managers or the workers, e.g. when hail wipes out a planting and the like, the workers' monetary losses shall be made good by the entire province. If someone is to blame for the losses, however, he shall be punished accordingly.

If someone wishes to attempt something on an estate that promises to be beneficial, and yet wishes to be insured against damages in case of failure, he shall tell the county or the province of his intention. And if certain experts who are asked to evaluate it approve the experiment, the state will undertake to insure against the losses. In order to prevent the experts from advising against such experiments out of sheer malice, or on the other hand from approving any experiment no matter how ill-conceived, certain rules of evaluation shall be set out, similar to those we shall encounter later when we speak of the censorship of books.

Nothing shall be paid in order to obtain permission to cultivate a piece of land. However, when several people offer to do this work, the choice among them shall be made in one of the ways described in the previous chapter.

As most other arts and crafts can only be properly practised in a social context, what has been said here also applies, with appropriate modifications, in large part to them as well.

CHAPTER 14
On commerce

In the best state, commerce may look forward to an even more thoroughgoing reorganization than the arts and crafts. Among merchants I count all people who stand between the producer of a good and those who are to use it (the consumers), and who draw a certain benefit for themselves from delivering these goods from the one to the other—thus not only the actual buyers and traders, but also their drivers, sailors, shipping agents, moneychangers, etc. It is striking how many such people there are, who furthermore spend most hours of the day in idleness, as, for example, the clerks in a store waiting for a customer to come. Furthermore, the fortunes of these citizens are subject to drastic change, so that they often amass immense wealth and then in no time at all are reduced to beggars, often taking hundreds of men down with them. Thus the question arises whether under more appropriate arrangements the number of the people thus occupied with commerce could be significantly reduced without causing any damage to the comfort of producers and consumers, and then whether their profits might not be made more regular.

I believe that both could very well be accomplished were commerce entrusted not to individuals but rather to the state (first of all to officials of the municipalities, then to those of the counties, the provinces, etc.), in such a way that in future the people who are employed in this work shall receive a fixed salary, roughly in the way that the so-called commision agents, shop-assistants and the like are today paid in a well-run trading house. This arrangement would have further advantages, it seems to me, namely: consumers would be able to find what they needed more reliably, at a lower price, and of better quality; the producers would receive income much more regularly; and an appropriate tax could be collected on the sale of goods, reducing the number of civil servants who would otherwise be occupied in collecting taxes, etc.

Every community must have its own trading (buying and selling) house. Everything made by a producer, whether it be an unfinished natural product or a finished good, shall be brought to this trading house, where he shall be paid a fair price (i.e. a price reflecting the labour that went into its production). Now whoever wants to obtain something shall only have to ask there, and buy it. If a trading house has a surplus of goods, it can send them to other municipalities, or else to the larger trading houses run by the county, which can then distribute them as needed to the municipalities, etc. It is clear that such an arrangement would make it possible significantly to reduce the personnel involved in commerce, for when the profit that is expected from commerce is to go not to an individual, but rather to a municipality, county, or even an entire province, no personnel will be hired beyond those required to deal with the business that comes up (and this business will decrease rather than increase, because of unification). At present, by contrast, the mere hope of pulling in some of the profit from already existing merchants is the reason why far more trading houses are founded than demand requires. For similar reasons, there will be fewer people in the unpleasant business of transporting goods from one place to another. No longer will people see the streets crowded, as they are today, with half-loaded or even empty wagons; nor will they see men and women making day-long journeys in order to bring a basketful of eggs or some other little thing to market. One or several wagons and ships belonging to the municipality will suffice for all of this. But from this it already follows that the costs of commerce will be less, and thus it would be sufficient to add a smaller premium to the prices of goods. Already on account of this, both consumers and producers should be better off; but also, through the unification of so many activities now done by individuals the municipality will be able to counterbalance losses in one transaction with advantages flowing from others. Further, it also has the means of compelling producers to deliver goods in proper condition, while at the same time being able to guarantee that such goods will always be purchased. Finally, it is obvious that under such arrangements no one would be able to enrich himself improperly through commerce, since the profit does not go into the coffers of individuals, but rather becomes the property of the municipality, the county, or the entire province. It is equally obvious that in this way it would be easiest to collect any taxes imposed on the consumption of goods.

One may nevertheless ask how I hope to prevent the many civil servants who must be employed by the state in such a business from misappropriating funds. But even today any good-sized trading house already knows how to do this, if only it is careful enough to prevent its agents from stealing. Hence I believe that the state, with far more means at its disposal for bringing to light any fraud, shall be all the more able to succeed in this. In the first place, an official can pay less than he claims to have paid only for goods whose price varies with their (vaguely defined) quality, e.g. grain of the best, middle or worst kind, etc. Then, in selling, fraud can only occur if the trader foists a faulty good on an unknowledgeable customer, or records a smaller payment than he received. A third sort of fraud, where worse goods are bought at the price of better for the sake of kickbacks, must soon come to light, since it must give rise to a deficit when the goods are resold at the price of the worse. It would be just as easy to discover any fraud involving weights and measures, stealing from the till, etc. Thus only the two sorts of fraud mentioned are to be feared. In the case of many goods, these sorts of fraud could be controlled if precise instructions were set out concerning how many grades were to be recognised, and what their characteristics were. Thus for example textiles, linens and the like might only be prepared at several fixed prices, and a symbol of the price actually woven into them (e.g. a thread of a certain colour on the margin). For goods that this does not apply to, it may be decreed that they are not to be bought or sold except at determined hours of the day in the presence of a municipal *comptroller*. One would not need to be an expert to fill this post, since he would only have to ensure that so and so much was actually paid for such and such goods, and that the transaction was recorded in the books. When, in addition to this arrangement, one ensures that frequently and at uncertain intervals, experts will come to verify everything (an easy enough measure to introduce), scarcely any possibilities for fraud will remain. It also goes without saying that the first discovery of even the slightest dishonesty in one of these civil servants shall cause him to lose his job and to be punished severely—indeed, even a strong suspicion of dishonesty may be grounds for dismissal here.

CHAPTER 15

On scholars

Not all who pursue higher studies must later become professional scholars, whose primary occupation is the production of scholarly works. Rather, they can follow the most varied paths in life; indeed for many occupations, e.g. serving as a judge, only people who have attended certain higher schools shall be considered. Those, however, who do choose the production of scholarly works for their principal occupation, whom I shall simply call *scholars*, must seek the approval of the state, and not simply of an individual municipality, but rather of the province, which shall also pay their living expenses for the time they intend wholly to devote to scholarly works. They shall also be accorded the right to request books and other aids required for their scholarly pursuits. However, when greater expenses are involved, the assent of several others shall be required. The annals will note a scholar's accomplishments, and will mention the cost of supporting his person as well as the outlay for the scholarly materials he used. Finally, scholars may not look upon these books and materials as their own property, but must return them to the province in as useable a condition as possible so that others may use them as well.

As scholars enter into a variety of associations for the sake of pursuing knowledge, the state not only tolerates, but rather seeks to support such associations as much as it can. By no means, however, will members of such a society be allowed to claim certain prerogatives or advantages over others who do not belong to it.

One way to counteract envy and resentful denigration of others (a temptation that is not, unfortunately, all that rare among scholars), is to stipulate that when recounting the progress of human knowledge one make a point of mentioning not only the discoverer of some new truth, but also the names of those who first gave the new doctrine a warm reception, and of those who opposed it, and attempted to suppress it through their mockery.

If a scholar endeavors to spread principles among the young, either by writing or oral instruction, that seem either false or dangerous to the government, he shall be asked to record his claims. He shall give the reasons that speak for their truth and the benefits of spreading them, with the utmost brevity and without any rhetorical dressing, and this essay shall be submitted to the Council of Elders. Should the Elders be unanimous in declaring that they are not convinced by these reasons, but rather still find these teachings to be incorrect and dangerous, then no one can find it unfair if the state forbids such a scholar to spread his views any farther. If it should emerge that he continues to do so in secret, perhaps through oral instruction, the state shall have the right to take away his opportunity to do so, e.g. by removing him from his professorship, etc. Treated thus, he cannot complain that he has been persecuted or hounded, in a way that could have been avoided, into a dishonest renunciation of his principles. Nor shall he find his ability to earn a living endangered, if he can bring himself to do some other useful work for which he is suited.

CHAPTER 16
On books and censorship

As books may never become the property of individuals, they shall be published at the expense of the state. From this it obviously follows that not everything anyone wants to publish shall in fact be printed. Rather, everything shall be first subjected to a preliminary examination, or censorship. A completely unconstrained freedom of the press, as urged by so many today, may well seem desirable in states that still have faulty institutions as a lesser evil to counteract greater ones. But that it can in no way be seen as the most perfect possible arrangement in a state becomes clear from the following considerations.

The printing of a book is not something that happens by itself. It requires a quite considerable expense of time and a no less considerable amount of useful materials. If the book is not merely to appear in print, but actually to be read by many people (and this is the desire of everyone who has something printed), one is also demanding that all these people spend their time to read it, time that may well have been put to better use. Finally, those who urge us to accept an unrestricted freedom of the press no doubt also wish it to be accompanied by an unrestricted freedom to read. Thus once a bad or dangerous book is printed and distributed, one could hardly prevent it causing incalculable damage. Think for instance of the harm that could be caused by just a few pages, were these maliciously to reveal a family's secrets when they should have remained forever hidden for the sake of the family and others; or if they were to impute I know not what disgraceful sins to the most righteous of men; if they distorted the true course of events by publishing a false version that many thousands will believe despite all denials; if they recommended the most abhorrent principles with sweet eloquence, and justified them with the most misleading fallacies, or inflamed the people's bodily desires through the most voluptuous depictions of vice, and so on. Can we make up for the damage caused by a bad book, the considerable time it has stolen from its typesetters, printers, and readers, the false ideas spread by it, the disgust it has caused many readers to feel even about better books, the damage to morals it causes—can we make up for all this merely by punishing its author in whatever way? Can such punishments even hinder the book from causing further damage, as long as one copy remains in the hands of the public? Can one even prevent similar books being written in the future through the warnings given through such punishment?

In my opinion, the following arrangements would be more appropriate. Before it is printed every book must be approved by certain specially appointed censors. These censors shall be entitled to strike out individual passages, or even to suppress an entire book, but only under the following headings:

a) *Licentious* or *harmful to morals*: when a book contains scenes depicting lewdness or other vices in a provocative way, or even defends such vices.

b) *Impassioned*: when a passionate tone, rather than measured words, dominates in a discussion of a topic that is still controversial, and therefore must be investigated in a calm, level-headed way.

c) *Defamatory*: when the good name of someone is attacked, and he is accused of crimes that have not yet been proven.

d) *Unworthy of consideration*: when a book serves neither for instruction nor for enjoyment, e.g. a theory that betrays the author's utter ignorance, or poems that are completely dreadful, etc.

Censors shall only be called to account when they call something good that *obviously* should have been suppressed, or suppress something that *obviously* should *not* have been according to these principles.

An author whose manuscript is either completely rejected or else has had passages struck out can appeal the judgment of the censors to several (e.g. five) others. These censors shall, simultaneously or in sequence, but in any case not knowing of the judgment of the others, be asked for their opinion. This is necessary in order to ensure that no censor suppress something good out of sheer malice.

If it has been shown that a censor has acted from such evil intent, he shall not only be removed from his post, but also branded with shame; he can even be removed from his post if this is merely suspected.

In order to be all the more certain that no book ever shall remain unprinted as long as it contains something useful, each book that even a single censor has recommended shall indeed be printed.

The names of the censors who were either for or against the printing of a book or a particular passage shall be made known in the book when it appears. Everyone shall be free to make recommendations for improvements in the current constitution, criticisms of existing institutions, objections to current religious opinions, etc., provided that they only do so in the measured tone of inquiry, and also in a scholarly style.

An author whose manuscript has been rejected shall be permitted to deposit it in the provincial library, where it shall be registered, and the names of the censors who rejected it recorded.

Sometimes today one has to publish writings accusing someone of crimes that have not yet been proven, because so far no other complainant who would be listened to can easily be found. But this is just a consequence of our faulty constitutions. In a well-constituted state it can never become necessary to raise a complaint against a criminal in the press. Rather, a written complaint delivered to the appropriate office will suffice.

Some call for a complete freedom of the press, but wish to hold the author or publisher responsible for any damages their book causes. But they seem not to have noticed that it is far easier for a censor to justify not having struck out a passage or not having suppressed a book than it is for the author. For the censors must let everything through that is not *obviously* to be banned under one of the above headings. The author, however, would be guilty no matter how well he wrote, whenever he failed to avoid anything that was even likely to prove offensive.

It is indeed surprising that although one hears many complaints about the obstacles that the *government* puts in the way of publishing a work, little is said about the arbitrary power granted to publishers. Is it not a greater evil that it is left entirely up to a publisher (under our current arrangements usually one man, who as a mere businessman pays attention only to his pecuniary interests) to decide whether a book shall be published, in what form it shall appear, and at what price? The worst books often find the most willing publishers, and are most richly rewarded, while the most worthy works sometimes remain unprinted, not because the government decrees it, but rather because no publisher thinks he can make a profit from them—or if they do appear, it is in the most dreadful form, and at an exorbitant price that puts them out of the reach of those who would most profit from them. And given the heaps of other, worthless, books that are presented alongside them, it is little wonder that they do not receive the attention they deserve. All of these evils would be counteracted by the measures I have indicated. Whether a book shall be printed or not, and what its fate shall be, will depend not on self-interest or mere chance, but rather on the word of a number of intelligent people who shall be motivated to give their true opinion for their honour's sake.

It would be advantageous in many ways to implement some further arrangements in connection with the censorship institutions described thus far. For instance, the censors might *recommend improvements* to the author (this would not be a duty of the censors, but it would be something they are allowed to do, and looked upon as a meritorious service); the author would of course be free either to accept or reject these suggestions. Should he accept the recommendations, it would be considered appropriate that the name of the censor who made these friendly suggestions not remain unmentioned. Every author who is not intoxicated with self-admiration will know how much it can profit a book when the author has the opportunity to learn, through the judgments others have conveyed to him before its publication, of mistakes in his work and possible improvements. The people entrusted with the business of censorship in a well-constituted state will as a rule be both insightful and knowledgeable, so it is to be expected that they will not overlook the faults of works they have been charged to examine. If they have reason to hope that an honest criticism of these faults will not be without benefit, they will read all the more attentively, and find it well worth their trouble to communicate their observations. Far more could be accomplished in this way before a book first appears than is accomplished today for the second edition of works with the help of reviews of the first. This is not to say, obviously, that reviews would not be appropriate in the best state, nor that they should not be written.

CHAPTER 17

On the fine arts

A sense for the production of the fine arts—the arts of poetry, rhetoric, painting, sculpture, musical composition, etc.— shall be nurtured as much as possible in the best state. One must not forget that these arts, appropriately used, not only enrich our lives through the enjoyment they afford, but also can and should cultivate and ennoble our feelings and our hearts.

Now the use of already existing works of art is one thing, the production of new ones quite another. The first shall be encouraged as much as possible in the best state. To this end, all genuinely successful (thus, among other things, morally edifying) works of poetry shall be spread to all corners whereever there is hope that someone may read and understand them. The greatest possible care shall be taken to ensure the preservation of valuable paintings, and excellent copies of these shall be made in an attempt to multiply people's enjoyment of them in all towns and provinces. Every family shall have portraits of its members, at the very least silhouettes. However, paintings and sculpture of great artistic merit, or at least of interest to more than a single family, shall be bought from the artist by the state, and displayed and used as public goods. Songs and musical compositions that are uplifting, or capable of improving our hearts through gentle emotions, or that put us in a joyful mood, shall be spread everywhere; and from tender youth onwards music shall be fruitfully used for the sake of moral improvement, amusement, and cheering the spirit. People shall sing when doing any kind of work whose nature permits it; in every school, singing shall enhance periods of rest.

Concerning the *second* matter, namely, the production of new works of art, one is not nearly so mild in one's judgments in the best state. Rather, people will agree with Horace in thinking that the only fate a mediocre work deserves is oblivion. For this reason, one will not so easily permit someone to make poetry or musical composition, etc., his primary business when he does not show promise of accomplishing something truly extraordinary. In my view, *dramatic performances* will not be put on by anyone in the best state, not even by dilettantes. Still less will one tolerate entire companies of people whose sole business is to imitate various attitudes and feelings, and who wish to be honoured for possessing the art of seeming to be what they are not. As I see things, people will judge that the so-called performance of a drama is an offense against good taste, very much like putting paint on a sculpture. On top of this, it will be judged dangerous to morals. Finally, one will come to think that the time spent by actors and others involved in the production, e.g. learning the roles, making the scenery, etc., is too much for the production of effects that can be produced far more easily and more perfectly with a little imagination.

CHAPTER 18
On nourishment

Asking whether the foods citizens use might be harmful to their health or life is considered a standing responsibility in the best state. It is the same with the question whether alongside the foods used hitherto there are other materials in the three kingdoms of nature from which healthy and tasty meals can be prepared. When physicians are sufficiently convinced that a certain fare is beneficial, and the only thing standing in the way of its introduction is custom, one shall be patient with the adults and commence its introduction with children. In a similar way, the foods that physicians declare to be harmful, as well as foods whose preparation requires the destruction of a considerable amount of other consumable materials, shall be taken out of use. The state shall take the greatest possible care to ensure the continual production of the ingredients for a healthy diet, and their use as food stuffs rather than for other non-essential purposes.

One will not wait to see whether an actual food shortage occurs in a given region. Instead, as soon as it appears that there is no more surplus, goods shall be brought from other regions, no matter how distant, to provide what is lacking. If the nature of the foodstuffs does not allow them to be transported over long distances, or if this would take too long, one proceeds as follows: first the path from the region with a surplus to the region where a shortage is feared is divided into several parts. The surplus of the former is then transferred to the part nearest to it, while that part simultaneously transfers to the next some of the foodstuffs it possesses (not in surplus, but in sufficient amount), and so on. It is clear that such an arrangement would make it possible to help in a single day a region threatened with a food shortage using the surplus in a region hundreds of miles away, provided that the business can be directed quickly enough, e.g. by using the telegraph.

Foodstuffs that are not available in quantities large enough to supply everyone who wants them, and that, moreover, are useful for soothing the weak or the sick, are not to be bought at will. Rather, the *Market Supervisor* (thus I will call the civil servant responsible for verifying the quality of foodstuffs and supervising sales) shall see to it that the members of the municipality whose doctors have instructed them to use these foods (by written prescription) receive a part of the stock first.

Should something remain after all these people find what they need, then others may buy as well. Foods that appear more stimulating to the palate on account of their rarity or for other reasons, and are therefore more eagerly sought, shall be subject to a tax, i.e. their price shall be raised in some proportion (e.g. doubled), so that the increase flows to the municipality rather than the producer.

These measures will, I hope, be found more fair and reasonable than providing common and similar provisions for all citizens, as some people have proposed. For tastes and dietary requirements differ greatly; so many different things can be used for food, and these prepared in so many different ways; and we have indeed seen that, in addition to increasing pleasure, a differentiated distribution of foods can further many other good ends.

A good many people have the bad habit of consuming more food and drink (especially the latter) than is necessary or even good for them, and yet not so much that they could reasonably be punished for one of these excesses. Yet in the end they cause more damage to themselves and the community through the daily repetition of this bad habit than others who are unmistakably guilty of gluttony, but only on rare occasions. As far as I can see, in the best state this problem could only be dealt with by *doctors*, who shall be charged with keeping an eye on all citizens of their municipality, and from time to time warning those who are approaching this fault, while doing what they can about it by rational persuasion. Should this fail, they shall lodge a complaint with the local judge of public morals.

CHAPTER 19

On dress

The principal purposes that clothes should serve are doubtless: protection against cold, rain, or excessive heat, covering the parts that modesty bids us to, and adornment. From this it follows that the materials for clothes, as well as their form, must be determined in part by the character of the country and the season, as well as by the sex, age, and bodily strength of those who wear them. Clothes must allow us to distinguish the sexes, and this in a completely obvious way, something that can be accomplished through the form, the colour, or both. Covering for the legs seems fitting and appropriate for women as well as men. Clothes that fit too tightly are bad for both health and morals. A certain variety in clothing, especially with respect to colours, should not be forbidden in the best state. It pleases the eye, makes people easier to recognise, and may have other advantages as well, e.g. making clothes available at a variety of prices, allowing people the pleasure of choosing their clothes according to their own taste, etc. It will also be good in many respects for single people to be distinguishable by their clothes from the married ones. It is even more certain that clothes should vary according to age, so that not only people's features, but also the fabric, the colour, or the cut of their clothes allow us to tell their age—of course, not to the very year. Materials that cost more to prepare than others that serve essentially the same purpose, e.g. ornamented fabrics that cost far more than plain ones, silk in countries where its production requires much land and labour, etc., shall be forbidden by the state.

CHAPTER 20

On housing

According to the principles set out above, a house can never be the property of an individual. Rather, it belongs to the municipality, and the occupant only pays a reasonable rent, roughly as much as is required to pay for its upkeep and the construction of a new house once this one has fallen down.

It is worth mentioning how extremely misguided our present housing arrangements are. A house in which five of six families live usually brings in enough rent to its owner to allow him to support his entire family, even after all costs of upkeep have been deducted. How unfair! Without doing any work at all, one family is allowed to live off five others, that is, lays claim to a sixth of their income! Can anyone deny that this is an atrocious practice, hardly better than that of the Robot system?[4]

No one will dispute that many improvements could be made in the contstruction of houses, through which they would be made healthier, more comfortable and pleasant, cheaper to build, and longer-lasting. One will make a special point of ensuring that all houses are dry, light, and conducive to health. In countries where the seasons require it, houses will be built so that some rooms can be used in winter, others in summer. Incidentally, neither splendor nor luxury shall be dominant in buildings used for housing. Only the public buildings shall be embellished and decorated with the rare treasures of the region. It would be appropriate to display *inscriptions* or *drawings* conveying something worth learning (e.g. moral sayings, pictures drawn from natural history, etc.) in all buildings, in every room, and generally everywhere possible, so that one only need diligently consider them in order to become familiar with the most important truths of worldly wisdom and the most useful knowledge.

---

[4]"*Robota*" is the Czech word for the unpaid labour peasants were required by law to perform for their landlords (ed.).

CHAPTER 21

On some measures concerning the differences between the sexes

It is essential that a good constitution provide an appropriate direction to the sex drive, with measures that ensure that this drive does not make people vicious and unhappy, but rather contributes a good deal to their true perfection and happiness in life.

On the one hand, people cannot be protected enough from an untimely awakening of the sex drive, especially through stimulation of their imagination. On the other hand, it is necessary to teach them about these matters, and to encourage them to acquire the status that allows one rightfully to satisfy this urge. I therefore think that:

a) in the best state young people shall be taught in school, namely, in the Sunday schools, as much as is useful to know about the wise arrangements God has made for the propagation of our kind, about the duties that spring from these, and especially about the misfortunes attaching to a too early awakening of this still slumbering urge. I also think

b) that in a well-constituted state books, pictures, songs and other items that stimulate the sex drive, fill the imagination with lascivious pictures, etc., shall nowhere and under no pretext be tolerated. Rather, instruction as well as the extremely helpful assistance of the fine arts shall make sure that worthy images and feelings are joined to correct ideas.

c) Should the prejudice arise among the people that celibacy, in and of itself, and not on account of external circumstances that may demand it, is a more perfect state than marriage, attempts shall be made to remove it through enlightenment.

d) Under present arrangements it is customary for young people, especially young men, to break from their parents in the years when they are on the verge of reaching maturity, and to associate only with other young people, principally of the same sex. This has many bad consequences for the formation of character, for one thoughtless and corrupt youth can lead hundreds of others astray. In the best state, therefore, it shall be considered ill-mannered for young people of one or the other sex, still less of both sexes, to associate without having older people in their midst. In public places of amusement, we shall see parents appear, accompanied by their children. The youths of both sexes can then form their own groups, but only in such a way that older people soon appear, supervise their games, talk or listen to them, and distribute praise and censure. Thus supported, the young people have the opportunity to get to know one another, and it is easier for those who were made for each other to meet.

e) It seems proper to me also that in the best state the young men shall court the young women, and the women allow themselves to be courted.

f) Every marriage in the best state must be preceded by a statutory period in which the two parties get to know one another.

g) The bond of marriage shall be regarded as indissoluble in and of itself, one that should never be formed with the intention of dissolving it later. Nevertheless, annulments shall be granted in certain cases for important reasons.

h) Poverty on one side or the other, or both, can never be a hindrance to marriage, for every healthy man who has learned something will be able to earn a living through his labour, while he shall receive support for the upbringing of his children from the municipality. For this reason, it is seen as an abomination when someone's circumstances, e.g. those of a servant, compel him to live in celibacy, even though he is a healthy adult. Accordingly, such arrangements shall not be tolerated by the state.

i) Second marriages will not be looked upon with reproach, as long as the first was dissolved by the death of one of the spouses, or through the lawful pronouncement of a judge.

j) Marriage shall be forbidden between people who live at close quarters, such as fathers and daughters, mothers and sons, siblings and the like. However, when such people live far away from one another, and did not know of their relatedness when they began to love one another, the state will present no obstacles to their marriage.

k) Children born outside of marriage will not atone for the sins of their parents, but rather shall be treated exactly like those born in wedlock.

l) In cases where the people are asked to vote, husband and wife have the right to cast only a single vote, and their combined voice counts for *two* votes; but should they not be able to agree, they have no vote at all.

m) As mothers generally deserve more of the credit than fathers for the life, health and upbringing of their children, it is not very fair that only the names of fathers, and not those of mothers, are carried on by their offspring. But as it is not possible to maintain both—for the composition of names would then grow *ad infinitum*—it might well be best for the sons to continue their father's surname, daughters, the mother's.

Chapter 22

On satisfying the desire for honour

An exceedingly strong drive in human nature is the desire for honour and distinction, a desire that causes as much good under proper direction as evil in unpropitious circumstances. One can be more successful by dealing with this drive through instruction than in any other way. For the strength of our longing for honour depends mostly upon the ideas we have been taught. Which things we will seek for the sake of honour depends still more on instruction. And instruction can bring us to regard as shameful things that shortly before we praised, and vice versa. It is therefore obvious that the influence of instruction and education on our desire for honour must be used in the best way in a well-constituted state. One works toward ensuring that this desire is awakened in everyone, but also toward preventing its becoming so strong that it suppresses all others, and makes a man sacrifice all other forms of happiness in order to enjoy honour, and indeed even makes him ready to commit the most atrocious offenses if he thinks the path of honour lies that way. With still greater effectiveness, however, one endeavors early on to impart to the young a true idea of where honour lies. The foolish concepts of honour that we, unfortunately, find so widespread in our current arrangements, the idea that it is honorable to hold more food and drink than others, to live more lavishly, to have amassed more wealth, or still better to have inherited it, to be no novice to the most varied debaucheries, to risk one's life for a trifle, etc.—such idiocies, I say, will hardly be known even by name under a suitable constitution. Here everyone will know that in order to find honour, one will at least have to seem to be moderate and sober, to have served mankind, to disburse little for one's own needs, allowing that much more for the good of others, and so on. It is quite justified that in the best state *wealth* shall be looked upon as honorable, but still more its *good employment*. For a) if one obtains more property not through mere chance (inheritance), but rather through one's own activity, the possession of wealth shall require uncommon diligence and skill; b) someone who is more wealthy can more easily be helpful to his fellow citizens, e.g. by loaning them money via the mediation of the state; c) finally, the state draws more income from him, as he pays more taxes, and bequeaths more to the state on his death. The objection that the more one person possesses the less others may own will still be valid in the best state; however, there no one's wealth can become so disproportionately large as to make this objection outweigh the reasons previously enumerated. Among the good uses of wealth shall be counted such things as supporting one's children, declining to accept money one is offered for rendering the state some service, making voluntary contributions, etc.

It is not enough, however, that an appropriate constitution provide for the spreading of *correct ideas* of genuine honour; its *institutions* must also be constituted in accordance with these ideas. Thus a citizen shall never be recognised as possessing the right to honour and shows of respect when this right cannot be defended by the strictest concepts of honour. The state declares in particular that no one has the right to shows of respect simply on account of his standing in society, or his official position. For just because he occupies a certain post does not entail that he is worthy of occupying it, and only the latter can earn him respect. This respect, however, can in no case be commanded, though it will surely be shown him without anyone commanding it as soon as his merit becomes more widely known. Outward shows of respect, displayed only when commanded and hence not given freely, can bring no joy to a reasonable person. Inestimable good, I venture to claim, will flow from this measure and from the equal salaries of civil servants mentioned above, or rather will flow from the abolition of the perverse institutions concerning these matters that still persist today! When no one draws a disproportionately greater income and is permitted to demand special shows of respect simply because he holds this or that post in society, or practices this or that occupation, the strongest incentive for seeking posts one is not suited for shall fall by the wayside. In future, people shall no longer throng to occupy an important post for reasons of self-interest or vanity. Rather, only those who believe themselves capable of filling it honorably will apply for it. But if the most important posts in a state are filled with worthy people, everyone will be better off for that reason alone. Accordingly, in the best state all *forms of address* bound up with official positions, i.e. appellations borrowed from a person's position and used with the intention of honoring him, shall be forbidden by law. Nor shall it be permitted that someone's position be mentioned along with his name, for instance when one wishes to distinguish him from others who bear the same name, or when it is necessary to explain why one brings his name up just now. Only a single *distinction of rank*, in my view, shall be prescribed by the state, namely, that in every case where several people have equally grounded claims to something, *women* shall have priority when there are people of both sexes, and when it is a matter of deciding between people of the same sex, the *older* people shall enjoy priority over the young. The priority accorded to women is required by the greater weakness of this sex and its characteristic sufferings, which should determine men, through a certain feeling of compassion, to think themselves called to offer their protection. That *age* is accorded a certain priority rests principally on the natural assumption that the longer someone has lived, the more services he has rendered. From these reasons, however, it follows that the female sex should not be accorded priority in the years of childhood or early youth, but rather beginning at the age of majority or maturity, and also that this priority does not extend over old men. Young women shall and must willingly give priority to old men. Finally, concerning the interactions between children and youths, it is again obvious that they shall imitate what they observe among their elders, i.e. boys and young men shall be taught willingly to accord priority to young women.

Chapter 23

On travel

Voyages are necessary partly for the maintenance of health, partly for the broadening of one's ideas, and so should not be neglected in the best state. Young people on the point of maturity should undertake *walking tours* under the supervision of older people. This holds for both sexes, though the two must be carefully separated on such occasions. *Hostels* shall be maintained by the state for such travelers, so that they do not have to pay when they travel with the state's permission (which shall be granted to everyone several times). That they shall not have to pay for seeing all the noteworthy things along the way goes without saying. Everyone will easily see why I wish all voyages of this sort, the principal purpose of which is educational (I am not speaking here of other travel, e.g. adults travelling on business, perhaps the state's), to be undertaken in the company of several others: travelling with company is not only more pleasant, but also less expensive, and bound up with fewer dangers. Moreover, people learn more when they point things out to one another, and when we discuss what we have seen with our companions it makes a more long-lasting impression on the mind.

CHAPTER 24
On amusements

A reasonable person amuses himself, whenever possible, in the company of others. He does this in part because knowing that others are sharing his enjoyment increases his own, in part because the presence of others serves to warn him against excesses, and finally because the conversation that can go along with most amusements enjoyed in company affords us many new joys and advantages. They provide, in particular, practice in thinking and speaking, thus clarifying our concepts through attempts to communicate them to others, instruction concerning the most varied matters, and reprimands which, if given and received in the best spirit, are most beneficial. Thus it is customary in the best state to enjoy almost all amusements in company, and someone who has the good fortune to belong to a household circle shall enjoy his amusements for the most part within this circle, sharing them with his family. To do the opposite, that is, to frequent public places of amusement unaccompanied by one's family, shall be considered something that can only lead to harm. There shall be no lack of public places where people, for the most part accompanied by their families, come together for amusements that can either not be enjoyed in the family circle at all, or at least not enjoyed to the same extent. The following are the most common amusements enjoyed at such places: newspapers, presenting the latest news of the country or outside, indeed from the whole world; readings from books written for the sake of entertainment; discourses on the most varied topics, provided that they are decent: puzzles to be solved; profound sayings to be considered; all manner of games and competitions, but not for money or improper preferment; moderate exercise; decent dancing, especially for younger people; music and song; finally, food and drink in pleasant company.

Since nothing that can be harmful for morals or health is tolerated, it is obvious that intoxicating drinks, smoking, taking snuff, and hunting for the fun of it shall be forbidden. All young people shall indeed learn how to carry a rifle, and will also shoot at targets for practice and amusement, and may occasionally—with permission of the hunter—hunt a wild animal when this is necessary. But a desire for the business of hunting, snaring birds and the like, shall be regarded as the mark of a morbid spirit, or at least of a mind run wild. It is still more obvious that in a well-constituted state the games that we customarily call *games of chance*, e.g. lotteries, shall not and cannot be tolerated. Is there anyone to whom the corrupting influence such competitions have on morals isn't utterly obvious? Mustn't one have lost all sound concepts of property rights when he finds nothing wrong with the thought that sheer chance shall decide who becomes the owner of a considerable sum of money or an estate, etc.?

Should the taste for an inferior sort of amusement (e.g. card playing) begin to spread among the people here and there, it is by no means appropriate to forbid it, since there is nothing wrong with it in itself, and since such a ban usually just makes the thing seem more desirable. Instead, one seeks to draw the attention of the citizens to certain other, hitherto less well known amusements, whereupon it is to be expected that they will soon freely choose the better over the worse.

Even where the faith that citizens profess does not demand that they set aside certain days for rest and recuperation, such days shall be introduced by the government. If however, a religion spreads such days too thickly throughout the year, one seeks to induce the people by means of enlightenment to address this flaw in their religious practice. One is still more careful to ensure that these days are used appropriately. Among other things, this means that those who perform tiring physical labour on other days shall take a break from that kind of work, and everyone shall enjoy an agreeable change of activities and occupations. Moreover, the mind shall be lifted up to contemplate God and moral truths, and finally people shall enjoy amusements, provided that they are not harmful or forbidden. In order to reach this goal all the better, a variety of such holidays shall have special purposes. Some shall be dedicated to thanking God for the gifts we have received, e.g. Thanksgiving, and many others; some shall be devoted to earnest reflection on the shortcomings and imperfections that our polity still has, and how these might be addressed, etc.

CHAPTER 25

On disputes between citizens

Should two citizens fall into conflict (e.g. over property or the fulfilling of a contract, etc.) and not be able to reach agreement, they shall choose one or several people to serve as arbitrators. Clearly, if they agree on the choice of arbitrators, and find their decision acceptable, the matter is resolved. Should the arbitrators bring to light on this occasion an offense committed by one or the other of the parties, or both (e.g. a *pactum turpe*[5]), it shall be their duty to report it to the appropriate authority. If the disputing parties cannot agree on the choice of arbitrators, then both or one of the parties (the one who believes he has been wronged) shall report this to the municipality, which shall then make the choice. They shall be permitted to appeal the decision of these arbitrators to others chosen by the county, but when the latter agree with the former, no further appeal shall be allowed. Should the latter reverse the decision of the former, however, a further appeal to provincial arbitrators shall be permitted, and so on, until two or more arbitrators concur, or those of a lower level change their judgment because of what they have learned through the appeals. The arbitrators shall judge based on considerations of *fairness*, according to what is *best for the whole*. The bizarre grounds for decision that are met with in large numbers in present constitutions will be unknown–for example, whether in a contract concerning payment *this word or that* was used (coin of the realm, hard cash, and the like) will have no influence on the decision concerning how much is to be paid.

If someone believes he has been injured by a municipality, or county, etc, he files a complaint with the officials of the municipality or county when it is reasonable to expect a fair decision from them, that is, when it is not these officials themselves who have mistreated him. Should this last case arise, he will complain in a way to be described shortly.

Some readers may perhaps be concerned that several of the measures I have described might give rise to continual squabbling and disputes. For example, above I said that each municipality would decide, for the most part, what property should belong to each of its members. One may well object that human nature is such that someone will tolerate

[5]A contract not in keeping with mandatory law (ed.)

great injuries so long as they are inflicted upon him by people he has been habituated from his youth to regard as beings of a higher kind, people whom, moreover, he does not personally know. But even the slightest injustice done him by a man he regards as his equal, whom he must encounter daily, etc. will cause him pain. I do not at all contest the correctness of this observation; but point out a) that someone who patiently bears injustice inflicted upon him, or who perhaps does not even notice that he has suffered injustice, nevertheless suffers, and would be happier if this injustice had not been inflicted on him; and b) that a small offense caused by an equal or by someone we encounter daily will only inflame us when we believe that it was done with evil intent. This will rarely be the case with the measures I have adduced. For because it is not a single individual but rather the entire municipality that must decide, hardly anyone of sound mind will imagine that the entire municipality bears ill will towards him.

CHAPTER 26

On the taxation of citizens and on public expenditures

A high rate of taxation must not be thought to be evil as such; it becomes so only when this revenue is improperly applied. One cannot reasonably complain that taxes are too high if they are used to meet the needs of citizens in a better way than would happen if they all kept their own money but also had to look after the satisfaction of their own needs. Indeed, it is very likely that under a proper constitution a far larger proportion of the national assets would be in the hands of the state (of communities, counties, etc.) than is the case in the present states.

It has already been said that a state, if properly constituted, would collect all money and other valuables left at the death of a citizen. As a rule the estates fall to the municipality in which the citizen has lived. Items of a kind that would benefit humanity much more if they were in the hands of the county or the state must be turned over to them. A handwritten essay suggesting improvements of not just the municipality, but the whole province would be of this sort. It goes without saying that this holds for objects, e.g. books, that were not the property of the departed. The taxation of the living must follow the principle that taxes are to be collected only from those who possess more than average or normal assets, that is, whose possessions have greater monetary value than they would receive if all national assets were equally divided among all individuals. A second principle is that they should not have to give up their entire surplus. Third, and finally, in order to avoid causing harm, it is better in doubtful cases to let citizens keep more for themselves than to make them give up too much. It is most meritorious and agreeable that citizens contribute their surplus to the common good of their own accord. Hence they should be constantly encouraged to pay such voluntary taxes, especially when considerable new public expenditures are incumbent. If even in our present condition such encouragements are not wholly ineffective, one may hope that in the best state they will be that much more productive.

There is another kind of taxation, indeed the most common, which occupies a middle ground between this wholly voluntary and the compulsory. It consists in requiring an appropriate contribution from those who want to enjoy certain dispensable goods that make life more pleasant, but are not absolutely necessary to maintain it, so-called *luxury goods*. Goods of this sort are foodstuffs more attractive to our taste, more beautiful fabrics for clothing, more sumptuous living quarters, animals kept for pleasure, e.g. horses, dogs, birds, etc. The results of this sort of taxation are:

a) that only those with surplus means are taxed and that in any case no one can complain about such a tax since they can easily avoid paying it if they really want to;

b) that it makes all necessities of life that much more affordable, and that everyone can obtain them more reliably and easily;

c) that a wealthier person cannot be reproached for buying such dispensable goods and can rest assured in the knowledge that in buying them he is useful to the state.

One could object that it is amiss to let the most dispensable products fetch the highest prices, since this could mislead people into placing the wrong value on them. My response is that this misunderstanding can easily be prevented through instruction and even mere common sense. Or who could possibly succumb to this absurdity if he is told from childhood that the state acts on the principle of taxing only dispensable goods, and of taxing them the higher the easier it is to get by without them. It is a still common objection that taxing dispensable goods makes the income uncertain, since the rich could conspire not to buy dispensable objects. But this concern falls away if all dispensable objects are taxed, so that a rich person cannot avoid paying taxes if wants to lead a more pleasant life. Moreover, if he does not pay during his lifetime, he must, after his death, leave all his assets to the state. This arrangement, as has been mentioned, allows a rich person to enjoy all agreeable things that nature offers without having to reproach himself; for he has earned them through his industry. He has not become rich by accident, he harms no one by his actions, and indeed performs a good deed.

Objects that are normally dispensable, but are necessary in special cases, for instance for the sick, and that nature or art produce only in the amount required for this need, are exempt from the tax and are not made available to people who do not need them. This includes wine in certain countries. Should they be available in great quantity, then the surplus shall be made available, but it shall be taxed like other dispensable goods.

How are these taxes to be collected? As far as at all possible directly from the consumer, who obtains his goods not directly from the producer, but from the state through trading houses. Foodstuffs that cannot be transported to a trading house because delays would spoil them and other objects that cannot be so traded for whatever reason should be sold in special places, where a market supervisor collects the appropriate tax from persons leaving the exit gate with the purchased goods.

To prevent cheating (smuggling and bootlegging) some goods can have a special seal attached during manufacture and a second one when they are sold. Moreover, every citizen would have not only the right, but also a duty to report any fraud concerning taxes owed to the state. He would be subject to punishment if he failed to do so while knowing of these transgressions. If this were done there would be no need to fear that the state would be cheated very often. With some goods it may be impossible to prevent this sort of cheating. The morals of the people might be better served if the state let it be known that everyone may obtain goods of this sort directly from the producer if this makes them more easily obtainable. It is sufficient if the state does not allow any traders to deliver goods from producer to consumer, except for the persons employed for this purpose by state or municipality. It would be easy to prevent the presence of such traders since everyone has to report his occupation and way of life to the judge of public morals and since everyone in town would have to know if someone were to ply such an illegal trade. The only remaining case, then, would be where someone brokers a trade as a favour to someone else, which could be also be declared legal.

Finally a third type of taxation may sometimes be necessary, namely the wholly compulsory sort, which occurs when the state precisely prescribes the amount that each citizen has to pay. One takes recourse to this sort of taxation only to supplement the other sources. The central government collects the whole sum from the provinces, they in turn from the counties, down to the municipalities, which collect from individual families.

Let us now list the most important expenditures that must be met with this income.

1) First of all, as I have suggested several times, it is the state that must meet all costs of the maintenance, care, education and instruction

of children and young people, whoever their parents. This is done because:

(a) No matter how diligent parents whose marriage is blessed with many children may be, one cannot assume that they will be able to increase their income through their industry to provide for all of them. Hence, inevitably, such a family must fall in need, unless arrangements are so poorly conceived as to allow any individual citizen to amass far more money than he needs to meet his living expenses.

(b) Only if parents receive what is needed to maintain their children not as charity but as a contribution they have a right to demand can they rejoice in their blessing. If this were not done it would not be surprising if each addition to the family caused them to view their future with more apprehension, and made them think of methods of preventing procreation.

(c) If it is the state that maintains its maturing citizens from the first moment of their lives, can we not expect that these citizens will be more loyal supporters? One could of course object that it is not fair to demand from people who have no children or perhaps even remain single that they should contribute to the maintenance of other people's children. Another objection might be that when children learn how little they cost their parents they would love them less. But these are trivial objections. What possible injustice could there be in obliging the childless to turn over part of what they can spare precisely because they themselves are childless to those that are blessed with children? Will not the efforts of these same children, once they are adults, be a benefit to those people? Can they not reasonably hope to be honoured as if they were their very parents? Must not every human being hope, in his old age, not to remain behind lonely and as the last person in God's creation? Must he not wish to be surrounded by younger, more robust persons who nourish and tend to him and support him in his last agony? Those who have no children of their own can expect this important service only from the children of others. It is only proper, therefore, that they should help to raise them. If this means nothing to you, you uncaring lot, tell us what you would do if the families with children, or who expect them later (and they are by far in the majority), unite to extinguish you from the face of the earth because you are pitiless, you small minded lot, and do not want to give up, as long as you live, anything that is yours? Finally, I fear nothing from the concern that these arrangements would diminish the love of children for their parents. The love of children for their parents does not stem from the calculation, which becomes possible only in later years, of how much they have cost their parents. It arises from altogether different conditions, conditions that will not be changed in the least by the way in which I picture the relation between parents and children in the best state. It will not change when adolescent children learn how much the state has contributed to their sustenance. They will understand that they owe infinitely more to their parents' love.

2) The state will underwrite all costs for the maintenance, cure and nursing of all sick, frail, old and insane, in short for all people who are incapable of providing for their own livelihood through labour. Even at the present time one more and more senses the fairness of this demand. No one, after all, can foresee whether he will not have to bear this fate. And every one must admit that in such unfortunate circumstances he would want the state to have such an arrangement in place.

3) The state will replace all losses that arise through accidents that are no one's fault if they are of the kind that can be made good through money or monetary value. That such an arrangement is most beneficial is self-evident. What a vast amount of human suffering would be remedied at once in this way, since the loss an individual suffers, when distributed over all people, is not felt at all. Should not reasonable people endeavour to limit as much as possible the power blind fate has over us? For this reason insurance companies have been founded in our country at this time, which is a commendable step in the right direction. But there are far more goods that people can lose through accidents and that, happily, are not irreplaceable than have been insured through these societies. A well-constituted state does not need special societies for this purpose. Rather it is the state itself that assumes the duty of compensating all citizens for their losses. But is the state entitled to force those who do not wish to participate, as would have to be the case if the victims were compensated from a special fund and not from the revenue that the state raises according to a law that applies equally to all citizens? This question surely can occur only to one who has learned the concepts of the schools. Sound common sense is satisfied to note that one is here forced into an obviously good thing and that in the opposite case, when it is left to each citizen to decide whether and which insurance society

he wishes to join, an infinite number of calculations would have to be made. Another objection has more weight, namely, that such insurance arrangements would render people careless and imprudent. But are not instruction and education means to assure that humanity does not lose the virtue of prudence, which is necessary even with all insurance arrangements in place? Can we not punish people for acts that are demonstrably negligent? And is it necessary, or in most cases even possible, fully to compensate a negligent person for the loss he has suffered, so that he has no incentive to be more cautious in the future?

4) The state assumes all costs for the production or transport of goods whenever they are so high that an individual could not obtain this good if he had to assume them, and where careful calculation shows that even with these many expenditures humanity as a whole, though not the public purse, stands to gain. What I have in mind happens most commonly where not enough goods can be provided to satisfy certain needs, and where the great expenditures did not arise because other useful goods had to be destroyed, but because the production or transport of this good required a lot of labour. For if the population continues to grow, and if moreover much work that used to require people is taken over by machines, it is easy to see that in time there will be many people who can be employed in any work whatever. Hence the cost of production or transportation of certain necessary goods may be so enormous that the foodstuffs consumed by the workers cost far more than the value of the good that has been supplied. Nonetheless, if the state has no occupation for these people where they can produce something of higher value, then it is better to employ them in this than in some other way. For when they supply the good in question, humanity gains something, even if the price that the state in the end charges to the consumer stands in no relation to the incurred costs. To be fair, we must admit that even in the present states much is done that can be compared to undertakings of this kind. Every road that the state builds, every bridge for which it assumes the cost can serve as an example. But how much more of this sort could be done but has not, and how much will become an urgent necessity as a consequence of increased population! Thus, for example, there are forests where the wood rots while elsewhere there is a great shortage because the cost of transportation is much too high to be borne by the individuals who need it. Here it will soon be necessary for the

state to take action and take it upon itself to transport the wood from those forests to more convenient locations.

5) The state will assume all costs of experiments and undertakings if they are of such a nature that an individual cannot be expected to venture them.

6) Obviously, expenditures connected with the production or use of goods that are not in any way the property of an individual, but are, in the view of the state, common goods, must also be borne by the state. Thus the cost of erecting and maintaining all buildings, roads, canals, etc., the printing of all books, the creation of pictures and monuments erected in public places, will be borne by the state.

7) Finally, it is the state that pays the cost of living of all who spend their time in the kind of work we cannot expect to be properly performed if their income depends on the good will of individuals. The state will pay these people according to a fixed rule and in turn bind them to their duty. In my opinion this group will include:

(a) all government officials mentioned in the beginning, if their obligations take up most of their time;

(b) all scholars engaged in publicly useful investigations or in the writing of beneficial works;

(c) all who are engaged in instruction and education;

(d) all physicians;

(e) all who have to look after the buying of goods from producers, their sale to consumers, their transport from place to place and storage;

(f) all those whom the state needs for supervisory positions (e.g. the supervisors of markets), or for keeping accounts or for other business that is of no immediate service to any one individual, but benefits the whole;

(g) all judges who perform their function perpetually and not merely occasionally, etc.

I expect that all these people will perform their occupational duties with more enjoyment and eagerness if their maintenance is assured. They will act with more assurance and will resist the whims of individuals more forcefully if they do not depend upon them and can be envisaged, not as their servants, but as servants of the whole. It is not the same with the people commonly called *ministers* or *teachers of religion*. Religious communities need them to provide public worship and spread religious concepts through instruction. Since the state may not force anyone to join a religious denomination, these people must not be paid or maintained by the state. Rather, citizens who confess one or another denomination can agree among themselves how to compensate these ministers, though they must in each case obtain the permission of the state. If several communities, or even counties and provinces have the same religion, then they can choose and maintain their ministers through decrees that make it appear as if they were public officials.

The salary scales for officials and other persons whom the state temporarily employs are functions of nothing but the time that would be spent in performing them with modest exertion, such that a servant of the state earns neither more nor less than anyone else who makes good use of his time. He should not earn more, for then people would throng to become public servants, and the private person who needs their services would be neglected. In the end, too, they may find ways of pressing the government to declare certain professions necessary even when they are not. Nor should he earn less, because it would be unjust to have those who work for the common good earn less than those who serve individuals.

The simplest way of balancing the state incomes and expenditures I have described, to avoid unnecessary transfers, invoices, etc. without making the overview over the whole unduly difficult is the following. Each municipality directly uses the contributions of its members to defray the cost of the expenditures it has to meet. The same holds for the voluntary taxes and all others that come into its hands. With this income the community seeks to cover the cost of maintaining the children living there, as well as the cost for the state officials living there, outlays for the local buildings, etc. If a municipality is not able to meet all its obligations, perhaps because of a great fire or a bad harvest etc., then it requests that the county cover its needs, while the neighbouring municipalities testify to its needs. It then receives what is required and issues *notes* acknowledging the debt. These notes circulate as paper money. They are used for payment. Printed on each is the name of the municipality that issued it, its value and the total amount of municipal debt at the time of their issue. A municipality that has received something from the state but later has to make some payment or other will redeem some of its notes. If a given municipality circulates a lot of notes, but cannot redeem them or, more properly, if its total debt goes beyond a certain point, then the state will investigate if the fault lies in the community itself. Has perhaps a certain spirit of indolence crept into it? If it is found to be so, they will be punished by losing certain non-essential goods, like food stuffs that serve only to make life more luxurious. But if the municipality is found innocent, if unavoidable bad luck, barrenness of the area, rough and inhospitable climate created the burden of debt, then a part of their notes are invalidated and their bearers compensated with paper money issued by the state.

Chapter 27
On rewards and punishments

It is the natural duty of all people to advance good and thwart evil as much as possible, no matter what state they live in, or whether they live in any state at all. It follows from this duty that whoever lives in a state whose government has the resolve to advance good and punish evil must bring whatever is good or evil in his fellow citizens to the attention of the proper agency. Such action should, however, generate some public benefit, like encouraging others, or cautioning against someone's appointment to office, or bettering the lot of people who suffer from his actions, or leading to his own betterment or to a penalty that deters others, etc. In modern states this duty is in no way acknowledged. People often find it against their conscience and say: I do not want to harm that man, etc. One anticipates much inconvenience and fears becoming known as an informer. This is why so many corrupt persons occupy the highest offices in the state. Everyone is persuaded of their bad conduct except for the office in charge of making their appointment, or else one knows about these things but suffers this mischief since no accuser steps forward. In a well-constituted state the duty to make such notifications must be taught and encouraged in the schools. It is not advisable, however, to accept anonymous information, since this may be motivated by mere malice, which would not only cause much trouble, but also forever leave a spot on the good name of an innocent accused. To allay the fear of revenge, which could keep someone from informing about a transgression, the following middle course can be taken: there will be an office where a sealed accusation can be deposited, with the name of the accuser in code. The supervisor of this office, who breaks the seal, is the only person to know the name of the accuser. He will then publish the code word and thus indicate that the information has been received. This prevents him from suppressing the accusation or betraying the name of the informant, since in both cases the crime would be easily detected. He then begins an investigation at the appropriate office, e. g. in the municipality where the accused person lives. The authenticity of the signature is easily ascertained since all signatures are deposited at the municipal offices and can be inspected by all administrative bodies. If a crime that was witnessed [but not reported] by several others is proven, then they, too, become liable to prosecution, especially if they belong to the class of persons entrusted with the supervision of others, e.g. men of the cloth. If an accused is found innocent, then his accuser is investigated, whether his accusation was public or covert. If he can prove that he had reasonable grounds for his suspicion, then he is released, otherwise his *calumny* will be made public and he shall be punished. If for some reason it is still thought appropriate, despite all these measures, to allow anonymous accusations, then they must trigger only secret investigations until more substantial suspicions come to light. What has here been said about *accusations* also holds, *mutatis mutandis*, for information regarding *meritorious acts*. For the state wishes to be informed of these as well. It is the duty of the office receiving the information to conduct further investigations. A citizen should not be deprived of a *reward* that he has earned, if his good deed is established either through such information or in some other way.

It transpires that a well-constituted state should not fail to recognise two kinds of meritorious action that accordingly deserve two types of reward. A wise state must, as far as possible, strive to reward anyone who has voluntarily served his fellow citizens for his work. This should be done even if the service was not performed from the purest moral motives and only accidentally produced a benefit for others, so long as it can be established that it was not done with evil intent. The state must proceed in this way in order to encourage good deeds in all, even those who cannot yet rise to pure and altruistic virtue. But if we reward even acts with self-serving motives if they benefit the common good, can we deny a reward to virtue that strives to improve the common good without selfish advantage or even with great sacrifice? Certainly not. But it is clear that the rewards must be different in the two cases. Actions of the first kind can be rewarded through *material advantages*. For example, if someone voluntarily takes on necessary heavy physical labour, then the municipality should pay him more than they usually would for the time spent. Now we have no reason to suppose that a man who has given proof of higher moral strength is altogether dead to sensory pleasure. He neither is nor should be, and having helped so many others to the enjoyment of earthly pleasures should himself taste the pleasures this earth offers. But the share of these that the state offers him *just like everyone else* cannot be considered a reward. Indeed, he would refuse any advantage at the expense of others, for instance an estate of special value, meals of exquisite taste, etc. How then can we reward him? Could one perhaps appoint him to an office that would enlarge the scope of his beneficial work? I think, however, that it should be a general principle that in a well constituted state *offices are never viewed as rewards*; they are never awarded in compensation for services to the country, no matter how meritorious. There are, however, offices that even in the best state are entrusted only to men of established honesty, great insight and other excellent qualities. And if his fellow citizens offer someone such an office he would indeed be honoured, and free to envisage this honour as a natural compensation for his virtues. I simply maintain that in considering someone for an appointment, citizens should not allow the thought of rewarding someone to enter into their deliberations. For if one must consider it an honour to be called to a certain office, then, presumably, it is a post with much authority. In filling it, it is incumbent that all who have a voice in this decision focus exclusively on one question: *who is most suitable for the post, who makes us expect that he will conduct the office with the most blessed success for humanity*? This question is so difficult in itself, and a correct answer requires an account of so many things, that we will necessarily be led astray if, instead of focusing on it alone we concern ourselves with a circumstance that should be taken into account only if we must choose between persons with exactly the same qualifications. For only in such rare cases is it permissible to appoint someone who considers the office a reward and rank him higher for that reason. But, as I said, such a case must be extremely rare given the great variety of people and the special knowledge that the proper conduct of each office requires. If the office is seen as a form of reward, this will not just distort the view of the electors, but even more mislead the appointee. If we declare that we award him this office to compensate him for his accomplishments, can he help concluding that we assign him no new duties and obligations with this office, but award him certain advantages and comforts he has so far done without? It is a common experience in all states where offices are dealt out as rewards that especially the most important responsibilities and offices are the most poorly managed. For nothing is more common than for people who have been awarded these titles to think of them only as means to lead a more comfortable life. The preceding makes it clear that a well-constituted state can reward the merit of a citizen with the *respect* of other citizens and nothing else. If the state takes care to make these merits known, then individuals can freely pay their respect daily and hourly as life offers opportunities, and on special occasions can demonstrate it publicly and communally. Hence making these merits public is the only thing the state is obliged to do.

The public occasions just mentioned include most prominently the *moral courts*. For just as several of the older states have found it beneficial from time to time to conduct special moral courts, the same will hold for the best state. It would be best if each municipality annually convened such courts. The municipality itself would elect the judges of public morals by simple majority in such a way that in the preceding year no one knows who they will be. The elected judges begin their work by asking the whole community and each individual citizen to give their honest judgement, whether praise or blame, about each of their fellow citizens, and to suggest what desserts they might be due. After this they read the names of all citizens (in the order of their house numbers) and the names of all family members aged fifteen years and older, and ask the people present for a judgement on each of them. Most importantly, they will ask how they all have occupied themselves, how diligent they have been, how frugally they have lived, etc. In the end, the elected judges of public morals render an account of their own conduct and, as every person has some faults, ask that theirs be pointed out. More prominent merits are honoured by a written *vote of thanks*, issued by the municipality, the county or an even higher level of government. To encourage others, this news will also be reported in the public gazettes. If the worthy man is still young, or if his parents, teachers or educators are still alive, and if there is good reason to suppose that it was the proper conduct of these persons that laid the foundations of his merits, then they too will be honoured by having a delegation convey the state's gratitude. When such a man has left this life, his memory will be honoured yet *more openly*. His portrait will be displayed at a suitable public place, his biography will be made available, and the memory of his deeds will be perpetuated in the historical annals. Permitting citizens still at a lower level of education and especially *younger* ones to decorate themselves by wearing a badge of honour would be an unobjectionable reward. This is so especially if it is made clear that by wearing his medal the decorated person meant to encourage others to emulate him. After what has been said we need no reminder that in the best state it is not only the *male* sex that one endeavours to reward. The merits of the *female* sex must be recognised and honoured as well. As was mentioned already, there will be special votes of thanks to mothers whose sons have distinguished themselves, likewise votes of thanks to mothers who have borne and raised many children who, if not achieving the extraordinary, have been upright citizens.

Just as no one who deserves a reward should remain unrewarded, so also no one who deserves punishment should remain unpunished. But obviously only those deserve punishment who have violated a law that they either *knew* or else *could* and *should* have known. In our contemporary states many may violate the laws because they do not know them and do not even have opportunities to learn them. In the best state the laws are not merely taught in school, but their appropriateness is shown. Violation of these laws will carry certain punishments which are, however, not always precisely determined. They are modified according to the specific circumstances (the moral depravity of the criminal, an increased tendency to this type of transgression in the population, etc.). The purpose of *announcing* punishments is always deterrence, but the purpose of *imposing* them can differ, depending on circumstances. It can be:

a) to maintain the future credibility and power of the announcement and the warning;

b) to make the warning and announcement stronger and more vivid by showing a concrete instance of them in a real case;

c) to make good in whole or part for the damage that was caused;

d) to deny the criminal the opportunity of committing further crimes of this or other kinds;

e) to change and improve his attitude, etc.

In a given case, the kind and severity of the punishment is to be determined through the character of these purposes. The most important circumstance is the *attitude of the lawbreaker*. A person who has sinned merely from rashness receives a mild punishment, while another who betrays an evil character will be punished severely, even for the theft of a few cents if it turns out that he acted with deliberation. People who betray an *evil character*, either through the nature of their crime, or through other circumstances that then come to light, are declared unsuitable for all higher offices until they give the most persuasive demonstration of a change of heart. For this reason every court will call on acquaintances and neighbours of the accused to testify to his character.

Since the law itself does not exactly determine a penalty, but at most sets certain limits, the schools will not dwell upon these penalties, for what would be the benefit of this? Whoever violates the law should be prepared to receive the maximum punishment. It is proper that a distinction is made between ascertaining the *facts*, and determining the deserved *punishment*. But I am inclined to believe that one should do exactly the opposite of what is now common in some states. There the investigation of fact is left to a *jury*, a group not of legal scholars but of persons of the same status as the accused, while the determination of the penalty is left to jurists. But the investigation of facts, of what precisely the accused has committed, the establishment of a fully valid proof is often extremely difficult, and can be left with assurance only to persons that are experienced in this sort of investigation. Once it has been brought to light what the criminal has done, however, sound common sense will be more unbiased than the learned in judging what punishment the criminal deserves. Thus only the first business requires special persons employed by the state (inquisitors or whatever one wants to call them). For the actual office of judge, several, perhaps twelve persons, from the criminal's municipality should suffice. To set a deadline by which the inquisitors must finish their investigation seems neither necessary nor possible as long as reasonably dependable and upright persons have been chosen for this office.

As a rule, each major crime that someone has committed will be made *public*, together with the punishment imposed. Exceptions are made only where the publicity itself would cause harm.

The punishments consist of the following:

a) *dismissal* from any higher office;

b) certain *fines* in the case of minor offences motivated by self-interest. The money thus collected will be used in part to compensate the victims, in part for other public purposes;

c) *incarceration*, where heavy or dangerous, but necessary, labour must be performed with slender fare. To make work *unnecessarily* more difficult, e.g. by attaching leg irons, etc. is considered cruel;

d) *corporeal punishment*, which is used only with children or very brutal persons, and which must never be life threatening;

e) *public humiliation*, for instance by publishing the crime through placards, or displaying the person on a stage;

f) *execution*, for there will be death penalties even in the best state, since there are crimes whose perpetrators will cause such general abhorrence that moral sense would be offended if they were allowed to live on. Further, such people themselves occasionally ask for an end to their life as a benefit. But I believe that executions should never be carried out before the eyes of the people. It is a horrific act that only dulls the moral sense. Let the criminal be killed in a dark dungeon by a machine, at a predetermined time during which the people mourn, pray, etc. Afterwards, as proof of the execution, the body of the convict may be displayed. Some states have claimed good results from forcing such people to complete inactivity, but so far I am unable to understand how this could be so. We will have to wait to see if this is confirmed by experience. As well, I cannot comprehend why a *confession*—if by this is meant an explicitly worded statement—should always be necessary fully to prove guilt. But I do consider it a duty never to impose punishment if there is some doubt that the crime has actually been committed. For this reason I consider cruel all pain inflicted upon the accused in order to force him to talk, unless he deserves this pain for crimes already proven.

Here are some examples of crimes and their punishments: I would impose the death penalty only for deliberate and planned murder. For theft the punishment would be double or threefold restitution, or work with slender fare, or corporeal punishment or public exhibition. If a female who does not sell her body as a profession becomes pregnant she is punished with nothing but the shame of the condition that she herself has caused. The man, however, will be punished by removal from office. But if he is of clean character and only submitted to weakness, he can be re-instated somewhere in a place where his transgression is not known. Or, depending on circumstances, he can receive corporeal punishment, or be sentenced to community labour. Adultery would be punished much more severely, especially if it transpires that the guilty party acted with premeditation and treated the other partner harshly. Drunkenness, if it is not habitual but due to carelessness, would lead to a fine, but if a dominating vice would be punished by dismissal from office, removal of children from the home, imprisonment and community labour etc. There would be no life sentences, but it is always made clear that a penalty will continue until there is clear evidence of reform. Unfortunately, with many this would never occur.

CHAPTER 28

On death

Just as one may not arbitrarily give away one's property when alive, so too one can not bequeath it to just anybody on death. However, the state shall allow objects to be left to any person if their value resides only in the relation to the person who wishes to bequeath them. Other objects, however, may only be thus bequeathed with permission of the state. There may be a concern that these provisions will often be violated, since persons close to the deceased might remove some of the goods. But in a well-constituted state this is surely not more likely than it is at present. On the contrary, in such a state it is nearly impossible for someone illegitimately to seize some good and possess it for long without being denounced. The reason is that the kind of excuse that serves in present conditions to forestall further inquiries and even remove all suspicion (i.e. one has found the thing, it was a present or a payment for some service etc.) has no purchase in a well-constituted state.

After his death a kind of judgement will be passed on each adult citizen, at least in his own community. He will be denied honourable burial if weighty grievances against him come to light. The difference between an honourable burial and another is merely that in the latter only near relatives will accompany the body. If much praise is heaped on a citizen, a monument may be erected for him, perhaps a stone on his grave, and a brief biography mentioning his merits will be inserted in the annals of the community or even the country. One makes every effort to preserve the memory of persons whose example will be an encouragement for many others.

It is not permissible, however, for funerals to become the occasion, in a misguided attempt to honour the dead, for destroying lots of useable goods. On the contrary, one seeks to convince everyone that emulating the virtues of the dead and finishing the noble tasks they were only able to begin is the most dignified way of honouring them. We gladly and often visit the resting places of the beloved dead. But the sadness felt at their loss is much softened through the common conviction that they still are, that they live in a more blessed state and that they know of us and that we shall see them again.

Index